Table of Contents

MW00442795

▶ **Use place value understanding and properties of operations to add and subtract.**

Measurement and Data

▶ **Measure and estimate lengths in standard units.**

Introduction

Core Standards for Math offers two-page lessons for every content standard in the *Common Core State Standards for Mathematics*. The first page of each lesson introduces the concept or skill being taught by providing step-by-step instruction and modeling and checks students' understanding through open-ended practice items. The second page includes multiple-choice practice items as well as problem-solving items.

Common Core State Standards for Mathematics: Content Standards

Content Standards define what students should understand and be able to do. These standards are organized into clusters of related standards to emphasize mathematical connections. Finally, domains represent larger groups of related standards. At the elementary (K–6) level, there are ten content domains. Each grade addresses four or five domains. The table below shows how the domains are placed across Grades K–6.

Domains	Grade Levels						
	K	1	2	3	4	5	6
Counting and Cardinality (CC)	●						
Operations and Algebraic Thinking (OA)	●	●	●	●	●	●	
Numbers and Operations in Base Ten (NBT)	●	●	●	●	●	●	
Measurement and Data (MD)	●	●	●	●	●	●	
Geometry (G)	●	●	●	●	●	●	●
Numbers and Operations—Fractions (NF)				●	●	●	
Ratios and Proportional Relationships (RP)							●
The Number System (NS)							●
Expressions and Equations (EE)							●
Statistics and Probability (SP)							●

The lessons in **Core Standards for Math** are organized by content standard. The content standard is listed at the top right-hand corner of each page. The entire text of the standards is provided on pages 266–268. The lesson objective listed below the content standard number indicates what part of the standard is emphasized in the lesson. You may choose to have students complete all the lessons for a particular standard or select lessons based on the more focused objectives.

Name_____

Lesson 1

COMMON CORE STANDARD CC.2.OA.1

Lesson Objective: Use bar models to represent a variety of addition and subtraction situations.

Algebra • Use Drawings to Represent Problems

You can use bar models to show problems.

There are 5 girls and 11 boys at the park.
How many more boys than girls are at the park?

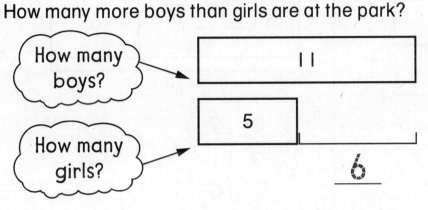

Write a number sentence. $11 - 5 = 6$

There are ___6___ more boys than girls.

Complete the bar model. Then write a number sentence to solve.

1. Nathan had 7 stamps. Then he got 9 more stamps.
   How many stamps does Nathan have now?

7	9

_____

____ + ____ = ____   ____ stamps

1. Eli has 13 marbles. Amber has 6 marbles. How many more marbles does Eli have than Amber?

13

6

- ○ 7
- ○ 8
- ○ 10
- ○ 19

2. There were 8 ants on a rock. Some more ants joined them. Then there were 13 ants on the rock. How many ants joined them?

- ○ 4
- ○ 5
- ○ 13
- ○ 22

3. Julian has 14 grapes. He gives 5 grapes to Lindsay. How many grapes does Julian have left?

_____	5

14

- ○ 19
- ○ 11
- ○ 10
- ○ 9

4. Sarah had 6 books. Her grandmother gave her 5 more books. How many books does Sarah have now?

- ○ 1
- ○ 10
- ○ 11
- ○ 13

5. Jared has 15 red cubes. He has 7 blue cubes. How many more red cubes than blue cubes does he have? Complete the bar model.

15

7

_____ more red cubes

_____

Name_____

Lesson **2**

COMMON CORE STANDARD CC.2.OA.1
Lesson Objective: Write equations to
represent and solve a variety of addition
and subtraction situations.

Algebra • Use Equations to Represent Problems

Some red fish and 9 green fish are in a tank.
The tank has 14 fish. How many red fish are there?

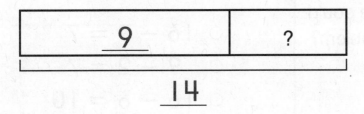

Write a number sentence.

Use a ■ for the missing number.

$$14 - 9 = ■$$

_____5_____ red fish in the tank.

Write a number sentence for the problem.
Use a ■ for the missing number. Then solve.

1. There are 13 trees in a park.
8 are pine trees. The rest are
oak trees. How many oak
trees are there?

So there are

_____

_____ oak trees.

8	?

13

1. There are 14 bees in an apple tree. There are 9 bees in a pear tree. How many more bees are in the apple tree than in the pear tree?

   Which number sentence could you use to solve the problem?

   ○ $9 + 14 = \blacksquare$

   ○ $\blacksquare + 9 = 14$

   ○ $9 = \blacksquare + 14$

   ○ $14 = 9 - \blacksquare$

2. There are 11 children at the park. Then 5 children go home. Which number sentence shows how many children are still at the park?

   ○ $8 - 4 = 4$

   ○ $11 - 5 = 6$

   ○ $11 + 5 = 16$

   ○ $11 + 6 = 17$

3. Lenny had 16 toy cars. He gave some cars to his sister. Now he has 9 cars. Which number sentence shows how many cars he gave to his sister?

   ○ $16 - 9 = 7$

   ○ $9 - 2 = 7$

   ○ $16 - 6 = 10$

   ○ $16 + 2 = 18$

PROBLEM SOLVING REAL WORLD

Write or draw to show how you solved the problem.

4. Tony has 7 blue cubes and 6 red cubes. How many cubes does he have in all?

   _____ cubes

Name_____

Lesson 3

COMMON CORE STANDARD CC.2.OA.1

Lesson Objective: Solve problems involving 2-digit addition by using the strategy *draw a diagram*.

Problem Solving • Addition

Hannah has 14 pencils. Juan has 13 pencils. How many pencils do they have in all?

Unlock the Problem

What do I need to find?

how many pencils

they have in all

What information do I need to use?

Hannah has __14__ pencils.

Juan has __13__ pencils.

Show how to solve the problem.

Hannah's 14 pencils	Juan's 13 pencils

____?____ pencils in all

$14 + 13 = \blacksquare$

_27_ pencils

Solve.

1. There are 21 peanuts in a bag. 16 more peanuts are put into the bag. How many peanuts are in the bag in all?

21 peanuts	16 peanuts

_____ peanuts in all

_____

_____ peanuts

1. James and Flora have 38 markers in all. Flora has 16 markers. How many markers does James have?

   ○ 22   ○ 54
   ○ 44   ○ 62

2. A pet store has two fish tanks. There are 48 fish in one tank and 23 fish in the other tank. How many fish are there in both tanks?

   ○ 25   ○ 71
   ○ 26   ○ 72

3. Miles puts 52 stickers in his notebook. Julie puts 29 stickers in her notebook. How many stickers do Miles and Julie put in their notebook in all?

   ○ 23   ○ 81
   ○ 71   ○ 94

4. There are 37 pencils in the pencil box. Ms. Marks hands out 18 of the pencils to the class. How many pencils are left in the pencil box?

   ○ 55   ○ 25
   ○ 29   ○ 19

5. Label the bar model. Write a number sentence with a ■ for the missing number. Solve.

   Tom has 23 red pens and 38 black pens. How many pens does Tom have?

   _____

   _____ pens

Name_____

Lesson 4

COMMON CORE STANDARD CC.2.OA.1

Lesson Objective: Represent addition situations with number sentences using a symbol for the unknown number.

Algebra • Write Equations to Represent Addition

Sara took 16 pictures.
Then she took 17 more pictures.
How many pictures did Sara take in all?

Use a bar model to show the problem.

16 pictures	17 pictures

____?____ pictures in all

Write a number sentence. Solve.

16 + 17 = ▨_____

____33____ pictures

Use a bar model to show the problem. Write a number sentence. Use a ▨ for the missing number. Then solve.

1. Josh has 18 basketball cards and 14 baseball cards. How many cards does he have altogether?

_____ basketball cards	_____ baseball cards

_____ cards altogether

_____

_____ cards

1. Gina scores 26 points in the game. Eric scores 31 points. Which number sentence can be used to find how many they score in all?

   ○ $26 + \blacksquare = 31$
   ○ $31 + \blacksquare = 55$
   ○ $26 + 31 = \blacksquare$
   ○ $31 + 62 = \blacksquare$

2. On a hike, Sierra sees 42 frogs and 27 turtles. Which number sentence can be used to find how many frogs and turtles Sierra sees in all?

   ○ $\blacksquare + 24 = 27$
   ○ $42 + 27 = \blacksquare$
   ○ $42 + 72 = \blacksquare$
   ○ $27 + \blacksquare = 42$

3. Tim and Liz collect stamps. Tim has 93 stamps. Liz has 32 stamps. How many stamps do Tim and Liz have in all?

   ○ 125
   ○ 115
   ○ 120
   ○ 105

4. Amber collects 49 pebbles at the beach. Meg collects 44 pebbles at the beach. How many pebbles do they collect in all?

   ○ 103
   ○ 93
   ○ 83
   ○ 5

PROBLEM SOLVING  REAL WORLD

Solve.

5. There are 21 children in Kathleen's class. 12 of the children are girls. How many children in her class are boys?

   _____ boys

Name_____

Lesson 5

COMMON CORE STANDARD CC.2.OA.1
Lesson Objective: Solve problems involving 2-digit subtraction by using the strategy *draw a diagram*.

Problem Solving • Subtraction

Katie had a box of 42 craft sticks. She used 26 craft sticks to make a sailboat. How many craft sticks were not used?

Unlock the Problem

What do I need to find?	**What information do I need to use?**
<u>how many craft sticks</u>	Katie had <u>42 craft sticks</u>.
were not used	She used <u>26 craft sticks</u>.

Show how to solve the problem.

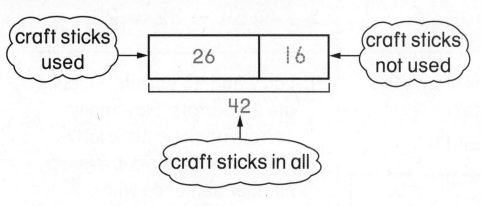

$$42 - 26 = \blacksquare$$

_____ 16 craft sticks

Write a number sentence with a ▤ for the missing number. Solve.

1. Ms. Lee took 35 purses to the fair. She sold 14 purses. How many purses does she have left?

14	?

35

_____   _____ purses

Core Standards for Math, Grade 2

1. Mrs. Dobbs has 38 stickers. She gives away 12 stickers. Which number sentence shows how many stickers she has left?

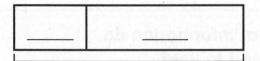

- $26 - 12 = 14$
- $12 + 26 = 38$
- $38 - 12 = 26$
- $12 - 6 = 6$

2. Which bar model shows the number sentence?

$$22 - 8 = 14$$

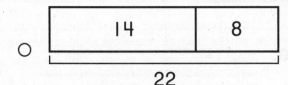

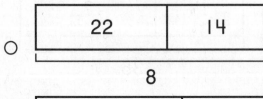

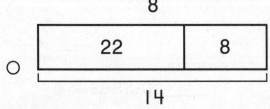

3. Alison makes 54 cookies. She gives away 32 cookies. Which number sentence shows how many cookies she has left?

- $54 + 32 = 86$
- $32 + 50 = 82$
- $32 - 12 = 20$
- $54 - 32 = 22$

4. Larry had 46 carrots. Rabbits ate 27 carrots. How many carrots does he have left? Label the bar model. Write a number sentence with a ■ for the missing number. Solve.

_____

_____

Name_____

Lesson 6
COMMON CORE STANDARD CC.2.OA.1
Lesson Objective: Represent subtraction situations with number sentences using a symbol for the unknown number.

Algebra • Write Equations to Represent Subtraction

37 birds were in the trees.
13 birds flew away.
How many birds are in the trees now?

The bar model shows the problem.

13	?

37

Use the bar model to write a number sentence.

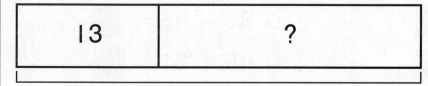

37 − 13 = ▨
_____

Subtract to find the missing part.

$$\begin{array}{r} 37 \\ -13 \\ \hline 24 \end{array}$$

So, the answer is __24__ birds.

Write a number sentence for the problem.
Use a ▨ for the missing number. Then solve.

1. Gina has 23 pens. 15 pens are
   blue and the rest are red. How
   many pens are red?

15	?

   23

   _____   _____ red pens

1. There were 27 children in a classroom. Then 18 children went outside. Which number sentence can be used to find how many children are in the classroom now?

   ○ $27 + 18 = $ ▮

   ○ $18 - 27 = $ ▮

   ○ $45 - 27 = $ ▮

   ○ $27 - 18 = $ ▮

2. Ms. Clark baked some cookies. She gave 25 cookies to her friends. Now she has 7 cookies. Which number sentence can be used to find how many cookies she baked?

   ○ ▮ $ + 25 = 7$

   ○ ▮ $ - 25 = 7$

   ○ ▮ $ + 7 = 25$

   ○ ▮ $ - 25 = 32$

3. Tom had 45 marbles. He gave 31 marbles to his sister. Which number sentence can be used to find how many marbles Tom has now?

   ○ $45 - 31 = $ ▮

   ○ $31 - 45 = $ ▮

   ○ $45 + 31 = $ ▮

   ○ $76 - 31 = $ ▮

4. There were 36 apples on a tree. Some apples fell down. Now there are 11 apples on the tree. Which number sentence can be used to find how many apples fell down?

   ○ $36 + $ ▮ $ = 11$

   ○ $11 - $ ▮ $ = 36$

   ○ $36 - $ ▮ $ = 11$

   ○ $25 - $ ▮ $ = 11$

PROBLEM SOLVING REAL WORLD

Solve. Write or draw to explain.

5. There were 21 children in the library. After 7 children left the library, how many children were still in the library?

_____ children

COMMON CORE STANDARD CC.2.OA.1
Lesson Objective: Analyze word problems to determine what operations to use to solve multistep problems.

Solve Multistep Problems

Mr. Wright had 34 blue pencils and 25 red pencils.
He gave 42 pencils to students. How many pencils
does he have now?

The first sentence tells you what Mr. Wright had.

 and

$$\begin{array}{r} 34 \\ +25 \\ \hline 59 \end{array}$$

The second sentence tells you that he gave
42 of the pencils to students.

$$\begin{array}{r} 59 \\ -42 \\ \hline 17 \end{array}$$

Mr. Wright has __17__ pencils now.

Solve the problem in steps. Show what you did.

1. Kara had 37 stickers. She gave
   11 stickers to Sam and 5 stickers
   to Jane. How many stickers does
   Kara have now?

   _____ stickers

1. There were 53 people in line at the movies. Then 17 people left the line. Later, 22 more people left. How many people are in line now?

   ○ 4   ○ 24
   ○ 14   ○ 58

2. Molly has 39 coins in her collection. Her sister has 26 coins. How many more coins are needed so they will have 85 coins in all?

   ○ 20   ○ 30
   ○ 21   ○ 65

3. Jack counted 48 ants on one log and 33 ants on another log. Some ants left. Then there were 54 ants in all. How many ants left?

   ○ 17   ○ 27
   ○ 21   ○ 81

4. There were 24 ducks on a pond. Then 27 more ducks came to the pond. Later, 14 ducks flew away. How many ducks are on the pond now?

   ○ 51   ○ 27
   ○ 37   ○ 21

PROBLEM SOLVING

Solve. Write or draw to explain.

5. Ava has 25 books. She gives away 7 books. Then Tom gives her 12 books. How many books does Ava have now?

   _____ books

Name_____

Lesson 8

COMMON CORE STANDARD CC.2.OA.2
Lesson Objective: Use doubles facts as a strategy for finding sums for near doubles facts.

Use Doubles Facts

Use doubles facts to help you find sums.

If you know 6 + 6,
you can find 6 + 7.

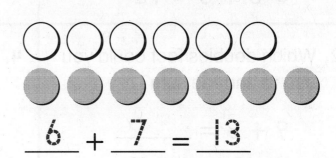

$$\underline{6} + \underline{6} = \underline{12}$$

7 is 1 more than 6.
So 6 + 7 is 1 more than 6 + 6.

$$\underline{6} + \underline{7} = \underline{13}$$

Write a doubles fact you can use to find the sum. Write the sum.

1. 4 + 5 = ____   ____ + ____ = ____

2. 5 + 6 = ____   ____ + ____ = ____

3. 7 + 8 = ____   ____ + ____ = ____

4. 8 + 9 = ____   ____ + ____ = ____

1. Which doubles fact could you use to find the sum?

$$4 + 5 = \rule{2cm}{0.4pt}$$

- ○ $3 + 3 = 6$
- ○ $4 + 6 = 10$
- ○ $5 + 5 = 10$
- ○ $6 + 6 = 12$

2. Which doubles fact could you use to find the sum?

$$9 + 8 = \rule{2cm}{0.4pt}$$

- ○ $8 + 8 = 16$
- ○ $7 + 7 = 14$
- ○ $9 + 1 = 10$
- ○ $10 + 10 = 20$

3. What is the sum?

$$7 + 6 = \rule{2cm}{0.4pt}$$

- ○ 11
- ○ 12
- ○ 13
- ○ 14

4. Maggie picked 3 apples. Lisa picked 4 apples. How many apples did they pick in all?

- ○ 6
- ○ 7
- ○ 8
- ○ 9

PROBLEM SOLVING

Solve. Write or draw to explain.

5. There are 6 ants on a log. Then 7 ants crawl onto the log. How many ants are on the log now?

_____ ants

Lesson 9

COMMON CORE STANDARD CC.2.OA.2

Lesson Objective: Recall sums for basic facts using properties and strategies.

Practice Addition Facts

Use what you know to find sums.

☆☆☆ ★★★★★

Add in any order. $3 + 5 = \underline{8}$

★★★★★ ☆☆☆

If you know $3 + 5$,
then you know $5 + 3$. $5 + 3 = \underline{8}$

☆☆☆☆☆ ★

Count on to add. To add 1, 2, or 3 to any
number, count on from that number. $5 + 1 = \underline{6}$

Write the sums.

1. $5 + 7 = \underline{}$ $7 + 5 = \underline{}$	2. $\underline{} = 5 + 1$ $\underline{} = 5 + 2$	3. $6 + 2 = \underline{}$ $6 + 3 = \underline{}$
4. $\underline{} = 9 + 5$ $\underline{} = 5 + 9$	5. $7 + 3 = \underline{}$ $3 + 7 = \underline{}$	6. $5 + 2 = \underline{}$ $5 + 3 = \underline{}$
7. $\underline{} = 3 + 6$ $\underline{} = 6 + 3$	8. $4 + 1 = \underline{}$ $1 + 4 = \underline{}$	9. $8 + 2 = \underline{}$ $8 + 3 = \underline{}$

1. What is the sum for both number sentences?

$$6 + 1 = \underline{\hspace{2cm}}$$

$$1 + 6 = \underline{\hspace{2cm}}$$

- ○ 4
- ○ 5
- ○ 6
- ○ 7

2. What is the sum?

$$8 + 7 = \underline{\hspace{2cm}}$$

- ○ 13
- ○ 14
- ○ 15
- ○ 16

3. Which of the following has the same sum?

$$2 + 9 = ?$$

- ○ 8 + 2
- ○ 9 + 2
- ○ 2 + 10
- ○ 3 + 9

4. Marco had 6 stamps. His mother gave him 3 more stamps. How many stamps does Marco have now?

- ○ 7
- ○ 8
- ○ 9
- ○ 10

PROBLEM SOLVING

Solve. Write or draw to explain.

5. Jason has 7 puzzles. Quincy has the same number of puzzles as Jason. How many puzzles do they have altogether?

_____ puzzles

Core Standards for Math, Grade 2

Name_____

Lesson 10

COMMON CORE STANDARD CC.2.OA.2

Lesson Objective: Recall sums for addition facts using the make a ten strategy.

Algebra • Make a Ten to Add

$8 + 5 = \underline{\ ?\ }$

Step ① Start with the greater addend.
Break apart the other addend to make a ten.

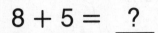

Step ② You need to add **2** to 8 to make a ten. So, break apart 5 as **2** and 3.

$8 + 2 = 10$ 3

Step ③ Add on the rest to the 10. $10 + \underline{\ 3\ } = \underline{\ 13\ }$

Step ④ Write the sum. $8 + 5 = \underline{\ 13\ }$

Show how you can make a ten to find the sum. Write the sum.

1. $7 + 6 = \underline{\ \ \ }$

3 3

$10 + \underline{\ \ \ } = \underline{\ \ \ }$

2. $9 + 2 = \underline{\ \ \ }$

1 1

$10 + \underline{\ \ \ } = \underline{\ \ \ }$

3. $4 + 8 = \underline{\ \ \ }$

2 2

$10 + \underline{\ \ \ } = \underline{\ \ \ }$

4. $5 + 9 = \underline{\ \ \ }$

$10 + \underline{\ \ \ } = \underline{\ \ \ }$

5. $8 + 6 = \underline{\ \ \ }$

$10 + \underline{\ \ \ } = \underline{\ \ \ }$

6. $4 + 9 = \underline{\ \ \ }$

$10 + \underline{\ \ \ } = \underline{\ \ \ }$

Core Standards for Math, Grade 2

I. How could you break apart the 7 to make a ten?

6 + 7

6 + _____ + _____

- ○ 2 + 5
- ○ 4 + 3
- ○ 5 + 2
- ○ 1 + 6

3. How could you break apart the 9 to make a ten?

8 + 9

8 + _____ + _____

- ○ 7 + 2
- ○ 4 + 5
- ○ 2 + 7
- ○ 3 + 6

2. What is the sum?

9 + 5 = _____

- ○ 11
- ○ 12
- ○ 13
- ○ 14

4. What is the sum?

4 + 8 = _____

- ○ 2
- ○ 12
- ○ 13
- ○ 16

PROBLEM SOLVING

Solve. Write or draw to explain.

5. There are 9 children on the bus. Then 8 more children get on the bus. How many children are on the bus now?

_____ children

Name_____

Lesson 11

COMMON CORE STANDARD CC.2.OA.2

Lesson Objective: Find sums of three addends by applying the Commutative and Associative Properties of Addition.

Algebra • Add 3 Addends

Add numbers in any order.
The sum stays the same.

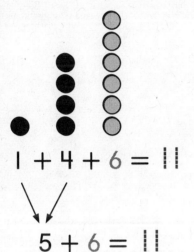 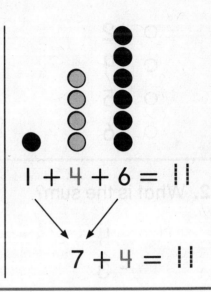

$1 + 4 + 6 = 11$ $1 + 4 + 6 = 11$ $1 + 4 + 6 = 11$

$5 + 6 = 11$ $1 + 10 = 11$ $7 + 4 = 11$

Solve two ways. Circle the two addends you add first.

1. $2 + 3 + 2 = $ _____ $2 + 3 + 2 = $ _____

2. $7 + 2 + 3 = $ _____ $7 + 2 + 3 = $ _____

3. $1 + 1 + 9 = $ _____ $1 + 1 + 9 = $ _____

4. $6 + 4 + 4 = $ _____ $6 + 4 + 4 = $ _____

1. What is the sum?

$$2 + 4 + 8 = \underline{\hspace{1cm}}$$

○ 12
○ 14
○ 15
○ 16

2. What is the sum?

$$\begin{array}{r} 4 \\ 3 \\ + 6 \\ \hline \end{array}$$

○ 13
○ 10
○ 9
○ 7

3. What is the sum?

$$\begin{array}{r} 4 \\ 5 \\ + 7 \\ \hline \end{array}$$

○ 9
○ 11
○ 16
○ 17

4. Ava grows 3 red flowers, 4 yellow flowers, and 4 purple flowers in her garden. How many flowers does Ava grow in all?

○ 7
○ 8
○ 10
○ 11

PROBLEM SOLVING  REAL WORLD

Choose a way to solve. Write or draw to explain.

5. Amber has 2 red crayons, 5 blue crayons, and 4 yellow crayons. How many crayons does she have in all?

_____ crayons

Name_____

Lesson 12

COMMON CORE STANDARD CC.2.OA.2
Lesson Objective: Use the inverse relationship
of addition and subtraction to recall basic facts.

Algebra • Relate Addition and Subtraction

Use addition facts to help you subtract.

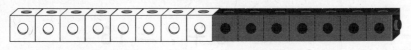

$8 + 7 = 15$

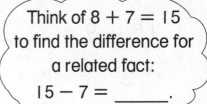

Think of $8 + 7 = 15$
to find the difference for
a related fact:

$15 - 7 =$ _____.

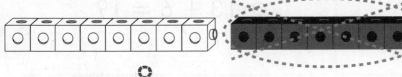

$15 - 7 = \underline{8}$

Write the sum and the difference for the related facts.

1. $6 + 3 =$ _____

    $9 - 6 =$ _____

2. $7 + 6 =$ _____

    $13 - 7 =$ _____

3. $6 + 8 =$ _____

    $14 - 8 =$ _____

4. $7 + 4 =$ _____

    $11 - 7 =$ _____

5. $8 + 4 =$ _____

    $12 - 4 =$ _____

6. $8 + 8 =$ _____

    $16 - 8 =$ _____

7. $9 + 7 =$ _____

    $16 - 7 =$ _____

8. $7 + 5 =$ _____

    $12 - 7 =$ _____

1. What is the difference for the related subtraction fact?

$$9 + 6 = 15$$

$$15 - 9 = \underline{\hspace{1cm}}$$

○ 3
○ 4
○ 5
○ 6

3. Which shows a related addition fact?

$$13 - 6 = 7$$

○ $6 + 7 = 13$
○ $7 + 13 = 20$
○ $7 - 6 = 1$
○ $13 + 6 = 19$

2. What is the sum for the related addition fact?

$$12 - 7 = 5$$

$$5 + 7 = \underline{\hspace{1cm}}$$

○ 11
○ 12
○ 13
○ 14

4. There are 11 brown birds and 5 red birds in a tree. How many more brown birds than red birds are there?

○ 5
○ 6
○ 7
○ 9

PROBLEM SOLVING  REAL WORLD

Solve. Write or draw to explain.

5. There are 13 children on the bus. Then 5 children get off the bus. How many children are on the bus now?

_____ children

Name_____

Lesson 13

COMMON CORE STANDARD CC.2.OA.2
Lesson Objective: Recall differences for basic facts using mental strategies.

Practice Subtraction Facts

Here are two ways to find differences.

$10 - 3 = \underline{\ ?\ }$

Count back 1, 2, or 3.

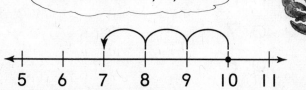

5 6 7 8 9 10 11

$10 - 1 = \underline{\ 9\ }$

$10 - 2 = \underline{\ 8\ }$

$10 - 3 = \underline{\ 7\ }$

Think of a related addition fact.

$3 + 7 = \underline{\ 10\ }$

$\underline{\ 7\ }$

So, $10 - 3 = \underline{\ 7\ }$.

Write the difference.

1. $13 - 5 = \underline{\qquad}$

2. $10 - 4 = \underline{\qquad}$

3. $12 - 3 = \underline{\qquad}$

4. $11 - 2 = \underline{\qquad}$

5. $9 - 3 = \underline{\qquad}$

6. $12 - 5 = \underline{\qquad}$

7. $16 - 8 = \underline{\qquad}$

8. $13 - 7 = \underline{\qquad}$

1. What is the difference?

$$15 - 7 = \underline{\hspace{2cm}}$$

- ○ 7
- ○ 8
- ○ 12
- ○ 15

2. What is the difference?

$$\underline{\hspace{2cm}} = 13 - 9$$

- ○ 4
- ○ 5
- ○ 6
- ○ 7

3. What is the difference?

$$16 - 7 = \underline{\hspace{2cm}}$$

- ○ 9
- ○ 8
- ○ 7
- ○ 6

4. Elena invited 8 friends to her party. 2 of them could not go. How many friends went to Elena's party?

- ○ 2
- ○ 4
- ○ 5
- ○ 6

PROBLEM SOLVING  REAL WORLD

Solve. Write or draw to explain.

5. Mr. Li has 16 pencils. He gives 9 pencils to some students. How many pencils does Mr. Li have now?

_____ pencils

Name_____

Lesson 14

COMMON CORE STANDARD CC.2.OA.2

Lesson Objective: Find differences on a
number line to develop the mental strategy
of decomposing to simplify facts.

Use Ten to Subtract

You can get to ten to help find differences.

$$13 - 7 = \underline{\ \ ?\ \ }$$

Step ① Start with the first number.

Step ② Subtract ones to get to 10.

$$13 - 3 = 10$$

Step ③ Subtract the rest from the 10.

    Think: I had 13. I subtracted 3 to get to 10.

             Now I subtract the 4 I have left. $10 - \underline{4} = \underline{6}$

Step ④ Write the difference. $13 - 7 = \underline{6}$

Show the tens fact you used. Write the difference.

1. $15 - 8 = \underline{\ \ \ \ \ }$

    5   3

   $10 - \underline{3} = \underline{\ \ \ \ \ }$

2. $12 - 4 = \underline{\ \ \ \ \ }$

    2   2

   $10 - \underline{\ \ \ \ } = \underline{\ \ \ \ \ }$

3. $11 - 7 = \underline{\ \ \ \ \ }$

   $10 - \underline{\ \ \ \ } = \underline{\ \ \ \ \ }$

4. $13 - 5 = \underline{\ \ \ \ \ }$

   $10 - \underline{\ \ \ \ } = \underline{\ \ \ \ \ }$

1. Which tens fact could you use to find the difference?

$$11 - 4 = \underline{\hspace{1cm}}$$

? ?

- ○ $10 - 5 = 5$
- ○ $10 - 4 = 6$
- ○ $10 - 3 = 7$
- ○ $10 - 2 = 8$

2. Which tens fact could you use to find the difference?

$$16 - 7 = \underline{\hspace{1cm}}$$

? ?

- ○ $10 - 4 = 6$
- ○ $10 - 3 = 7$
- ○ $10 - 2 = 8$
- ○ $10 - 1 = 9$

3. Mr. Brown picked 12 plums. He gave 8 plums away. How many plums did he have left?

- ○ 3
- ○ 4
- ○ 5
- ○ 6

4. Which number makes the number sentence true?

$$13 - 5 = 8$$

$$10 - \underline{\hspace{1cm}} = 8$$

- ○ 2
- ○ 3
- ○ 4
- ○ 6

PROBLEM SOLVING

Solve. Write or draw to explain.

5. Carl read 15 pages on Monday night and 9 pages on Tuesday night. How many more pages did he read on Monday night than on Tuesday night?

_____ more pages

COMMON CORE STANDARD CC.2.OA.3
Lesson Objective: Classify numbers up to 20 as even or odd.

Algebra • Even and Odd Numbers

These are even numbers.
They show pairs with no cubes left over.

4 is even.   6 is even.   8 is even.   10 is even.

These are odd numbers.
They show pairs with 1 cube left over.

3 is odd.   5 is odd.   7 is odd.   9 is odd.

Count out the number of cubes.
Make pairs. Then write even or odd.

1.
15 _____

2.
11 _____

3.
12 _____

4.
13 _____

5.
16 _____

6.
14 _____

1. The Morris family has an even number of dogs and an odd number of cats. Which could be the number of pets in the Morris family?

   ○ 1 dog and 2 cats
   ○ 1 dog and 3 cats
   ○ 2 dogs and 2 cats
   ○ 2 dogs and 1 cat

2. Elsa shades a pair of ten frames to show an even number. Which could be Elsa's ten frames?

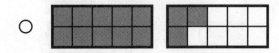

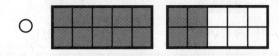

○

PROBLEM SOLVING

3. Mr. Dell has an odd number of sheep and an even number of cows on his farm. Circle the choice that could tell about his farm.

   9 sheep and 10 cows

   10 sheep and 11 cows

   8 sheep and 12 cows

Name_____

Lesson 16

COMMON CORE STANDARD CC.2.OA.3
Lesson Objective: Write equations with
equal addends to represent even numbers.

Algebra • Represent
Even Numbers

An even number of cubes will make two equal groups.

Count 8 cubes. Put the cubes into two equal groups. Do the two groups
have equal numbers of cubes? To check, match one to one.

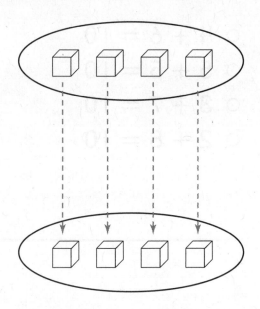

$$8 = \underline{\quad 4 \quad} + \underline{\quad 4 \quad}$$

How many cubes are there in all? Complete the addition
sentence to show the equal groups.

1. _____ = _____ + _____

2. _____ = _____ + _____

3. _____ = _____ + _____

4. _____ = _____ + _____

Core Standards for Math, Grade 2

1. The frames show two groups for 8. Which addition sentence shows the groups?

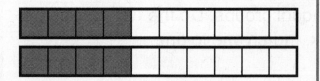

- ○ 1 + 7 = 8
- ○ 2 + 6 = 8
- ○ 3 + 5 = 8
- ○ 4 + 4 = 8

2. Mary and Ana each have the same number of stickers. They have 10 stickers altogether. Which addition sentence shows the number of stickers Mary and Ana each have?

- ○ 4 + 6 = 10
- ○ 5 + 5 = 10
- ○ 3 + 7 = 10
- ○ 2 + 8 = 10

PROBLEM SOLVING

Solve. Write or draw to explain.

3. The seats in a van are in pairs. There are 16 seats. How many pairs of seats are there?

_____ pairs of seats

Name_____

Lesson 17

COMMON CORE STANDARD CC.2.OA.4
Lesson Objective: Solve problems involving
equal groups by using the strategy *act it out*.

Problem Solving • Equal Groups

Clarence puts grapes in 4 rows.
He puts 5 grapes in each row.
How many grapes does Clarence have?

Unlock the Problem

What do I need to find?

<u>how many grapes</u>
_____

Clarence has

**What information do
I need to use?**

Clarence has ___4___ rows of
grapes.

He puts ___5___ grapes in each row.

Show how to solve the problem.

○○○○○
○○○○○
○○○○○
○○○○○

Clarence has ___20___ grapes.

Draw to show what you did.

1. Rachel puts her markers in 3 rows.
   Each row has 3 markers.
   How many markers does Rachel have?

Rachel has _____ markers.

Name_____

1. Ms. Green put 4 stamps on each card. How many stamps will she put on 5 cards?

   ○ 20
   ○ 16
   ○ 9
   ○ 8

2. Gina has 4 mice cages. There are 4 mice in each cage. How many mice does Gina have?

   ○ 8
   ○ 10
   ○ 12
   ○ 16

3. Eric puts his dimes in 5 rows. He puts 3 dimes in each row. How many dimes does he have in all?

   ○ 5
   ○ 8
   ○ 12
   ○ 15

4. Rachel puts 4 pencils in each box. How many pencils will she put in 3 boxes?

   ○ 16
   ○ 12
   ○ 7
   ○ 4

5. Rob puts 3 counters in each row. How many counters in all does he put in 4 rows? Draw to show your work.

_____ counters

COMMON CORE STANDARD CC.2.OA.4

Lesson Objective: Write equations using repeated addition to find the total number of objects in arrays.

Algebra • Repeated Addition

Find the total number of cats.

- Circle each row.

- Count how many rows.

  ___3___ equal rows

- Count how many in one row.

  ___4___ cats in one row

- Write an addition sentence. Add the number of cats in each row.

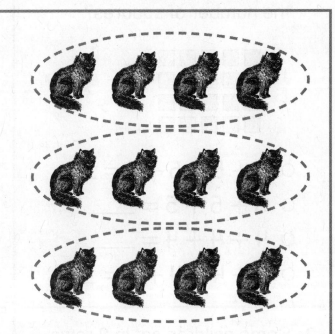

$$\underline{4} + \underline{4} + \underline{4} = \underline{12}$$

Find the number of shapes in each row.
Complete the addition sentence to find the total.

1. ● ● ● ● ●
    ● ● ● ● ●
    ● ● ● ● ●

    3 rows of _____

    ___ + ___ + ___ = ___

2. ✗ ✗ ✗ ✗
    ✗ ✗ ✗ ✗
    ✗ ✗ ✗ ✗
    ✗ ✗ ✗ ✗

    4 rows of _____

    ___ + ___ + ___ + ___ = ___

Core Standards for Math, Grade 2

1. Which could you use to find the number of squares?

- ○ 5 + 5 + 5 + 5 = ___
- ○ 5 + 5 + 5 = ___
- ○ 4 + 4 + 4 = ___
- ○ 4 + 4 + 4 + 4 = ___

3. Which could you use to find the number of circles?

- ○ 3 + 3 + 3 = ___
- ○ 3 + 3 + 3 + 3 = ___
- ○ 5 + 5 + 5 = ___
- ○ 5 + 5 + 5 + 5 = ___

2. Some children sat in 2 rows. There were 3 children in each row. How many children were there in all?

- ○ 1
- ○ 2
- ○ 5
- ○ 6

4. Mr. Henry has 4 rows of trees. There are 2 trees in each row. How many trees does he have in all?

- ○ 10
- ○ 8
- ○ 6
- ○ 2

PROBLEM SOLVING

Solve. Write or draw to explain.

5. A classroom has 3 rows of desks. There are 5 desks in each row. How many desks are there altogether?

_____ desks

Name_____

Explore 3-Digit Numbers

COMMON CORE STANDARD CC.2.NBT.1
Lesson Objective: Write 3-digit numbers
that are represented by groups of tens.

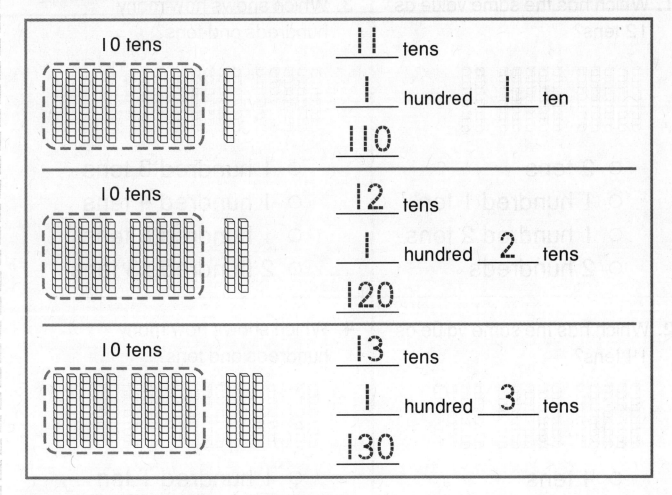

10 tens

____11____ tens

____1____ hundred ____1____ ten

110

10 tens

____12____ tens

____1____ hundred ____2____ tens

120

10 tens

____13____ tens

____1____ hundred ____3____ tens

130

Circle tens to make 1 hundred.
Write the number in different ways.

1. _____ tens

   _____ hundred _____ tens

   _____

2. _____ tens

   _____ hundred _____ tens

   _____

1. Which has the same value as
   12 tens?

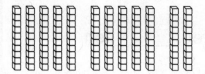

- ○ 2 tens
- ○ 1 hundred 1 ten
- ○ 1 hundred 2 tens
- ○ 2 hundreds

2. Which has the same value as
   14 tens?

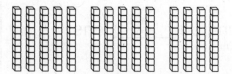

- ○ 4 tens
- ○ 40 tens
- ○ 1 hundred 4 tens
- ○ 1 hundred 14 tens

3. Which shows how many
   hundreds and tens?

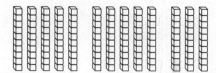

- ○ 1 hundred 3 tens
- ○ 1 hundred 4 tens
- ○ 1 hundred 8 tens
- ○ 2 hundreds 3 tens

4. Which shows how many
   hundreds and tens?

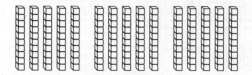

- ○ 1 hundred 1 ten
- ○ 1 hundred 5 tens
- ○ 5 hundreds 1 ten
- ○ 5 hundreds 5 tens

PROBLEM SOLVING REAL WORLD

Solve. Write or draw to explain.

5. Millie has a box of 1 hundred cubes.
   She also has a bag of 70 cubes.
   How many trains of 10 cubes
   can she make?

_____ trains of 10 cubes

Name_____

Lesson **20**

COMMON CORE STANDARD CC.2.NBT.1
Lesson Objective: Use concrete and pictorial models to represent 3-digit numbers.

Model 3-Digit Numbers

Show 243.

Hundreds	Tens	Ones

With blocks:

In a chart:

Hundreds	Tens	Ones
2	4	3

With a quick picture:

Write how many hundreds, tens, and ones.
Show with 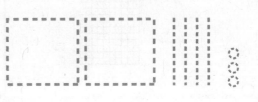. Then draw a quick picture.

1. 138

Hundreds	Tens	Ones

2. 217

Hundreds	Tens	Ones

3. 352

Hundreds	Tens	Ones

4. 174

Hundreds	Tens	Ones

1. Kelly uses blocks to make the number 102. Which shows 102?

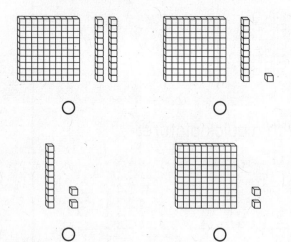

○   ○

○   ○

2. What number is shown with these blocks?

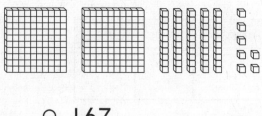

○ 167

○ 252

○ 257

○ 262

3. Which chart shows how many hundreds, tens, and ones are in 241?

○
Hundreds	Tens	Ones
4	2	1

○
Hundreds	Tens	Ones
2	4	1

○
Hundreds	Tens	Ones
1	4	2

○
Hundreds	Tens	Ones
2	1	4

4. Which chart shows how many hundreds, tens, and ones are in 423?

○
Hundreds	Tens	Ones
4	2	3

○
Hundreds	Tens	Ones
4	3	2

○
Hundreds	Tens	Ones
2	4	3

○
Hundreds	Tens	Ones
3	4	2

PROBLEM SOLVING

5. Write the number that matches the clues.

- My number has 2 hundreds.

- The tens digit is 9 more than the ones digit.

Hundreds	Tens	Ones

My number is _____.

Name_____

Lesson 21

COMMON CORE STANDARD CC.2.NBT.1

Lesson Objective: Apply place value concepts to write 3-digit numbers that are represented by pictorial models.

Hundreds, Tens, and Ones

How many are there in all?

Hundreds	Tens	Ones

____3____ hundreds ____2____ tens ____5____ ones

Write how many in the chart.

Hundreds	Tens	Ones
3	2	5

Write the number as hundreds plus tens plus ones.

_300_ + _20_ + _5_

3 hundreds 2 tens 5 ones is the same as __325__.

Write how many hundreds, tens, and ones are in the model. Write the number in two ways.

1.

Hundreds	Tens	Ones

____

____ + ____ + ____

2.

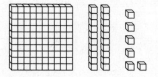

Hundreds	Tens	Ones

____

____ + ____ + ____

1. Count the hundreds, tens, and ones. Which number does the picture show?

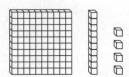

○ 441   ○ 141

○ 414   ○ 114

2. Which is a way to write the number shown with these blocks?

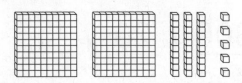

○ 200 + 20 + 5

○ 200 + 30 + 5

○ 300 + 20 + 5

○ 500 + 30 + 2

3. Liz has 248 beads. How many hundreds are in this number?

○ 2 hundreds

○ 4 hundreds

○ 6 hundreds

○ 8 hundreds

4. Ray sold 362 tickets to the show. Which is another way to write the number 362?

○ 6 hundreds 3 tens 2 ones

○ 3 hundreds 6 tens 3 ones

○ 3 hundreds 6 tens 2 ones

○ 2 hundreds 6 tens 3 ones

PROBLEM SOLVING REAL WORLD

5. Write the number that answers the riddle. Use the chart.

A model for my number has 6 ones blocks, 2 hundreds blocks, and 3 tens blocks.

What number am I?

Hundreds	Tens	Ones

_____

Core Standards for Math, Grade 2

Name______________________________

Lesson 22

COMMON CORE STANDARD CC.2.NBT.1

Lesson Objective: Use place value to describe the values of digits in numbers to 1,000.

Place Value to 1,000

The value of each digit in 426 is shown by its place in the number.

Hundreds	Tens	Ones
4 hundreds	2 tens	6 ones

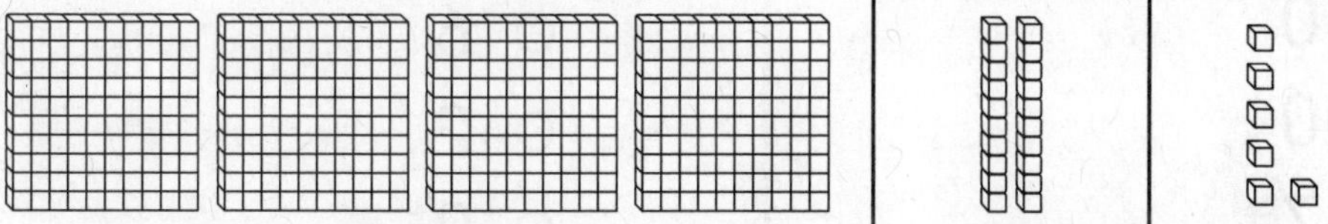

400	20	6

426

Circle the value or the meaning of the underlined digit.

1. 7<u>8</u>2	800	80	8
2. <u>3</u>52	3 hundreds	3 tens	3 ones
3. 7<u>4</u>2	4	40	400
4. 41<u>9</u>	9 hundreds	9 tens	9 ones
5. <u>5</u>84	500	50	5

1. A classroom has 537 books. What is the value of the digit 5 in 537?

  ○ 5
  ○ 50
  ○ 500
  ○ 537

3. Miss Brown drove 280 miles during summer vacation. What digit is in the tens place in the number 280?

  ○ 8
  ○ 6
  ○ 2
  ○ 0

2. There are 203 birds. What is the value of the digit 3 in the number 203?

  ○ 3
  ○ 30
  ○ 200
  ○ 300

4. Which number has the digit 6 in the hundreds place?

  ○ 68
  ○ 196
  ○ 362
  ○ 610

PROBLEM SOLVING

5. Write the 3-digit number that answers the riddle.
  • I have the same hundreds digit as ones digit.
  • The value of my tens digit is 50.
  • The value of my ones digit is 4.   The number is _____.

Name_____

Lesson 23

COMMON CORE STANDARDS CC.2.NBT.1a, CC.2.NBT.1b

Lesson Objective: Understand that each group of 10 tens is equivalent to 1 hundred.

Group Tens as Hundreds

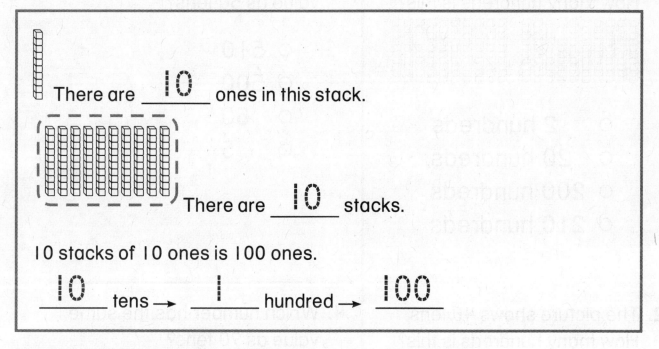

There are ___10___ ones in this stack.

There are ___10___ stacks.

10 stacks of 10 ones is 100 ones.

___10___ tens → ___1___ hundred → ___100___

Write how many tens. Circle groups of 10 tens.
Write how many hundreds. Write the number.

1.

_____ tens

_____ hundreds

_____ blocks

2.

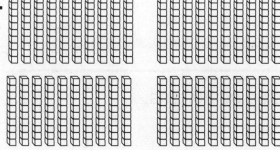

_____ tens

_____ hundreds

_____ blocks

1. The picture shows 20 tens. How many hundreds is this?

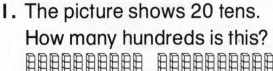

- ○ 2 hundreds
- ○ 20 hundreds
- ○ 200 hundreds
- ○ 210 hundreds

2. The picture shows 40 tens. How many hundreds is this?

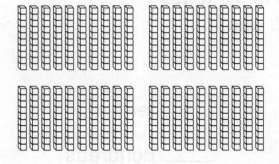

- ○ 410 hundreds
- ○ 400 hundreds
- ○ 40 hundreds
- ○ 4 hundreds

3. Which number has the same value as 50 tens?

- ○ 510
- ○ 500
- ○ 50
- ○ 5

4. Which number has the same value as 90 tens?

- ○ 910
- ○ 900
- ○ 90
- ○ 9

5. Write the number that has the same value as 30 tens.

_____

Lesson 24

COMMON CORE STANDARD CC.2.NBT.2

Lesson Objective: Extend counting sequences within 100, counting by 1s, 5s, and 10s.

Counting Patterns Within 100

You can count different ways.

Count by fives.

5, 10, 15, 20, 25, 30, 35

Count by tens.

10, 20, 30, 40, 50, 60

Count by fives.

1. 5, 10, 15, 20, _____ , _____ , _____

2. 20, 25, 30, 35, _____ , _____ , _____

3. 55, 60, 65, 70, _____ , _____ , _____

Count by tens.

4. 10, 20, 30, _____ , _____ , _____

5. 30, 40, 50, 60, _____ , _____ , _____

47
Core Standards for Math, Grade 2

1. Which group of numbers shows counting by fives?

   ○ 28, 27, 26, 25, 24

   ○ 35, 36, 37, 38, 39

   ○ 40, 50, 60, 70, 80

   ○ 55, 60, 65, 70, 75

3. Which group of numbers shows counting by ones?

   ○ 44, 45, 46, 47, 48

   ○ 25, 30, 35, 40, 45

   ○ 20, 30, 40, 50, 60

   ○ 10, 15, 20, 25, 30

2. Which group of numbers shows counting by tens?

   ○ 40, 41, 42, 44, 44

   ○ 50, 60, 70, 80, 90

   ○ 60, 65, 70, 75, 80

   ○ 70, 69, 68, 67, 66

4. Which group of numbers shows counting back by ones?

   ○ 30, 40, 50, 60, 70

   ○ 25, 30, 35, 30, 35

   ○ 16, 15, 14, 13, 12

   ○ 11, 12, 13, 14, 15

PROBLEM SOLVING

5. Tim counts his friends' fingers by fives.
   He counts six hands. What numbers does he say?

   5, _____ , _____ , _____ , _____ , _____

Lesson 25

COMMON CORE STANDARD CC.2.NBT.2

Lesson Objective: Extend counting sequences within 1,000, counting by 1s, 5s, 10s, and 100s.

Counting Patterns Within 1,000

You can count in different ways.
Look for a pattern to use.

Count by tens.

500, 510, 520, 530, 540, 550

Count by hundreds.

300, 400, 500, 600, 700, 800

Count by tens.

1. 410, 420, 430, _____ , _____

2. 730, 740, _____ , _____ , _____

3. 250, 260, _____ , _____ , _____

Count by hundreds.

4. 100, 200, 300, _____ , _____

5. 500, 600, _____ , _____ , _____

1. Which group of numbers shows counting by tens?

   ○ 610, 611, 612

   ○ 630, 640, 650

   ○ 635, 640, 645

   ○ 692, 691, 690

3. Which group of numbers shows counting by hundreds?

   ○ 500, 510, 520

   ○ 505, 510, 515

   ○ 400, 401, 402

   ○ 400, 500, 600

2. Which group of numbers shows counting by fives?

   ○ 340, 345, 350

   ○ 360, 361, 362

   ○ 430, 440, 450

   ○ 500, 600, 700

4. Which group of numbers shows counting back by ones?

   ○ 256, 257, 258

   ○ 225, 230, 235

   ○ 218, 217, 216

   ○ 190, 200, 210

PROBLEM SOLVING

5. Lee has a jar of 100 pennies.
   She adds groups of 10 pennies to the jar.
   She adds 5 groups. What numbers does she say?

   _____ , _____ , _____ , _____ , _____

Lesson 26

COMMON CORE STANDARD CC.2.NBT.3
Lesson Objective: Use place value to describe the values of digits in 2-digit numbers.

Understand Place Value

0, 1, 2, 3, 4, 5, 6, 7, 8, and 9 are digits.
A digit's place in a number shows
the value of the digit.

52 has two digits.

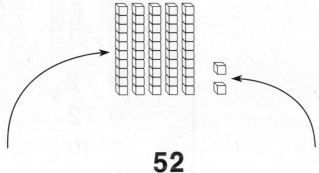

52

The digit __5__ is in the tens place.

The digit 5 shows __5__ tens.

Its value is __50__.

The digit __2__ is in the ones place.

The digit 2 shows __2__ ones.

Its value is __2__.

Circle the value of the underlined digit.

1. 2̲7	**2.** 1̲8	**3.** 5̲6
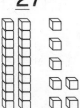	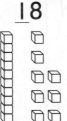	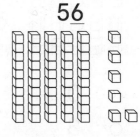
20 2	1 10	60 6
4. 3̲0	**5.** 7̲5	**6.** 4̲1
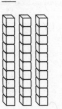	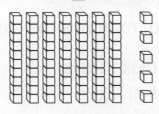	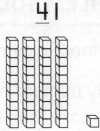
30 3	5 50	4 40

Name_____

1. What is the value of the underlined digit?

2̲7

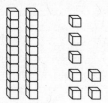

- ○ 2
- ○ 7
- ○ 20
- ○ 70

3. What is the value of the underlined digit?

48̲

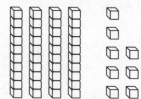

- ○ 8
- ○ 12
- ○ 40
- ○ 80

2. Lucas has 53 toy cars. What is the value of the digit 3 in the number 53?

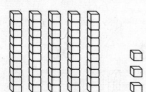

- ○ 0
- ○ 3
- ○ 10
- ○ 30

4. Ben has 62 crackers. What is the value of the 6 in this number?

- ○ 6
- ○ 8
- ○ 20
- ○ 60

PROBLEM SOLVING REAL WORLD

Write the 2-digit number that matches the clues.

5. My number has a tens digit that is 8 more than the ones digit. Zero is not one of my digits.

My number is _____.

Expanded Form

Show tens and ones in 43.

Tens	Ones

How many tens? __4__ tens　　　How many ones? __3__ ones

__43__ is __4__ tens __3__ ones

__43__ is __40__ + __3__

Describe the number in two ways.

1. 35

____ tens ____ ones

____ + ____

2. 63

____ tens ____ ones

____ + ____

3. 57

____ tens ____ ones

____ + ____

4. 19

____ tens ____ ones

____ + ____

1. Which shows another way to describe 27?

   ○ 20 + 7
   ○ 20 + 70
   ○ 2 + 7
   ○ 70 + 2

3. Which shows another way to describe 52?

   ○   5 + 2
   ○   20 + 5
   ○   50 + 2
   ○   500 + 2

2. Which shows another way to describe 65?

   ○ 5 tens 6 ones
   ○ 6 tens 0 ones
   ○ 6 tens 5 ones
   ○ 6 tens 6 ones

4. Which shows another way to describe 78?

   ○ 80 + 7
   ○ 70 + 8
   ○ 7 + 8
   ○ 80 + 70

PROBLEM SOLVING REAL WORLD

5. Circle the ways to write the number shown by the model.

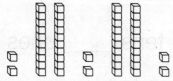

   4 tens 6 ones   40 + 6   64

   6 tens 4 ones   60 + 4   46

Name_____

Lesson 28

COMMON CORE STANDARD CC.2.NBT.3
Lesson Objective: Write 2-digit numbers in
word form, expanded form, and standard form.

Different Ways to Write Numbers

You can write numbers in different ways.

20 + 6   twenty-six

2 tens 6 ones   26

ones	teen words		tens	
1 one	11 eleven	1 ten 1 one	10 ten	1 ten
2 two	12 twelve	1 ten 2 ones	20 twenty	2 tens
3 three	13 thirteen	1 ten 3 ones	30 thirty	3 tens
4 four	14 fourteen	1 ten 4 ones	40 forty	4 tens
5 five	15 fifteen	1 ten 5 ones	50 fifty	5 tens
6 six	16 sixteen	1 ten 6 ones	60 sixty	6 tens
7 seven	17 seventeen	1 ten 7 ones	70 seventy	7 tens
8 eight	18 eighteen	1 ten 8 ones	80 eighty	8 tens
9 nine	19 nineteen	1 ten 9 ones	90 ninety	9 tens

Write the number another way.

1. twenty

_____

2. 37

_____ tens _____ ones

3. 40 + 5

_____

4. eighty-one

_____

5. 56

_____

6. 9 tens 2 ones

_____

7. 1 ten 8 ones

_____

8. seventy-three

_____ tens _____ ones

Name_____

1. Which is another way to write thirty-eight?

   ○ 8 tens 3 ones
   ○ 38
   ○ 3 + 8
   ○ 83

2. Which is another way to write 10 + 9?

   ○ 9 tens 10 ones
   ○ 91
   ○ nineteen
   ○ ninety

3. Which is another way to write 5 tens 6 ones?

   ○ 60 + 5
   ○ fifty
   ○ 65
   ○ 50 + 6

4. Which is another way to write 72?

   ○ 7 tens 2 ones
   ○ seventy
   ○ 7 + 2
   ○ 7 + 20

PROBLEM SOLVING REAL WORLD

5. A number has the digit 3 in the ones place and the digit 4 in the tens place. Which of these is another way to write this number? Circle it.

   3 + 4   40 + 3   30 + 4

Lesson 29

COMMON CORE STANDARD CC.2.NBT.3
Lesson Objective: Apply place value concepts to find equivalent representations of numbers.

Algebra • Different Names for Numbers

Here are some ways to show 28.

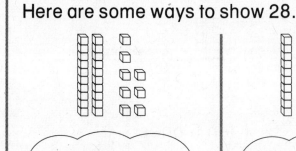 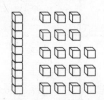 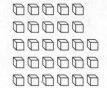

Describe the tens and ones with words and addition.

Describe the tens and ones with words and addition.

Describe the tens and ones with words and addition.

__2__ tens __8__ ones

__20__ + __8__

__1__ ten __18__ ones

__10__ + __18__

__0__ tens __28__ ones

__0__ + __28__

Describe the blocks in two ways.

1. 32

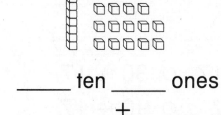

____ ten ____ ones

____ + ____

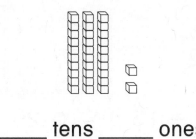

____ tens ____ ones

____ + ____

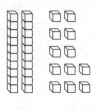

____ tens ____ ones

____ + ____

2. 47

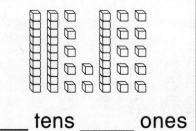

____ tens ____ ones

____ + ____

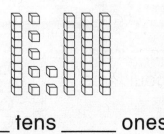

____ tens ____ ones

____ + ____

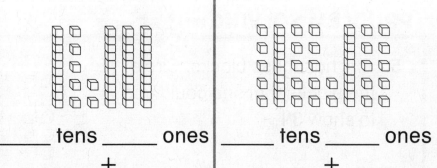

____ tens ____ ones

____ + ____

1. The blocks show 29. How many tens and ones are there?

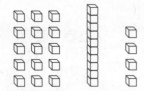

- ○ 2 tens 3 ones
- ○ 1 ten 19 ones
- ○ 1 ten 14 ones
- ○ 1 ten 9 ones

3. The blocks show 30. How many tens and ones are there?

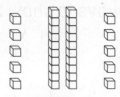

- ○ 1 ten 5 ones
- ○ 1 ten 10 ones
- ○ 2 tens 5 ones
- ○ 2 tens 10 ones

2. The blocks show 33. There are 2 tens and 13 ones. Which shows the number as tens plus ones?

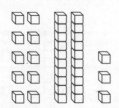

- ○ 20 + 3
- ○ 30 + 13
- ○ 20 + 13
- ○ 40 + 3

4. The blocks show 47. There are 3 tens and 17 ones. Which shows the number as tens plus ones?

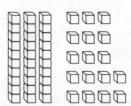

- ○ 20 + 17
- ○ 30 + 17
- ○ 30 + 7
- ○ 40 + 17

PROBLEM SOLVING REAL WORLD

5. Toni has these blocks. Circle the blocks that she could use to show 34.

Name_____

Lesson 30

COMMON CORE STANDARD CC.2.NBT.3
Lesson Objective: Solve problems by finding different combinations of tens and ones to represent 2-digit numbers using the strategy *find a pattern*.

Problem Solving • Tens and Ones

Anya has 25 toys. She can put them away in boxes of 10 toys or as single toys. What are the different ways Anya can put away the toys?

Unlock the Problem

What do I need to find?

the different ways

Anya can put away the toys

What information do I need to use?

She can put them away in

boxes of 10 toys or as

single toys.

Look for a pattern.

2 tens + 5 ones

1 ten + 15 ones

0 tens + 25 ones

Boxes of 10 toys	Single toys
2	5
1	15

Find a pattern to solve.

1. Mr. Moore is buying 29 apples. He can buy them in packs of 10 apples or as single apples. What are the different ways Mr. Moore can buy the apples?

Packs of 10 apples	Single apples
2	
1	
0	

1. Jon wants to buy 21 apples. What choice is missing from the list?

Bags of 10 apples	Single apples
2	1
1	11

○ 0 bags, 21 apples

○ 0 bags, 11 apples

○ 1 bag, 21 apples

○ 2 bags, 2 apples

2. Ms. Brice can buy markers in packs of 10 or as single markers. Which of these is a way she can buy 47 markers?

○ 4 packs, 17 markers

○ 3 packs, 17 markers

◉ 2 packs, 7 markers

○ 1 pack, 27 markers

3. Ann needs 12 folders for school. What choice is missing from the list?

Packs of 10 folders	Single folders
0	12

○ 2 packs, 0 folders

○ 2 packs, 1 folder

○ 1 pack, 12 folders

○ 1 pack, 2 folders

4. Jeff can carry his pears in bags of 10 pears or as single pears. Which of these is a way he can carry his 36 pears?

○ 2 bags, 26 pears

○ 6 bags, 3 pears

○ 3 bags, 6 pears

○ 1 bag, 16 pears

5. Stamps are sold in packs of 10 stamps or as single stamps. Leah wants to buy 26 stamps. What are all of the different ways she can buy the stamps?

Packs of 10 stamps	Single stamps

Name_____

Lesson 31

COMMON CORE STANDARD CC.2.NBT.3
Lesson Objective: Read and write 3-digit
numbers in word form.

Number Names

You can write a number using words.

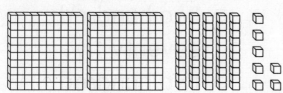

257

What is shown with the
hundreds blocks?

___two hundred___

What is shown with the
tens and ones blocks?

___fifty-seven___

So you write 257 as ___two hundred fifty-seven___ .

Write the number using words.

1. 163

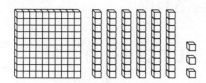

_____

2. 427

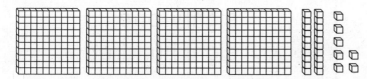

_____

Write the number.

3. two hundred nine

_____

4. five hundred seventy-nine

_____

1. There are five hundred twenty-three children at the school. Which shows this number?

   ○ 520
   ○ 523
   ○ 530
   ○ 532

3. Which is another way to write the number 275?

   ○ two hundred seventy-five
   ○ two hundred seventy
   ○ two hundred fifty-seven
   ○ two hundred five

2. Vin has three hundred forty pieces in his puzzle. Which shows this number?

   ○ 304
   ○ 314
   ○ 340
   ○ 341

4. Which is another way to write the number 618?

   ○ six hundred eight
   ○ six hundred eighteen
   ○ six hundred eighty-one
   ○ eight hundred sixteen

5. Write the number 454 using words.

_____

Name_____

Different Forms of Numbers

COMMON CORE STANDARD CC.2.NBT.3
Lesson Objective: Write 3-digit numbers in expanded form and in standard form.

There is more than one way to show and write a number.

three hundred sixty-two

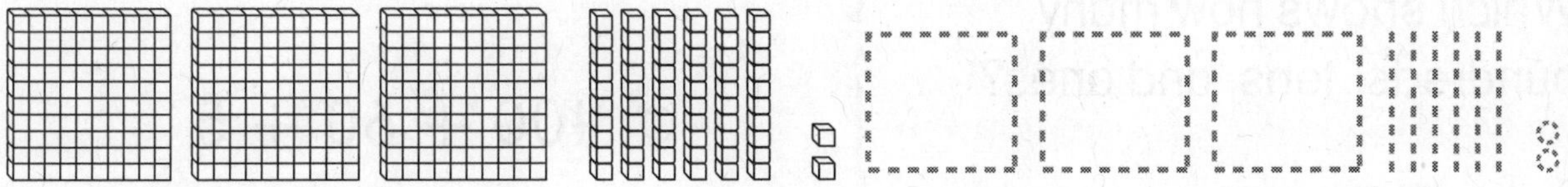

__3__ hundreds __6__ tens __2__ ones

$$\underline{300} + \underline{60} + \underline{2}$$
$$\underline{362}$$

Read the number and draw a quick picture.
Then write the number in different ways.

1. four hundred thirty-two

_____ hundreds _____ tens _____ ones

_____ + _____ + _____

_____

2. two hundred seventy-five

_____ hundreds _____ tens _____ ones

_____ + _____ + _____

_____

1. Look at the picture.

Which shows how many hundreds, tens, and ones?

- ○ 2 hundreds 4 tens 3 ones
- ○ 3 hundreds 3 tens 4 ones
- ○ 3 hundreds 2 tens 4 ones
- ○ 2 hundreds 3 tens 4 ones

2. Claudia has four hundred sixty-five stickers in her collection. Which is another way to write the number?

- ○ 400 + 60 + 5
- ○ 400 + 600 + 5
- ○ 40 + 60 + 5
- ○ 4 + 6 + 5

PROBLEM SOLVING REAL WORLD

Write the number another way.

3. 200 + 30 + 7

_____

4. 895

_____

Name_____

Lesson 33

COMMON CORE STANDARD CC.2.NBT.3

Lesson Objective: Apply place value concepts to find equivalent representations of numbers.

Algebra • Different Ways to Show Numbers

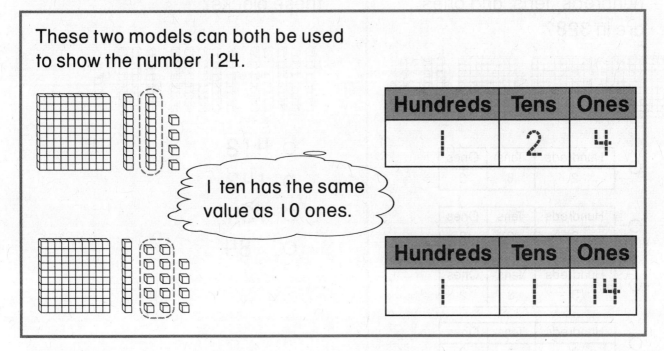

These two models can both be used to show the number 124.

I ten has the same value as 10 ones.

Hundreds	Tens	Ones
1	2	4

Hundreds	Tens	Ones
1	1	14

Write how many hundreds, tens, and ones are in the model.

1. 132

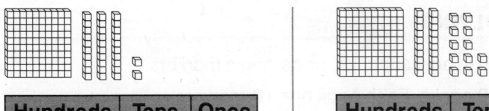

Hundreds	Tens	Ones

Hundreds	Tens	Ones

2. 246

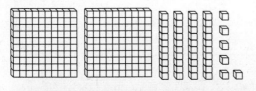

Hundreds	Tens	Ones

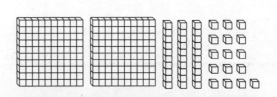

Hundreds	Tens	Ones

1. Which shows how many hundreds, tens, and ones are in 328?

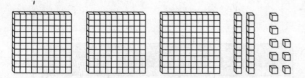

○
Hundreds	Tens	Ones
2	8	3

○
Hundreds	Tens	Ones
3	2	8

○
Hundreds	Tens	Ones
3	8	2

○
Hundreds	Tens	Ones
8	2	3

2. What number is shown with these blocks?

○ 413

○ 143

○ 134

○ 84

PROBLEM SOLVING REAL WORLD

Markers are sold in boxes, packs, or as single markers.

Each box has 10 packs. Each pack has 10 markers.

3. Draw pictures to show two ways to buy 276 markers.

Name_____

Lesson 34

COMMON CORE STANDARD CC.2.NBT.4
Lesson Objective: Solve problems involving
number comparisons by using the strategy
make a model.

Problem Solving • Compare Numbers

At the zoo, there are 137 birds and 142 reptiles.
Are there more birds or more reptiles at the zoo?

Unlock the Problem

What do I need to find?

I need to find if there are

more _**birds**_ or _**reptiles**_ .

**What information do
I need to use?**

There are __137__ birds.

There are __142__ reptiles.

Show how to solve the problem.

Birds   Reptiles

The number of hundreds is the same.
There are more tens in the number of reptiles.

There are more _**reptiles**_ at the zoo.

Draw quick pictures to model the numbers.

1. There are 153 birds and 149 fish at the nature center.
   Are there more birds or more fish?

   There are more _____ .

Name_____

1. There are 174 markers in a bin. Which number is greater than 174?

- ○ 138
- ○ 154
- ○ 147
- ○ 179

2. There are 213 books in the classroom. Which number is less than 213?

- ○ 231
- ○ 205
- ○ 276
- ○ 250

3. There are 332 puzzle pieces in a box. Which number is greater than 332?

- ○ 286
- ○ 241
- ○ 391
- ○ 323

4. There are 409 pennies in a jar. Which number is less than 409?

- ○ 390
- ○ 419
- ○ 437
- ○ 526

5. Tim has 128 paper clips. Draw a quick picture to show a number that is greater than the number of paper clips.

Lesson 35

COMMON CORE STANDARD CC.2.NBT.4
Lesson Objective: Compare 3-digit numbers using the >, =, and < symbols.

Algebra • Compare Numbers

To compare 3-digit numbers, first compare hundreds.

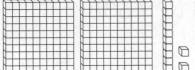

2̲12 has more hundreds than 1̲12.

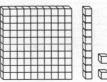

$212 \; \large{>} \; 112$

If hundreds are equal, then compare tens.

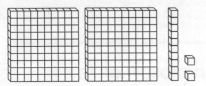

21̲2 has fewer tens than 22̲1.

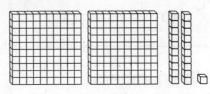

$212 \; \large{<} \; 221$

If hundreds and tens are equal, then compare ones.

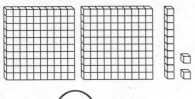

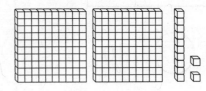

$21\underline{2} \; \large{=} \; 21\underline{2}$

Compare the numbers. Write >, <, or =.

1. 317 ◯ 326

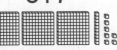 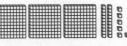

2. 582 ◯ 634

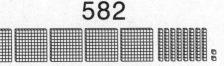 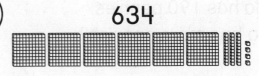

1. Compare the numbers.
Use >, <, or =.

Hundreds	Tens	Ones
2	4	1
2	1	4

241 ◯ 214

>   <   =
◯   ◯   ◯

2. Compare the numbers.
Use >, <, or =.

Hundreds	Tens	Ones
4	1	4
4	4	0

414 ◯ 440

>   <   =
◯   ◯   ◯

3. Compare the numbers.
Use >, <, or =.

638 ◯ 638

>   <   =
◯   ◯   ◯

4. Which of the following is greater than 357?

◯ 140

◯ 272

◯ 346

◯ 481

PROBLEM SOLVING

Solve. Write or draw to explain.

5. Toby has 178 pennies.
Bella has 190 pennies.
Who has more pennies?

_____ has more pennies.

Name ______________________

Lesson 36

COMMON CORE STANDARD CC.2.NBT.5

Lesson Objective: Record 2-digit addition using the standard algorithm.

2-Digit Addition

Add 27 and 36.

STEP 1

Model 27 and 36.
Add the ones.

7 + 6 = 13

	Tens	Ones
	☐	
	2	7
+	3	6

STEP 2

If you can make a 10, regroup 10 ones for 1 ten.

13 ones = 1 ten 3 ones

	Tens	Ones
	1	
	2	7
+	3	6
		3

STEP 3

Add the tens.
Remember to add the regrouped ten.

1 + 2 + 3 = 6

	Tens	Ones
	1	
	2	7
+	3	6
	6	3

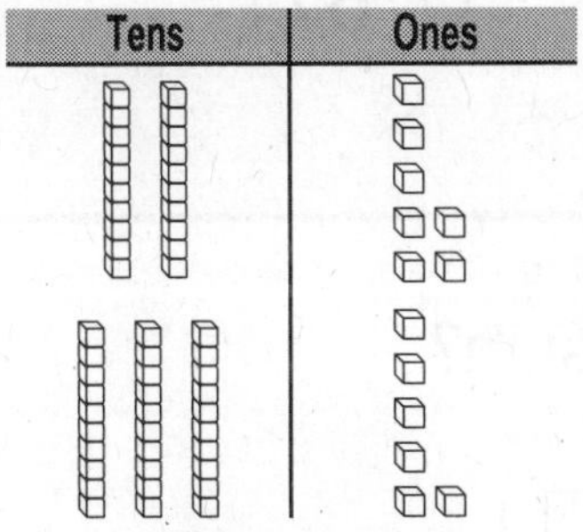

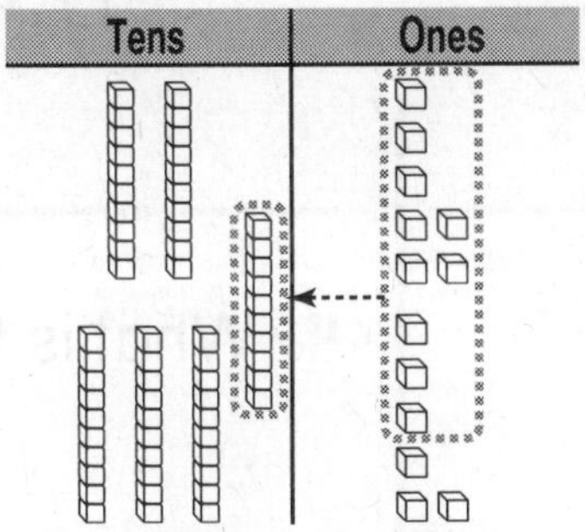

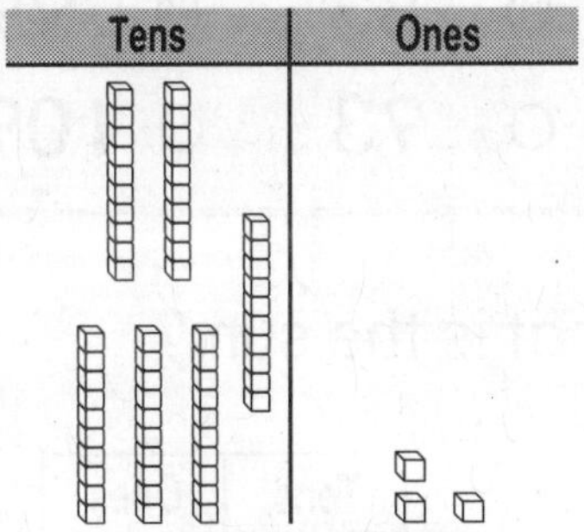

Regroup if you need to. Write the sum.

1.

	Tens	Ones
	☐	
	5	4
+	2	9

2.

	Tens	Ones
	☐	
	1	7
+	6	1

3.

	Tens	Ones
	☐	
	4	1
+	2	9

4.

	Tens	Ones
	☐	
	3	5
+	3	2

Name_____

1. What is the sum?

Tens	Ones
☐	
7	5
+ 2	4

○ 83   ○ 99
○ 93   ○ 109

2. What is the sum?

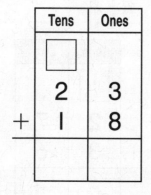

Tens	Ones
☐	
2	3
+ 1	8

○ 41   ○ 31
○ 40   ○ 30

3. What is the sum?

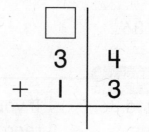

```
 ☐ | 
 3 | 4
+1 | 3
```

○ 37   ○ 47
○ 44   ○ 57

4. What is the sum?

```
 ☐ | 
 2 | 6
+2 | 5
```

○ 41   ○ 60
○ 51   ○ 61

PROBLEM SOLVING  REAL WORLD

Solve. Write or draw to explain.

5. Angela drew 16 flowers on her paper in the morning. She drew 25 more flowers in the afternoon. How many flowers did she draw in all?

_____ flowers

Lesson 37

COMMON CORE STANDARD CC.2.NBT.5
Lesson Objective: Practice 2-digit addition
with and without regrouping.

Practice 2-Digit Addition

Eliza sold 47 pencils in one week.
She sold 65 pencils the next week.
How many pencils did she sell in both weeks?

Add 47 and 65. Add the ones. $7 + 5 = 12$	Regroup. 12 ones = 1 ten and 2 ones	Add the tens. $1 + 4 + 6 = 11$

☐
  4 | 7
+ 6 | 5
	1
	  4 | 7
	+ 6 | 5
	    | 2
		1
		  4 | 7
		+ 6 | 5
		11 | 2

Write the sum.

1. ☐

   4 3
+ 6 9

2. ☐

   7 6
+ 5 8

3. ☐

   3 8
+ 4 2

4. ☐

   8 5
+ 6 8

5. ☐

   8 2
+ 4 7

6. ☐

   8 1
+ 1 7

7. ☐

   2 7
+ 8 6

8. ☐

   5 1
+ 3 8

1. What is the sum?

$$\begin{array}{r} 58 \\ + 44 \\ \hline \end{array}$$

○ 92
○ 98
○ 102
○ 112

2. Elizabeth collected 72 markers. Tori collected 52 markers. How many markers did they collect in all?

$$\begin{array}{r} 72 \\ + 52 \\ \hline \end{array}$$

○ 114
○ 124
○ 130
○ 136

3. Tony found 31 shells on the beach. Andy found 27 shells. How many shells did they find in all?

$$\begin{array}{r} 31 \\ + 27 \\ \hline \end{array}$$

○ 46
○ 48
○ 54
○ 58

4. What is the sum?

$$\begin{array}{r} 88 \\ + 39 \\ \hline \end{array}$$

○ 117
○ 127
○ 131
○ 139

PROBLEM SOLVING

Solve. Write or draw to explain.

5. There are 45 books on the shelf. There are 37 books on the table. How many books in all are on the shelf and the table?

_____ books

Name_____

Lesson 38

COMMON CORE STANDARD CC.2.NBT.5

Lesson Objective: Rewrite horizontal addition problems vertically in the standard algorithm format.

Rewrite 2-Digit Addition

Add. $43 + 19 = ?$

STEP 1	STEP 2	STEP 3
What is the tens digit in 43? __4__	What is the tens digit in 19? __1__	Add the ones. Regroup if you need to.
Write 4 in the tens column. Write the ones digit, 3, in the ones column.	Write 1 in the tens column. Write the ones digit, 9, in the ones column.	Add the tens.

STEP 1

Tens	Ones
□ 4	3
+	

STEP 2

Tens	Ones
□ 4	3
+ 1	9

STEP 3

Tens	Ones
1 4	3
+ 1	9
6	2

Rewrite the numbers. Then add.

1. $26 + 9$

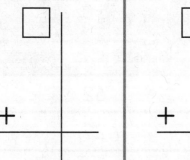

2. $16 + 43$

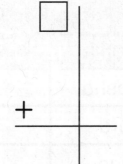

3. $32 + 38$

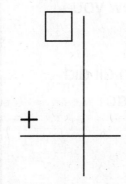

4. $23 + 26$

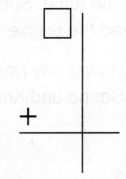

1. What is the sum of 34 + 56?

- ○ 100
- ○ 90
- ○ 80
- ○ 74

3. What is the sum of 18 + 64?

- ○ 92
- ○ 84
- ○ 82
- ○ 72

2. What is the sum of 39 + 32?

- ○ 71
- ○ 68
- ○ 61
- ○ 51

4. What is the sum of 40 + 56?

- ○ 97
- ○ 96
- ○ 90
- ○ 86

PROBLEM SOLVING

Use the table. Show how you solved the problem.

5. How many pages in all did Sasha and Kara read?

Pages Read This Week	
Child	**Number of Pages**
Sasha	62
Kara	29
Juan	50

_____ pages

Name_____

Lesson 39

COMMON CORE STANDARD CC.2.NBT.5
Lesson Objective: Break apart a 1-digit subtrahend to subtract it from a 2-digit number.

Algebra • Break Apart
Ones to Subtract

To subtract a one-digit number, break it apart.

Break apart ones in 7.

- Use 4 because 44 has a 4 in the ones place.
- The other part is 3.

Start at 44.
Subtract 4, and then subtract 3.

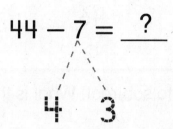

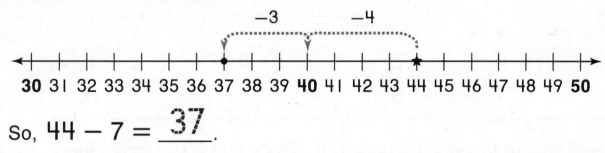

So, $44 - 7 = \underline{37}$.

Break apart ones to subtract. Write the difference.

1. $42 - 8 = \underline{}$

2. $47 - 8 = \underline{}$

3. $43 - 5 = \underline{}$

4. $41 - 8 = \underline{}$

1. Break apart ones to subtract. What is the difference?

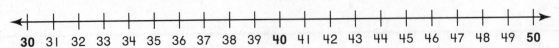

$$42 - 8 = \underline{\hspace{1cm}}$$

50	46	44	34
○	○	○	○

2. Break apart ones to subtract. What is the difference?

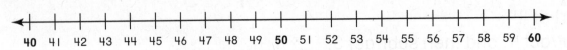

$$56 - 7 = \underline{\hspace{1cm}}$$

63	51	49	41
○	○	○	○

3. Harrison had 61 cars. He gave 6 cars to his brother. How many cars does Harrison have now?

- ○ 67
- ○ 57
- ○ 55
- ○ 54

4. Tracy had 33 stamps. She gave 5 stamps to her friend. How many stamps does Tracy have now?

- ○ 30
- ○ 28
- ○ 25
- ○ 18

5. Sam wants to subtract 9 from 47. How should he break apart the 9? Explain.

_____

_____

Lesson **40**

COMMON CORE STANDARD CC.2.NBT.5

Lesson Objective: Break apart a 2-digit subtrahend to subtract it from a 2-digit number.

Algebra • Break Apart Numbers to Subtract

To subtract a two-digit number, break it apart.

First break apart 16 into tens and ones.

Now break apart ones in 6.

• Use 4 because 54 has a 4 in the ones place.

• The other part is 2.

$54 - 16 = \underline{\ ?\ }$

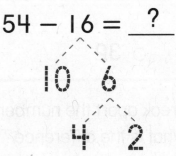

Use the number line to subtract the three parts.

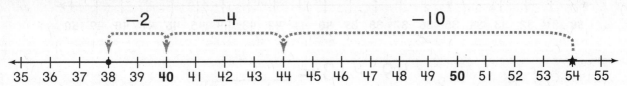

So, $54 - 16 = \underline{\ 38\ }$.

Break apart the number you are subtracting.
Write the difference.

30 31 32 33 34 35 36 37 38 39 **40** 41 42 43 44 45 46 47 48 49 **50** 51 52 53 54 55 56 57 58 59 **60**

1. $51 - 16 = \underline{\ \ \ }$

2. $57 - 18 = \underline{\ \ \ }$

3. $54 - 17 = \underline{\ \ \ }$

4. $52 - 18 = \underline{\ \ \ }$

1. Break apart the number you are subtracting.
   What is the difference?

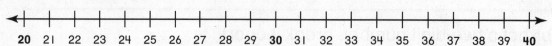

$$38 - 16 = \underline{\hspace{1cm}}$$

○ 32   ○ 22   ○ 12   ○ 2

2. Break apart the number you are subtracting.
   What is the difference?

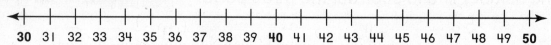

$$49 - 13 = \underline{\hspace{1cm}}$$

○ 62   ○ 46   ○ 42   ○ 36

3. Miles had 54 baseball cards. He gave 18 baseball cards to Greyson. How many baseball cards does Miles have now?

   ○ 44
   ○ 40
   ○ 38
   ○ 36

4. Last week Brooke made 28 bags for the festival. This week she made 14 bags. How many more bags did Brooke make last week than this week?

   ○ 52
   ○ 44
   ○ 14
   ○ 4

5. Break apart the number you are subtracting.
   Write the difference.

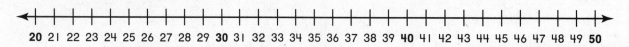

$$47 - 15 = \underline{\hspace{1cm}}$$

Name_____

Model and Record 2-Digit Subtraction

Subtract.

$$\begin{array}{r} 54 \\ -\ 15 \\ \hline \end{array}$$

Are there enough ones to subtract 5? __no__

Tens	Ones
5	4
− 1	5

Regroup 1 ten as 10 ones.
Write the new number of tens and ones.

Tens	Ones
4	14
5	4
− 1	5

Subtract the ones.

14 ones − 5 ones = __9__ ones
Write that number in the ones place.
Subtract the tens.
4 tens − 1 ten = __3__ tens
Write that number in the tens place.

Tens	Ones
4	14
5	4
− 1	5
3	9

Draw a quick picture to solve. Write the difference.

1.

Tens	Ones
4	3
− 1	6

Tens	Ones

2.

Tens	Ones
3	1
− 1	7

Tens	Ones

Core Standards for Math, Grade 2

1. What is the difference?

Tens	Ones
□	□
4	7
− 1	6

- ○ 21
- ○ 29
- ○ 30
- ○ 31

3. What is the difference?

Tens	Ones
□	□
6	1
− 2	8

- ○ 43
- ○ 33
- ○ 32
- ○ 23

2. What is the difference?

Tens	Ones
□	□
2	4
− 1	7

- ○ 17
- ○ 8
- ○ 7
- ○ 5

4. Miguel read 36 pages today. He read 15 pages yesterday. How many more pages did he read today than yesterday?

- ○ 21
- ○ 23
- ○ 31
- ○ 51

PROBLEM SOLVING

Solve. Write or draw to explain.

5. Kendall has 63 stickers. Her sister has 57 stickers. How many more stickers does Kendall have than her sister?

_____ more stickers

Lesson 42

COMMON CORE STANDARD CC.2.NBT.5
Lesson Objective: Record 2-digit
subtraction using the standard algorithm.

2-Digit Subtraction

Subtract.
$$\begin{array}{r} 54 \\ -28 \\ \hline \end{array}$$

Are there enough
ones to subtract 8? __no__

Tens	Ones
5	4
− 2	8

Regroup 1 ten as 10 ones.
Write the new number
of tens and ones.

Tens	Ones
4̷5	1̷4
− 2	8

Subtract the ones.
14 ones − 8 ones = __6__ ones
Write that number in the ones place.

Tens	Ones
4	14
5̷	4̷
− 2	8
	6

Subtract the tens.
4 tens − 2 tens = __2__ tens
Write that number in the tens place.

Tens	Ones
4	14
5̷	4̷
− 2	8
2	6

Regroup if you need to. Write the difference.

1.

Tens	Ones
7	2
− 4	5

2.

Tens	Ones
5	1
− 1	3

3.

Tens	Ones
3	8
− 1	6

Name_____

1. Regroup if you need to.
What is the difference?

Tens	Ones
□	□
7	4
− 3	5

○ 49
○ 41
○ 39
○ 38

3. Regroup if you need to.
What is the difference?

Tens	Ones
□	□
8	6
− 2	8

○ 58
○ 59
○ 60
○ 68

2. Regroup if you need to.
What is the difference?

Tens	Ones
□	□
6	2
− 1	9

○ 81   ○ 41
○ 43   ○ 33

4. There were 43 cows in a field.
Then 16 cows went in a barn.
How many cows were still in
the field?

○ 59
○ 37
○ 29
○ 27

PROBLEM SOLVING REAL WORLD

Solve. Write or draw to explain.

5. Mrs. Paul bought 32 erasers.
She gave 19 erasers to students.
How many erasers does she still have?   _____ erasers

Core Standards for Math, Grade 2

Lesson 43

COMMON CORE STANDARD CC.2.NBT.5

Lesson Objective: Practice 2-digit subtraction with and without regrouping.

Name_____

Practice 2-Digit Subtraction

Clay scored 80 points. Meg scored 61 points.
How many more points did Clay score than Meg?

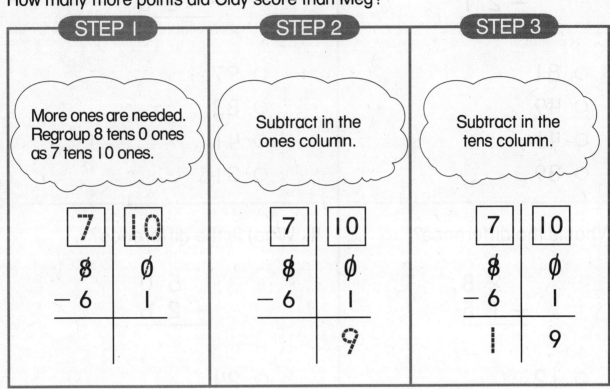

STEP 1

More ones are needed. Regroup 8 tens 0 ones as 7 tens 10 ones.

STEP 2

Subtract in the ones column.

STEP 3

Subtract in the tens column.

Write the difference.

1.	2.	3.
6 0 −2 7	3 7 −2 2	6 1 −4 8

4.	5.	6.
7 0 −2 6	3 7 −1 9	5 5 −1 4

1. What is the difference?

$$\begin{array}{r} 6\ 0 \\ -\ 2\ 1 \\ \hline \end{array}$$

- ○ 81
- ○ 49
- ○ 41
- ○ 39

3. What is the difference?

$$\begin{array}{r} 6\ 7 \\ -\ 2\ 6 \\ \hline \end{array}$$

- ○ 97
- ○ 83
- ○ 41
- ○ 31

2. What is the difference?

$$\begin{array}{r} 2\ 8 \\ -\ 1\ 5 \\ \hline \end{array}$$

- ○ 12
- ○ 13
- ○ 14
- ○ 15

4. What is the difference?

$$\begin{array}{r} 5\ 0 \\ -\ 2\ 6 \\ \hline \end{array}$$

- ○ 24
- ○ 25
- ○ 36
- ○ 76

PROBLEM SOLVING

Solve. Write or draw to explain.

5. Julie has 42 sheets of paper.
   She gives 17 sheets to Kari.
   How many sheets of paper
   does Julie have now?

_____ sheets of paper

Name _____

Lesson 44

COMMON CORE STANDARD CC.2.NBT.5
Lesson Objective: Rewrite horizontal
subtraction problems vertically in the
standard algorithm format.

Rewrite 2-Digit Subtraction

$62 - 38 = ?$

Rewrite 62 first.

	62

The 6 is in the tens place. Write it in the tens column.

The 2 is in the ones place. Write it in the ones column.

Tens	Ones
□	□
6	2
−	

Then rewrite 38.

	38

The 3 is in the tens place. Write it in the tens column.

The 8 is in the ones place. Write it in the ones column.

Tens	Ones
□	□
6	2
− 3	8

Now the ones digits are in a column and the tens digits are in a column.

Subtract. Write the difference.

Tens	Ones
5	12
6̸	2̸
− 3	8
2	4

Rewrite the subtraction problem. Find the difference.

1. $56 - 24$

Tens	Ones
□	□
−	

2. $74 - 37$

Tens	Ones
□	□
−	

3. $43 - 15$

Tens	Ones
□	□
−	

Core Standards for Math, Grade 2

1. Which shows a different way to write the subtraction problem?

$$72 - 43$$

○ $$\begin{array}{r} 72 \\ -43 \\ \hline \end{array}$$

○ $$\begin{array}{r} 72 \\ -34 \\ \hline \end{array}$$

○ $$\begin{array}{r} 27 \\ -43 \\ \hline \end{array}$$

○ $$\begin{array}{r} 27 \\ -34 \\ \hline \end{array}$$

2. Which shows a different way to write the subtraction problem?

$$97 - 21$$

○ $$\begin{array}{r} 97 \\ -12 \\ \hline \end{array}$$

○ $$\begin{array}{r} 97 \\ -21 \\ \hline \end{array}$$

○ $$\begin{array}{r} 79 \\ -12 \\ \hline \end{array}$$

○ $$\begin{array}{r} 79 \\ -21 \\ \hline \end{array}$$

3. Which shows the answer to the subtraction problem?

$$59 - 12$$

○ 71

○ 57

○ 47

○ 41

PROBLEM SOLVING

Solve. Write or draw to explain.

4. Jimmy went to the toy store. He saw 23 wooden trains and 41 plastic trains. How many more plastic trains than wooden trains did he see?

_____ more plastic trains

Core Standards for Math, Grade 2

Add to Find Differences

Count up to solve. 34 − 27 = ?
Start at 27. Count up 3 to 30.

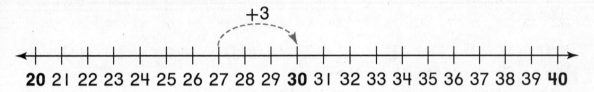

20 21 22 23 24 25 26 27 28 29 **30** 31 32 33 34 35 36 37 38 39 **40**

To get to 34 from 30, count up 4 more.

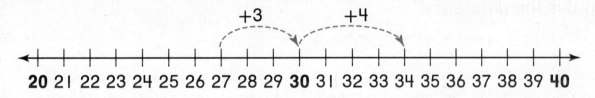

20 21 22 23 24 25 26 27 28 29 **30** 31 32 33 34 35 36 37 38 39 **40**

So, 34 − 27 = **7**.

7 was added to get to 34.

Count up to find the difference.

1. 41 − 37 = _____

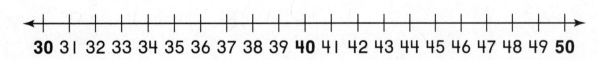

30 31 32 33 34 35 36 37 38 39 **40** 41 42 43 44 45 46 47 48 49 **50**

2. 43 − 38 = _____

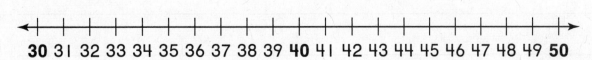

30 31 32 33 34 35 36 37 38 39 **40** 41 42 43 44 45 46 47 48 49 **50**

1. Use the number line. Count up to find the difference.
What is the difference?

$$84 - 75 = \underline{}$$

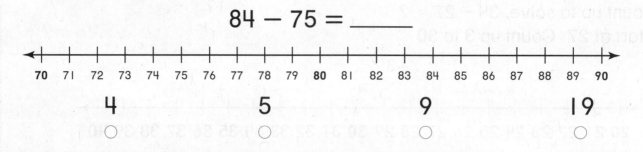

4 ⃝   5 ⃝   9 ⃝   19 ⃝

2. Use the number line. Count up to find the difference.
What is the difference?

$$43 - 37 = \underline{}$$

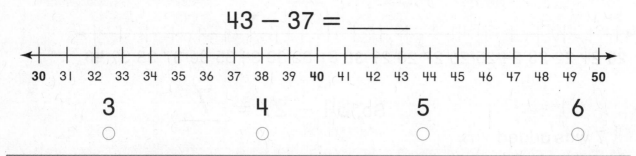

3 ⃝   4 ⃝   5 ⃝   6 ⃝

3. Use the number line. Count up to find the difference.
What is the difference?

$$66 - 58 = \underline{}$$

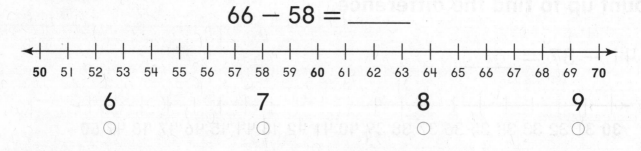

6 ⃝   7 ⃝   8 ⃝   9 ⃝

4. Amy needs to subtract 49 from 58. Explain how
she can solve the problem by counting up.

_____

_____

_____

Name_____

Lesson 46

COMMON CORE STANDARD CC.2.NBT.6
Lesson Objective: Find a sum by breaking apart a 1-digit addend to make a 2-digit addend a multiple of 10.

Break Apart Ones to Add

Sometimes when you are adding, you can break apart ones to make a ten.

$37 + 8 = \underline{\quad ? \quad}$

Look at the two-digit addend, 37. What digit

is in the ones place? $\underline{\quad 7 \quad}$

Decide how many you need to add to the ones digit to make 10.

$7 + \underline{\quad 3 \quad} = 10$, and $37 + \underline{\quad 3 \quad} = 40$

Break apart that number from the one-digit addend, 8.

$8 - 3 = 5$

Finally, write the new number sentence. $40 + 5 = \underline{\quad 45 \quad}$

Break apart ones to make a ten.
Then add and write the sum.

1. $28 + 6 = \underline{\quad\quad}$

2. $34 + 7 = \underline{\quad\quad}$

1. Break apart ones to make a ten. What is the sum?

$$17 + 8 = \underline{\quad}$$

- ○ 13
- ○ 15
- ○ 24
- ○ 25

3. Break apart ones to make a ten. What is the sum?

$$89 + 5 = \underline{\quad}$$

- ○ 104
- ○ 94
- ○ 84
- ○ 83

2. Break apart ones to make a ten. What is the sum?

$$57 + 4 = \underline{\quad}$$

- ○ 31
- ○ 41
- ○ 51
- ○ 61

4. Break apart ones to make a ten. What is the sum?

$$32 + 9 = \underline{\quad}$$

- ○ 41
- ○ 40
- ○ 31
- ○ 30

PROBLEM SOLVING  REAL WORLD

Solve. Write or draw to explain.

5. Jimmy had 18 toy airplanes. His mother bought him 7 more toy airplanes. How many toy airplanes does he have now?

_____ toy airplanes

Name_____

Lesson 47

COMMON CORE STANDARD CC.2.NBT.6
Lesson Objective: Use compensation to
develop flexible thinking for 2-digit addition.

Use Compensation

This is a way to add 2-digit numbers.
Take ones from one addend to make the other addend a tens number.

$27 + 38 = \underline{\quad?\quad}$

First, find the addend with the greater ones digit. $\underline{\quad 38 \quad}$

How many ones would you need to add to make it a tens number?

$38 + \underline{\quad} = 40$ Add $\underline{\quad 2 \quad}$ to make $\underline{\quad 40 \quad}$.

Next, take that many ones away from the other addend.

$27 - 2 = 25$ The two new addends are $\underline{\quad 25 \quad}$ and $\underline{\quad 40 \quad}$.

Write the new addition sentence to find the sum.

$\underline{\quad 25 \quad} + \underline{\quad 40 \quad} = \underline{\quad 65 \quad}$

Show how to make one addend the next tens number.
Complete the new addition sentence.

1. $28 + 16 = ?$

   $\underline{\quad} + \underline{\quad} = \underline{\quad}$

2. $37 + 24 = ?$

   $\underline{\quad} + \underline{\quad} = \underline{\quad}$

1. Which shows a way to find the sum?

$$41 + 29$$

- ○ $40 + 10 = 50$
- ○ $50 + 20 = 70$
- ○ $40 + 20 = 60$
- ○ $50 + 30 = 80$

3. Which shows a way to find the sum?

$$66 + 16$$

- ○ $60 + 16 = 76$
- ○ $70 + 16 = 86$
- ○ $60 + 12 = 72$
- ○ $70 + 12 = 82$

2. Which shows a way to find the sum?

$$38 + 18$$

- ○ $30 + 16 = 46$
- ○ $30 + 18 = 48$
- ○ $40 + 16 = 56$
- ○ $40 + 18 = 58$

4. Which shows a way to find the sum?

$$17 + 23$$

- ○ $10 + 20 = 30$
- ○ $10 + 23 = 33$
- ○ $17 + 20 = 37$
- ○ $10 + 30 = 40$

PROBLEM SOLVING REAL WORLD

Solve. Write or draw to explain.

5. The oak tree at the school was 34 feet tall.
Then it grew 18 feet taller.
How tall is the oak tree now?

_____ feet tall

Break Apart Addends as Tens and Ones

Lesson Objective: Apply place-value concepts when using a break-apart strategy for 2-digit addition.

$25 + 46 = ?$

Break apart 25 into tens and ones.   Break apart 46 into tens and ones.

25   46

20 + 5 +   40 + 6

Then, add the tens from the two addends.

Add the ones from the two addends.

$$\underline{20} + \underline{40} = \underline{60}$$
$$\underline{5} + \underline{6} = \underline{11}$$
$$\underline{60} + \underline{11} = \underline{71}$$

Add the two sums.

So, $25 + 46 = \underline{71}$.

Break apart the addends to find the sum.

1.   12   +   48 = ?

___ + ___ + ___ + ___

Add the tens.   ___ + ___ = ___

Add the ones.   ___ + ___ = ___

How many in all? ___ + ___ = ___

So, $12 + 48 = $ ___.

Core Standards for Math, Grade 2

Name_____

1. Which shows how to break apart the addends to find the sum?

$$57 + 37$$

○ $50 + 30 + 7 + 7$
○ $50 + 20 + 7$
○ $20 + 14 + 7$
○ $30 + 7 + 7$

3. Which shows how to break apart the addends to find the sum?

$$45 + 18$$

○ $40 + 10 + 5$
○ $50 + 10 + 8 + 5$
○ $40 + 10 + 5 + 8$
○ $40 + 5 + 8$

2. Which shows how to break apart the addends to find the sum?

$$25 + 17$$

○ $20 + 10 + 7$
○ $20 + 10 + 5 + 7$
○ $30 + 10 + 5$
○ $20 + 7 + 5$

4. Which shows how to break apart the addends to find the sum?

$$49 + 23$$

○ $40 + 20 + 9 + 3$
○ $40 + 20 + 9$
○ $40 + 20 + 10$
○ $40 + 9 + 3$

5. Break apart the addends to find the sum.

$$67 \longrightarrow \underline{} + \underline{}$$

$$+ 28 \longrightarrow \underline{} + \underline{}$$

$$\underline{} + \underline{} = \underline{}$$

Lesson **49**

COMMON CORE STANDARD CC.2.NBT.6
Lesson Objective: Draw quick pictures and
record 2-digit addition using the standard
algorithm.

Model and Record 2-Digit Addition

Model 33 + 19.

How many ones
are there in all? __12__ ones

Can you make a ten? __yes__

Tens	Ones
	3 3
+	1 9

Regroup 10 ones as 1 ten.
Write a 1 in the tens column
to show the regrouped ten.

How many ones are left
after regrouping? __2__ ones

Write that number in the ones place.

Tens	Ones
	3 3
+	1 9
	2

How many tens
are there in all? __5__ tens

Write that number
in the tens place.

Tens	Ones
1	
	3 3
+	1 9
5	2

Draw quick pictures to help you solve. Write the sum.

1.

Tens	Ones
	4 7
+	2 5

Tens	Ones

2.

Tens	Ones
	3 6
+	4 6

Tens	Ones

1. What is the sum?

Tens	Ones
☐	
1	6
+ 1	8

Tens	Ones

○ 23   ○ 33
○ 24   ○ 34

3. What is the sum?

Tens	Ones
☐	
3	4
+ 2	6

Tens	Ones

○ 54   ○ 60
○ 56   ○ 70

2. What is the sum?

Tens	Ones
☐	
5	9
+ 2	7

Tens	Ones

○ 86   ○ 76
○ 85   ○ 75

4. What is the sum?

Tens	Ones
☐	
4	4
+ 2	8

Tens	Ones

○ 52   ○ 68
○ 62   ○ 72

PROBLEM SOLVING REAL WORLD

Choose a way to solve.
Write or draw to explain.

5. There were 37 children at the park
on Saturday and 25 children at the
park on Sunday. How many children
were at the park on those two days?

_____ children

COMMON CORE STANDARD CC.2.NBT.6
Lesson Objective: Find sums of three 2-digit numbers.

Algebra • Find Sums
for 3 Addends

You can add three numbers in different ways.
Start by adding the ones first.

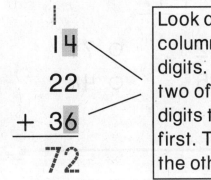

$\begin{array}{r} 14 \\ 22 \\ +\ 36 \\ \hline 72 \end{array}$	Look at the column of ones digits. Choose two of the digits to add first. Then add the other digit.

$$4 + 6 = 10$$
$$10 + 2 = 12$$

Then add the tens.

$$1 + 1 + 2 + 3 = 7$$

$\begin{array}{r} 14 \\ 22 \\ +\ 36 \\ \hline 72 \end{array}$	Start at the top of the ones column. Add the first two digits, and then add the third digit.

$$4 + 2 = 6$$
$$6 + 6 = 12$$

Then add the tens.

$$1 + 1 + 2 + 3 = 7$$

Add.

1.
$$\begin{array}{r} 18 \\ 25 \\ +\ 32 \\ \hline \end{array}$$

2.
$$\begin{array}{r} 40 \\ 37 \\ +\ 16 \\ \hline \end{array}$$

3.
$$\begin{array}{r} 13 \\ 21 \\ +\ 34 \\ \hline \end{array}$$

4.
$$\begin{array}{r} 26 \\ 22 \\ +\ 23 \\ \hline \end{array}$$

1. What is the sum?

$$
\begin{array}{r}
58 \\
24 \\
+\ \ 3 \\
\hline
\end{array}
$$

○ 95   ○ 82

○ 85   ○ 27

3. What is the sum?

$$
\begin{array}{r}
54 \\
31 \\
+\ 17 \\
\hline
\end{array}
$$

○ 102   ○ 71

○ 85   ○ 48

2. What is the sum?

$$
\begin{array}{r}
62 \\
28 \\
+\ 11 \\
\hline
\end{array}
$$

○ 115   ○ 98

○ 101   ○ 91

4. What is the sum?

$$
\begin{array}{r}
48 \\
35 \\
+\ 24 \\
\hline
\end{array}
$$

○ 117   ○ 107

○ 111   ○ 99

PROBLEM SOLVING

Solve. Write or draw to explain.

5. Liam has 24 yellow pencils,
   15 red pencils, and 9 blue pencils.
   How many pencils does he have
   altogether?

_____ pencils

Core Standards for Math, Grade 2

Algebra • Find Sums for 4 Addends

You can add 4 numbers in different ways.
One way is to add pairs of digits in the ones column.

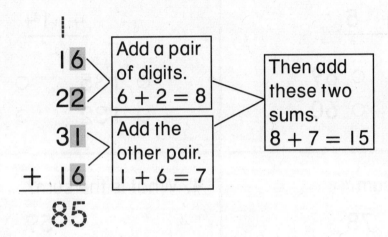

Then add the digits in the tens column.

Add.

1.

```
   43
   57
   32
 +  2
```

2.

```
   24
   21
   19
 + 32
```

3.

```
   21
   14
   20
 + 42
```

1. What is the sum?

$$
\begin{array}{r}
34 \\
20 \\
11 \\
+\ 5 \\
\hline
\end{array}
$$

- ○ 78   ○ 69
- ○ 70   ○ 60

3. What is the sum?

$$
\begin{array}{r}
63 \\
27 \\
31 \\
+\ 14 \\
\hline
\end{array}
$$

- ○ 135   ○ 125
- ○ 132   ○ 121

2. What is the sum?

$$
\begin{array}{r}
78 \\
43 \\
12 \\
+\ 4 \\
\hline
\end{array}
$$

- ○ 147   ○ 137
- ○ 143   ○ 127

4. What is the sum?

$$
\begin{array}{r}
59 \\
52 \\
24 \\
+\ 31 \\
\hline
\end{array}
$$

- ○ 174   ○ 162
- ○ 166   ○ 156

PROBLEM SOLVING

Solve. Show how you solved the problem.

5. Kinza jogs 16 minutes on Monday,
13 minutes on Tuesday, 9 minutes
on Wednesday, and 20 minutes on
Thursday. What is the total number
of minutes she jogged?

_____ minutes

Name_____

Lesson 52

COMMON CORE STANDARD CC.2.NBT.7

Lesson Objective: Draw quick pictures to represent 3-digit addition.

Draw to Represent 3-Digit Addition

Add 213 and 124.
Draw quick pictures of 213 and 124.

Count the hundreds, tens, and ones.

___3___ hundreds ___3___ tens ___7___ ones

Hundreds	Tens	Ones

Write the number. ___337___

Draw quick pictures. Write how many hundreds, tens, and ones in all. Write the number.

1. Add 135 and 214.

Hundreds	Tens	Ones

_____ hundreds _____ tens _____ ones

_____

2. Add 121 and 143.

Hundreds	Tens	Ones

_____ hundreds _____ tens _____ ones

_____

Core Standards for Math, Grade 2

1. Add 164 and 124. What is the sum?

Hundreds	Tens	Ones
☐	|||||	○○○○
☐	||	○○○○

○ 140   ○ 248   ○ 288   ○ 298

2. Add 206 and 271. What is the sum?

Hundreds	Tens	Ones
☐ ☐		○○○○○ ○
☐ ☐	||||||||	○

○ 165   ○ 477   ○ 475   ○ 487

PROBLEM SOLVING

Solve. Write or draw to explain.

3. A farmer sold 324 lemons and 255 limes.
   How many pieces of fruit did the farmer
   sell altogether?

   _____ pieces of fruit

Lesson 53

COMMON CORE STANDARD CC.2.NBT.7

Lesson Objective: Apply place value concepts when using a break apart strategy for 3-digit addition.

Break Apart 3-Digit Addends

743
+ 124

Break apart each addend.
Write the value of each digit.

$743 = \underline{700} + \underline{40} + \underline{3}$

$124 = \underline{100} + \underline{20} + \underline{4}$

Add the hundreds, tens, and ones.
Then add these sums together.

Hundreds	Tens	Ones

$743 \longrightarrow \underline{700} + \underline{40} + \underline{3}$

$+124 \longrightarrow \underline{100} + \underline{20} + \underline{4}$

$\underline{800} + \underline{60} + \underline{7} = \underline{867}$

Break apart the addends to find the sum.

Hundreds	Tens	Ones

1. $253 \longrightarrow$ _____ + _____ + _____

$+ 536 \longrightarrow$ _____ + _____ + _____

_____ + _____ + _____ = _____

1. Which shows 681 broken apart
   into hundreds, tens, and ones?

   ○ 500 + 10 + 8
   ○ 500 + 80 + 1
   ○ 600 + 10 + 8
   ○ 600 + 80 + 1

2. Break apart the addends into hundreds,
   tens, and ones. What is the sum?

   $$371$$
   $$+ 148$$

   ○ 223   ○ 419   ○ 519   ○ 529

PROBLEM SOLVING REAL WORLD

Solve. Write or draw to explain.

3. There are 126 crayons in a bucket.
   A teacher puts 144 more crayons
   in the bucket. How many crayons
   are in the bucket now?

   _____ crayons

Name_____

Lesson **54**

COMMON CORE STANDARD CC.2.NBT.7

Lesson Objective: Record 3-digit addition using the standard algorithm with possible regrouping of ones.

3-Digit Addition: Regroup Ones

Add.

$$318 + 256$$

Hundreds	Tens	Ones
	☐	
3	1	8
+ 2	5	6

Add the ones.

$8 + 6 = \underline{14}$

Do you need to regroup? __yes__

Regroup 10 ones as 1 ten.

Hundreds	Tens	Ones
	☐	
3	1	8
+ 2	5	6
		4

Add the tens.

$1 + 1 + 5 = \underline{7}$

Add the hundreds.

$3 + 2 = \underline{5}$

Hundreds	Tens	Ones
	1	
3	1	8
+ 2	5	6
5	7	4

Write the sum.

1.

Hundreds	Tens	Ones
	☐	
5	2	6
+ 1	4	2

2.

Hundreds	Tens	Ones
	☐	
4	5	7
+ 3	3	5

1. What is the sum?

Hundreds	Tens	Ones
	☐	
3	7	5
+ 2	1	6

○ 691   ○ 581

○ 591   ○ 159

2. What is the sum?

Hundreds	Tens	Ones
	☐	
1	4	9
+ 1	2	8

○ 267   ○ 278

○ 277   ○ 377

3. What is the sum?

Hundreds	Tens	Ones
	☐	
3	6	7
+ 1	2	8

○ 239   ○ 495

○ 485   ○ 595

4. What is the sum?

Hundreds	Tens	Ones
	☐	
4	5	5
+ 2	3	5

○ 600   ○ 650

○ 610   ○ 690

PROBLEM SOLVING  REAL WORLD

Solve. Write or draw to explain.

5. In the garden, there are 258 yellow daisies and 135 white daisies. How many daisies are in the garden altogether?

_____ daisies

Core Standards for Math, Grade 2

COMMON CORE STANDARD CC.2.NBT.7

Lesson Objective: Record 3-digit addition using the standard algorithm with possible regrouping of tens.

3-Digit Addition: Regroup Tens

Add.   271
     + 158

Add the ones.

1 + 8 = ___9___

Hundreds	Tens	Ones
2	7	1
+ 1	5	8
		9

Add the tens.

7 + 5 = __12__

Do you need to regroup? __yes__

Regroup 12 tens as 1 hundred 2 tens.

Hundreds	Tens	Ones
1		
2	7	1
+ 1	5	8
	2	9

Add the hundreds.

1 + 2 + 1 = __4__

Hundreds	Tens	Ones
1		
2	7	1
+ 1	5	8
4	2	9

Write the sum.

1.

Hundreds	Tens	Ones
2	6	4
+ 1	4	5

2.

Hundreds	Tens	Ones
2	3	2
+ 6	0	6

1. What is the sum?

Hundreds	Tens	Ones
☐	☐	
1	9	2
+ 3	5	6

○ 448   ○ 544
○ 458   ○ 548

3. What is the sum?

Hundreds	Tens	Ones
☐	☐	
1	8	3
+ 2	5	6

○ 439   ○ 349
○ 433   ○ 339

2. What is the sum?

Hundreds	Tens	Ones
☐	☐	
3	9	1
+ 2	9	6

○ 697   ○ 685
○ 687   ○ 587

4. What is the sum?

$$\begin{array}{r} 363 \\ + 254 \\ \hline \end{array}$$

○ 671   ○ 617
○ 651   ○ 607

PROBLEM SOLVING

Solve. Write or draw to explain.

5. There are 142 blue toy cars and
293 red toy cars at the toy store.
How many toy cars are there in all?

_____ toy cars

Name_____

Lesson 56

COMMON CORE STANDARD CC.2.NBT.7
Lesson Objective: Record 3-digit addition using the standard algorithm with possible regrouping of both ones and tens.

Addition: Regroup Ones and Tens

Sometimes, you may need to regroup more than once.

$$189$$
$$+ 623$$

Step 1 Add the ones.
There are 12 ones in all.
Regroup 12 ones as 1 ten 2 ones.

```
  1
  1 8 9
+ 6 2 3
      2
```

Step 2 Add the tens.
There are 11 tens in all.
Regroup 11 tens as 1 hundred 1 ten.

```
  1 1
  1 8 9
+ 6 2 3
  1 2
```

Step 3 Add the hundreds.
There are 8 hundreds in all.

```
  1 1
  1 8 9
+ 6 2 3
  8 1 2
```

Write the sum.

1.
```
  2 7 8
+ 4 6 5
```

2.
```
  1 5 7
+ 7 7 1
```

3.
```
  3 6 4
+ 4 1 9
```

1. What is the sum?

$$139$$
$$+379$$

○ 518   ○ 508
○ 500   ○ 418

2. What is the sum?

$$158$$
$$+162$$

○ 210   ○ 310
○ 220   ○ 320

3. What is the sum?

$$243$$
$$+457$$

○ 600   ○ 700
○ 690   ○ 790

4. What is the sum?

$$275$$
$$+168$$

○ 453   ○ 433
○ 443   ○ 343

PROBLEM SOLVING

Solve. Write or draw to explain.

5. Saul and Luisa each scored 167 points
on a computer game. How many points
did they score in all?

_____ points

Name_____

Lesson 57

COMMON CORE STANDARD CC.2.NBT.7
Lesson Objective: Solve problems
involving 3-digit subtraction by using the
strategy *make a model.*

Problem Solving • 3-Digit Subtraction

There were 237 books on the shelves.

Mr. Davies took 126 books off the shelves.

How many books were still on the shelves?

Unlock the Problem

What do I need to find?

how many books
_____

were still on the shelves

**What information do
I need to use?**

There were ___237___ books on
the shelves.

Mr. Davies took ___126___ books
off the shelves.

Show how to solve the problem.

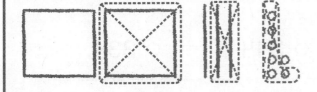

There were ___111___ books still on the shelves.

Make a model to solve. Then draw
a quick picture of your model.

1. Mr. Cho has 256 pencils.
   Then he sells 132 pencils.
   How many pencils does
   he have now?

_____ pencils

1. There were 487 cars in a parking lot.
Then 156 cars left. How many cars are
in the parking lot now?

  ○ 231   ○ 321   ○ 331   ○ 336

2. Helen counted 381 leaves on her porch.
There were 129 red leaves. How many
leaves were not red?

  ○ 262   ○ 252   ○ 250   ○ 249

3. There were 614 boxes at a post office.
Then people took 280 boxes home. How
many boxes are still at the post office?

  ○ 434   ○ 420   ○ 344   ○ 334

4. Michael collected 525 bottle caps. His sister
collected 413 bottle caps. How many more
bottle caps did Michael collect than his sister?
Draw a quick picture to help you solve the
problem. Then write your answer.

_____ more bottle caps

Name_____

3-Digit Subtraction: Regroup Tens

Subtract.

$$463 - 317$$

Are there enough ones to subtract 7? __no__

Regroup 1 ten as 10 ones.

Hundreds	Tens	Ones
4	6	3
− 3	1	7

There are __13__ ones

and __5__ tens.

Subtract the ones.

$$13 - 7 = \underline{6}$$

Hundreds	Tens	Ones
	5	13
4	6	3
− 3	1	7
		6

Subtract the tens.

$$5 - 1 = \underline{4}$$

Subtract the hundreds.

$$4 - 3 = \underline{1}$$

Hundreds	Tens	Ones
	5	13
4	6	3
− 3	1	7
1	4	6

Solve. Write the difference.

1.

Hundreds	Tens	Ones
8	6	2
− 3	2	8

2.

Hundreds	Tens	Ones
6	7	8
− 2	4	5

1. What is the difference?

Hundreds	Tens	Ones
	☐	☐
7	9	5
− 5	3	7

○ 257   ○ 267

○ 258   ○ 268

2. What is the difference?

Hundreds	Tens	Ones
	☐	☐
5	5	7
− 4	1	9

○ 138   ○ 148

○ 142   ○ 156

PROBLEM SOLVING

Solve. Write or draw to explain.

3. There were 985 pencils. Some pencils were sold. Then there were 559 pencils left. How many pencils were sold?

_____ pencils

Name_____

Lesson 59

COMMON CORE STANDARD CC.2.NBT.7

Lesson Objective: Record 3-digit subtraction using the standard algorithm with possible regrouping of hundreds.

3-Digit Subtraction: Regroup Hundreds

Subtract.   326
           − 174

Subtract the ones.

$6 - 4 = \underline{2}$

Are there enough tens to subtract 7 tens? _no_

Regroup 1 hundred as 10 tens.

Hundreds	Tens	Ones
2	12	
3̸	2̸	6
− 1	7	4
		2

Now there are _12_ tens

and _2_ hundreds.

Subtract the tens.

$12 - 7 = \underline{5}$

Subtract the hundreds.

$2 - 1 = \underline{1}$

Hundreds	Tens	Ones
2	12	
3̸	2̸	6
− 1	7	4
1	5	2

Solve. Write the difference.

1.

Hundreds	Tens	Ones
6	7	9
− 2	6	1

2.

Hundreds	Tens	Ones
5	2	5
− 2	9	3

Name_____

1. What is the difference?

$$847$$
$$-392$$

○ 559   ○ 539
○ 555   ○ 455

3. What is the difference?

$$548$$
$$-276$$

○ 262   ○ 372
○ 272   ○ 374

2. What is the difference?

$$413$$
$$-152$$

○ 261   ○ 345
○ 341   ○ 565

4. What is the difference?

$$924$$
$$-460$$

○ 584   ○ 464
○ 544   ○ 440

PROBLEM SOLVING

Solve. Write or draw to explain.

5. There were 537 people in the parade. 254 of these people were playing an instrument. How many people were not playing an instrument?

_____ people

Subtraction: Regroup Hundreds and Tens

COMMON CORE STANDARD CC.2.NBT.7
Lesson Objective: Record 3-digit subtraction using the standard algorithm with possible regrouping of both hundreds and tens.

You may need to regroup more than once.

$$282$$
$$-198$$

Regroup 1 ten as 10 ones. Subtract the ones.	Regroup 1 hundred as 10 tens. Subtract the tens.	Subtract the hundreds.
$$\begin{array}{r} 7\;12 \\ 2\;\not8\;\not2 \\ -1\;9\;8 \\ \hline 4 \end{array}$$	$$\begin{array}{r} 17 \\ 1\;7\;12 \\ \not2\;\not8\;\not2 \\ -1\;9\;8 \\ \hline 8\;4 \end{array}$$	$$\begin{array}{r} 17 \\ 1\;7\;12 \\ \not2\;\not8\;\not2 \\ -1\;9\;8 \\ \hline 8\;4 \end{array}$$

Solve. Write the difference.

1.
$$\begin{array}{r} 481 \\ -176 \\ \hline \end{array}$$

2.
$$\begin{array}{r} 746 \\ -28 \\ \hline \end{array}$$

3.
$$\begin{array}{r} 331 \\ -148 \\ \hline \end{array}$$

4.
$$\begin{array}{r} 395 \\ -131 \\ \hline \end{array}$$

5.
$$\begin{array}{r} 524 \\ -265 \\ \hline \end{array}$$

6.
$$\begin{array}{r} 748 \\ -603 \\ \hline \end{array}$$

Name_____

1. What is the difference?

$$
\begin{array}{r}
7\ 2\ 5 \\
-\ 2\ 8\ 4 \\
\hline
\end{array}
$$

   ○ 441   ○ 541
   ○ 449   ○ 545

3. What is the difference?

$$
\begin{array}{r}
8\ 5\ 2 \\
-\ 6\ 7\ 6 \\
\hline
\end{array}
$$

   ○ 276   ○ 176
   ○ 186   ○ 174

2. What is the difference?

$$
\begin{array}{r}
5\ 6\ 1 \\
-\ 1\ 9\ 3 \\
\hline
\end{array}
$$

   ○ 358   ○ 458
   ○ 368   ○ 468

4. What is the difference?

$$
\begin{array}{r}
6\ 3\ 7 \\
-\ 4\ 5\ 8 \\
\hline
\end{array}
$$

   ○ 175   ○ 189
   ○ 179   ○ 271

PROBLEM SOLVING

Solve.

5. Mia's coloring book has 432 pages.
She has already colored 178 pages.
How many pages in the book are
left to color?

_____ pages

Regrouping with Zeros

Subtract 138 from 305.

There are not enough ones to subtract 8.

Since there are 0 tens, regroup 3 hundreds as 2 hundreds 10 tens.

Hundreds	Tens	Ones

$$
\begin{array}{r}
2\ 10 \\
\cancel{3}\ \cancel{0}\ 5 \\
-\ 1\ 3\ 8 \\
\end{array}
$$

Then regroup 10 tens 5 ones as 9 tens 15 ones.

Subtract the ones.

$$15 - 8 = 7$$

Hundreds	Tens	Ones

$$
\begin{array}{r}
9 \\
2\ \cancel{10}\ 15 \\
\cancel{3}\ \cancel{0}\ \cancel{5} \\
-\ 1\ 3\ 8 \\
\hline
7 \\
\end{array}
$$

Subtract the tens.

$$9 - 3 = 6$$

Subtract the hundreds.

$$2 - 1 = 1$$

Hundreds	Tens	Ones

$$
\begin{array}{r}
9 \\
2\ \cancel{10}\ 15 \\
\cancel{3}\ \cancel{0}\ \cancel{5} \\
-\ 1\ 3\ 8 \\
\hline
1\ 6\ 7 \\
\end{array}
$$

So, $305 - 138 = \underline{167}$.

Solve. Write the difference.

1.
$$
\begin{array}{r}
8\ 0\ 1 \\
-\ 3\ 7\ 5 \\
\hline
\end{array}
$$

2.
$$
\begin{array}{r}
6\ 9\ 3 \\
-\ 2\ 4\ 1 \\
\hline
\end{array}
$$

3.
$$
\begin{array}{r}
9\ 0\ 7 \\
-\ 6\ 2\ 4 \\
\hline
\end{array}
$$

Core Standards for Math, Grade 2

1. What is the difference?

$$
\begin{array}{r}
3\ 0\ 6 \\
-\ 1\ 2\ 7 \\
\hline
\end{array}
$$

○ 289   ○ 179

○ 189   ○ 171

3. What is the difference?

$$
\begin{array}{r}
4\ 4\ 8 \\
-\ 2\ 6\ 3 \\
\hline
\end{array}
$$

○ 185   ○ 285

○ 195   ○ 291

2. What is the difference?

$$
\begin{array}{r}
9\ 0\ 2 \\
-\ 5\ 3\ 8 \\
\hline
\end{array}
$$

○ 464   ○ 374

○ 382   ○ 364

4. What is the difference?

$$
\begin{array}{r}
7\ 0\ 4 \\
-\ 3\ 5\ 5 \\
\hline
\end{array}
$$

○ 459   ○ 349

○ 449   ○ 341

PROBLEM SOLVING

Solve.

5. There are 303 students. There are 147 girls. How many boys are there?

_____ boys

Count On and Count Back by 10 and 100

10 less than 234

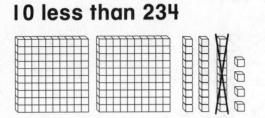

2 hundreds 2 tens 4 ones.

$$224$$

Notice what digit changes.

100 less than 234

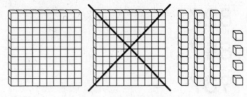

1 hundred 3 tens 4 ones.

$$134$$

10 more than 234

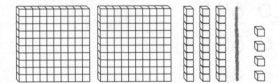

2 hundreds 4 tens 4 ones.

$$244$$

100 more than 234

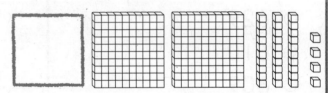

3 hundreds 3 tens 4 ones.

$$334$$

Write the number.

1. 10 more than 719

_____

2. 10 less than 246

_____

3. 100 more than 291

_____

4. 100 less than 687

_____

5. 10 less than 568

_____

6. 100 more than 649

_____

1. Which number is 10 more than 837?

   ○ 827
   ○ 847
   ○ 937
   ○ 947

3. Which number is 100 more than 326?

   ○ 226
   ○ 336
   ○ 426
   ○ 436

2. Which number is 10 less than 619?

   ○ 629
   ○ 610
   ○ 609
   ○ 519

4. Which number is 100 less than 541?

   ○ 641
   ○ 531
   ○ 451
   ○ 441

PROBLEM SOLVING

Solve. Write or draw to explain.

5. Sarah has 128 stickers. Alex has 10 fewer stickers than Sarah. How many stickers does Alex have?

   _____ stickers

Name_____

Lesson 63

COMMON CORE STANDARD CC.2.NBT.8
Lesson Objective: Extend number patterns by counting on by tens or hundreds.

Algebra • Number Patterns

Find a counting pattern.

421, 431, 441, 451, ■, ■

Which digit changes from
number to number?

The ___tens___ digit changes.

How does it change?

by ___one___ each time

Look at the chart. Find
the next two numbers
in the pattern.

401	402	403	404	405	406	407	408	409	410
411	412	413	414	415	416	417	418	419	420
421	422	423	424	425	426	427	428	429	430
431	432	433	434	435	436	437	438	439	440
441	442	443	444	445	446	447	448	449	450
451	452	453	454	455	456	457	458	459	460
461	462	463	464	465	466	467	468	469	470
471	472	473	474	475	476	477	478	479	480
481	482	483	484	485	486	487	488	489	490
491	492	493	494	495	496	497	498	499	500

The next two numbers are __461__ and __471__.

Look at the digits to find the next two numbers.

1. 937, 947, 957, 967, ■, ■

The next two numbers are _____ and _____ .

2. 135, 235, 335, 435, ■, ■

The next two numbers are _____ and _____ .

1. Look at the pattern. What number comes next?

321, 331, 341, 351

- ○ 311
- ○ 352
- ○ 361
- ○ 362

2. Rico wrote this number pattern. What two numbers come next in Rico's pattern?

183, 283, 383, 483

- ○ 493, 503
- ○ 683, 783
- ○ 484, 485
- ○ 583, 683

3. Look at the pattern. What two numbers come next in the pattern?

467, 477, 487, 497

- ○ 507, 517
- ○ 517, 527
- ○ 587, 597
- ○ 597, 697

4. Beth wrote a number pattern starting with 325. She counted on by hundreds. Which of the following numbers comes next in her number pattern?

- ○ 225
- ○ 335
- ○ 415
- ○ 425

PROBLEM SOLVING REAL WORLD

5. What are the missing numbers in the pattern?

431, 441, 451, 461, , 481, 491,

The missing numbers are _____ and _____.

Lesson 64

COMMON CORE STANDARD CC.2.NBT.9
Lesson Objective: Model 2-digit addition with regrouping.

Model Regrouping for Addition

Add 18 and 25.
Show 18 and 25 with ▭▭▭▭ and ▢.
Count the ones.
How many ones are there in all? _**13**_ ones

Can you make a ten? _**yes**_

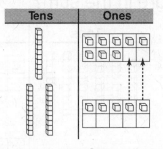

Trade 10 ones
for 1 ten.
This is called
regrouping.

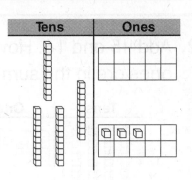

Count the tens. How many
tens are there in all? _**4**_ tens
Count the ones. How many
ones are there in all? _**3**_ ones

_**4**_ tens _**3**_ ones is the same as _**43**_ .

Write how many tens and ones in the sum.
Write the sum.

1. Add 46 and 19.

Tens	Ones

_____ tens _____ ones

_____

2. Add 45 and 27.

Tens	Ones

_____ tens _____ ones

_____

3. Add 58 and 38.

Tens	Ones

_____ tens _____ ones

_____

Core Standards for Math, Grade 2

1. Add 65 and 9. How many tens are in the sum?

Tens	Ones

■ tens 4 ones

○ 5   ○ 7
○ 6   ○ 8

2. Add 45 and 16. How many ones are in the sum?

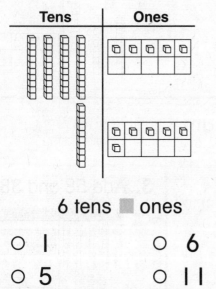

Tens	Ones

6 tens ■ ones

○ 1   ○ 6
○ 5   ○ 11

3. Add 29 and 17. What is the sum?

Tens	Ones

○ 36   ○ 39
○ 37   ○ 46

4. Add 28 and 39. What is the sum?

Tens	Ones

○ 57   ○ 67
○ 66   ○ 69

5. Draw a quick picture to add 42 and 29. Write the sum.

_____

Core Standards for Math, Grade 2

Model Regrouping for Subtraction

Subtract 37 from 65.

Are there enough ones to subtract 7? ___no___
So, you will need to regroup.

Trade 1 ten for 10 ones.

_____

Subtract the ones. Then subtract the tens.

15 ones − 7 ones = ___8___ ones

5 tens − 3 tens = ___2___ tens

___2___ tens ___8___ ones is the same as ___28___.

The difference is ___28___.

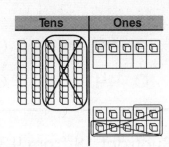

Draw to show the regrouping. Write the tens and ones that are in the difference. Write the number.

1. Subtract 18 from 43.

Tens	Ones

_____ tens _____ ones

_____

2. Subtract 19 from 55.

Tens	Ones

_____ tens _____ ones

_____

1. Subtract 16 from 52. What is the difference?

Tens	Ones

○ 69   ○ 36

○ 44   ○ 34

3. Subtract 27 from 43. What is the difference?

Tens	Ones

○ 70   ○ 16

○ 24   ○ 14

2. Subtract 14 from 43. Which shows the tens and ones in the difference?

Tens	Ones

○ 2 tens 9 ones

○ 3 tens 1 one

○ 5 tens 7 ones

○ 8 tens 7 ones

PROBLEM SOLVING

Choose a way to solve. Write or draw to explain.

4. Mr. Ortega made 51 cookies. He gave 14 cookies away. How many cookies does he have now?

_____ cookies

Name_____

Lesson 66

COMMON CORE STANDARD CC.2.MD.1

Lesson Objective: Make an inch ruler and use it to measure the lengths of objects.

Make and Use a Ruler

Use a paper strip. Mark the sides of a color tile.
Mark 6 tiles. Color each part.

Each part is about ____I inch____ long.

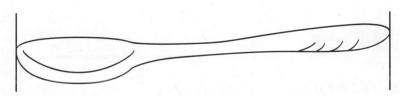

Line up the left edge of the bracelet with
the first mark. Count the inches.

The bracelet is about __5__ inches long.

Measure the length with your ruler. Count the inches.

1.

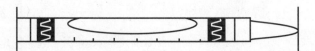

about _____ inches

2.

about _____ inches

Core Standards for Math, Grade 2

1. Each square tile is about 1 inch long. How long is the ribbon?

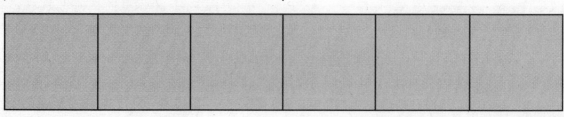

- ○ about 1 inch
- ○ about 2 inches
- ○ about 3 inches
- ○ about 4 inches

2. Each square tile is about 1 inch long. How long is the string?

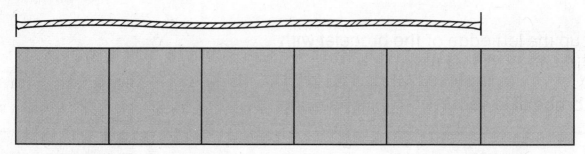

- ○ about 3 inches
- ○ about 4 inches
- ○ about 5 inches
- ○ about 6 inches

PROBLEM SOLVING

3. Use your ruler. Measure the width of this page in inches.

about _____ inches

Name _____

Lesson 67

COMMON CORE STANDARD CC.2.MD.1
Lesson Objective: Measure the lengths of objects to the nearest inch using an inch ruler.

Measure with an Inch Ruler

1. Line up one end with 0.

2. Find the inch mark closest to the other end.

3. Read the number of inches at that mark.

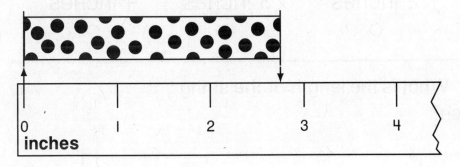

The ribbon is about ___3___ inches long.

Measure the length to the nearest inch.

1.

_____ inches

2.

_____ inches

3.

_____ inches

1. Use an inch ruler. What is the length of the marker to the nearest inch?

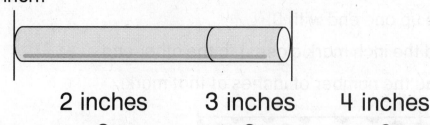

1 inch	2 inches	3 inches	4 inches
○	○	○	○

2. Use an inch ruler. What is the length of the string to the nearest inch?

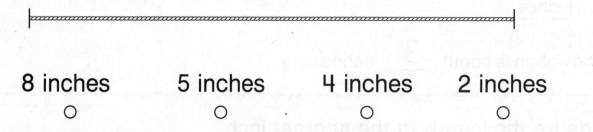

8 inches	5 inches	4 inches	2 inches
○	○	○	○

3. Use an inch ruler. What is the length of the bead to the nearest inch?

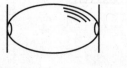

1 inch	2 inches	3 inches	4 inches
○	○	○	○

PROBLEM SOLVING REAL WORLD

4. Measure the string. What is its total length?

_____ inches

Lesson 68

COMMON CORE STANDARD CC.2.MD.1
Lesson Objective: Select appropriate tools for measuring different lengths.

Choose a Tool

Use an inch ruler to measure short lengths.

Use a yardstick to measure greater lengths.

Use a measuring tape to measure lengths that are not flat.

Choose the best tool for measuring the real object. Then measure and record the length.

1. a pencil

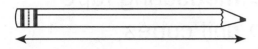

Tool: _____

Length: _____

2. a chalkboard

Tool: _____

Length: _____

1. Sam wants to measure the distance around a soup can. Which is the best tool for Sam to use?

   ○ yardstick
   ○ measuring tape
   ○ large paper clip
   ○ inch ruler

2. Taylor wants to measure the length of the school hallway. Which is the best tool for him to use?

   ○ inch ruler
   ○ centimeter ruler
   ○ yardstick
   ○ unit cubes

3. Stacey wants to measure some paintbrushes to find one that is 6 inches long. Which is the best tool for her to use?

   ○ inch ruler
   ○ paper clip
   ○ yardstick
   ○ unit cubes

4. Angelina wants to measure the distance around her basketball. Which is the best tool for her to use?

   ○ inch ruler
   ○ measuring tape
   ○ unit cubes
   ○ yardstick

5. Draw a picture of something you would use a centimeter ruler to measure.

Lesson 69

COMMON CORE STANDARD CC.2.MD.1
Lesson Objective: Measure lengths of objects to the nearest centimeter using a centimeter ruler.

Measure with a Centimeter Ruler

Line up the left end of the ribbon with the zero mark on the ruler.

Which centimeter mark is closest to the other end of the ribbon?

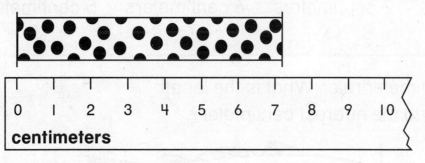

The ribbon is about ___7___ centimeters long.

Measure the length to the nearest centimeter.

1.

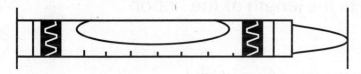

_____ centimeters

2.

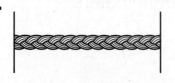

_____ centimeters

3.

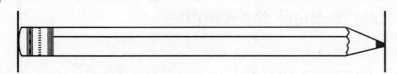

_____ centimeters

1. Use a centimeter ruler. What is the length of the pen cap to the nearest centimeter?

8 centimeters ○   7 centimeters ○   6 centimeters ○   5 centimeters ○

2. Use a centimeter ruler. What is the length of the fish to the nearest centimeter?

8 centimeters ○   10 centimeters ○   12 centimeters ○   16 centimeters ○

3. Use a centimeter ruler. What is the length of the ribbon to the nearest centimeter?

5 centimeters ○   7 centimeters ○   8 centimeters ○   9 centimeters ○

PROBLEM SOLVING REAL WORLD

4. Draw a string that is about 8 centimeters long. Then use a centimeter ruler to check the length.

Name_____

Lesson 70

COMMON CORE STANDARD CC.2.MD.2

Lesson Objective: Measure the lengths of objects in both inches and feet to explore the inverse relationship between size and number of units.

Measure in Inches and Feet

The real folder is about 12 inches wide.
The real folder is also about 1 foot wide.

12 inches is the same as 1 foot.

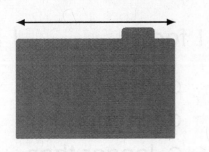

Measure to the nearest inch.
Then measure to the nearest foot.

Find the real object.	Measure.
1. desk	____ inches ____ feet
2. rug	____ inches ____ feet
3. map	____ inches ____ feet

1. Which of the following makes the sentence correct?

   I foot is _____ I inch.

   ○ the same as
   ○ shorter than
   ○ longer than

2. Mia measures the length of a book to the nearest inch. It is about 12 inches long. How long is the book?

   ○ 1 foot
   ○ 2 feet
   ○ 6 feet
   ○ 12 feet

3. Lee has a string that is 3 inches long. Pat has a string that is 3 feet long. Which of the following is correct?

   ○ Lee's string is longer.
   ○ Pat's string is longer.
   ○ Both strings are the same length.

PROBLEM SOLVING

4. Jake has a piece of yarn that is 4 feet long. Blair has a piece of yarn that is 4 inches long. Who has the longer piece of yarn? Explain.

   _____

   _____

   _____

   _____

Centimeters and Meters

COMMON CORE STANDARD CC.2.MD.2
Lesson Objective: Measure the lengths of objects in both centimeters and meters to explore the inverse relationship between size and number of units.

You can measure longer
lengths in meters.

I meter is the same as
100 centimeters.

The real board is about 100 centimeters tall.
So, the real board is about I meter tall.

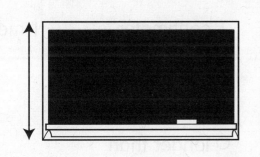

Measure to the nearest centimeter.
Then measure to the nearest meter.

Find the real object.	Measure.
desk _(image of desk)_	_____ centimeters _____ meters
door _(image of door)_	_____ centimeters _____ meters
classroom floor _(image of classroom floor)_	_____ centimeters _____ meters

1.

2.

3.

Core Standards for Math, Grade 2

1. Which makes the sentence correct?

I centimeter is _____ I meter.

○ the same as

○ shorter than

○ longer than

2. Tina measures the length of a table to the nearest meter. It is about I meter long. About how many centimeters long is the table?

○   I centimeter

○   5 centimeters

○   10 centimeters

○   100 centimeters

3. Which is the best choice for the length of a real bookshelf?

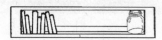

○ I centimeter   ○ 10 centimeters   ○ I meter   ○ 10 meters

PROBLEM SOLVING  REAL WORLD

4. Sally will measure the length of a wall in both centimeters and meters. Will there be fewer centimeters or fewer meters? Explain.

_____

_____

_____

Estimate Lengths in Inches

COMMON CORE STANDARD CC.2.MD.3
Lesson Objective: Estimate the lengths of
objects by mentally partitioning the lengths
into inches.

The bead is 1 inch long. How many beads will fit on the string?
Four beads will fit on the string.

About how long is the string? The string is about _____4_____ inches long.

Circle the best estimate for the length of the string.

1.

2 inches   4 inches   6 inches

2.

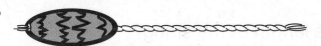

1 inch   3 inches   5 inches

3.

1 inch   2 inches   4 inches

4.

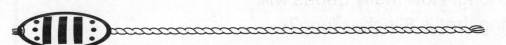

5 inches   8 inches   10 inches

Core Standards for Math, Grade 2

1. Lily has some beads that are 1 inch long each.
   She wants to put them on a string.

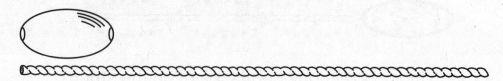

Which is the best estimate for the length of the string?

5 inches   3 inches   2 inches   1 inch
   ○   ○   ○   ○

2. Leo has some beads that are 1 inch long each.
   He wants to put them on a string.

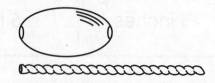

Which is the best estimate for the length of the string?

1 inch   2 inches   3 inches   4 inches
   ○   ○   ○   ○

PROBLEM SOLVING REAL WORLD

Solve. Write or draw to explain.

3. Ashley has some beads. Each bead
   is 2 inches long. How many beads will
   fit on a string that is 8 inches long?

   _____ beads

Lesson 73

COMMON CORE STANDARD CC.2.MD.3
Lesson Objective: Estimate the lengths of objects in feet.

Estimate Lengths in Feet

About how many rulers will fit along the length
of a real whiteboard?

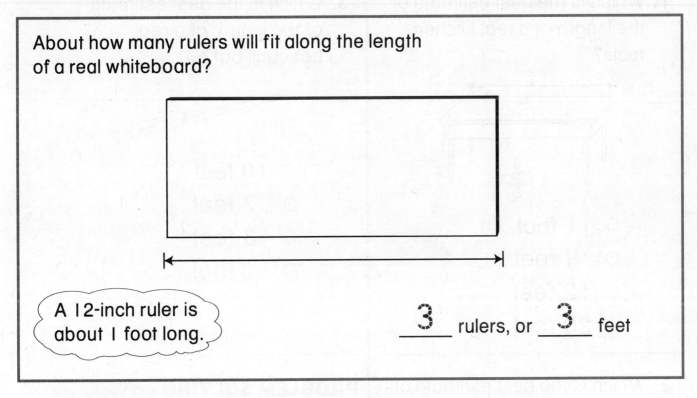

A 12-inch ruler is
about 1 foot long.

___3___ rulers, or ___3___ feet

**Find each object. Estimate how many 12-inch rulers
will be about the same length as the object.**

1. chalkboard

Estimate: _____ rulers, or _____ feet

2. poster

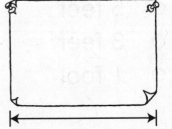

Estimate: _____ rulers, or _____ feet

1. Which is the best estimate of the length of a real kitchen table?

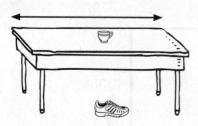

- ○ 1 foot
- ○ 4 feet
- ○ 12 feet
- ○ 20 feet

2. Which is the best estimate of the length of a real folder?

- ○ 10 feet
- ○ 5 feet
- ○ 3 feet
- ○ 1 foot

3. Which is the best estimate of the length of a real baseball bat?

- ○ 10 feet
- ○ 7 feet
- ○ 3 feet
- ○ 1 foot

PROBLEM SOLVING

Solve. Write or draw to explain.

4. Mr. and Mrs. Baker place 12-inch rulers along the length of a rug. They each line up 3 rulers along the edge of the rug. What is the length of the rug?

about _____ feet

Lesson 74

COMMON CORE STANDARD CC.2.MD.3
Lesson Objective: Estimate lengths of
objects in centimeters by comparing them to
known lengths.

Estimate Lengths in Centimeters

The ribbon is about 8 centimeters long. How can you find
the most reasonable estimate for the length of the string?

ribbon

string

1 centimeter

(6 centimeters)

10 centimeters

Think: 1 centimeter is
not reasonable because
the string is much longer
than 1 cube.

Think: 10 centimeters is
not reasonable because
the string is shorter than
the ribbon.

1. The rope is about 7 centimeters long. Circle the
best estimate for the length of the yarn.

rope

yarn

5 centimeters   9 centimeters   14 centimeters

2. The pencil is about 10 centimeters long. Circle the
best estimate for the length of the ribbon.

pencil

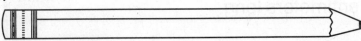

ribbon

5 centimeters   9 centimeters   12 centimeters

1. The length of the string is about 3 centimeters.

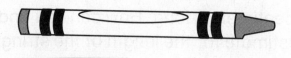

Which is the best estimate for the length of
the crayon?

1 centimeter	2 centimeters	4 centimeters	7 centimeters
○	○	○	○

2. The pencil is about 8 centimeters long.

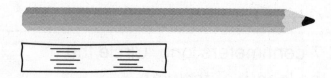

Which is the best estimate for the length of
the ribbon?

1 centimeter	4 centimeters	9 centimeters	12 centimeters
○	○	○	○

PROBLEM SOLVING REAL WORLD

3. The string is about 6 centimeters long. Draw
a pencil that is about 12 centimeters long.

Name _____

Lesson 75

COMMON CORE STANDARD CC.2.MD.3
Lesson Objective: Estimate the lengths of
objects in meters.

Estimate Lengths in Meters

Estimate the length of the chalk tray.

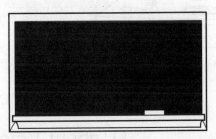

The chalk tray is about the same
length as 2 meter sticks.

So, the chalk tray is about _____2_____ meters long.

Find the real object.
Estimate its length in meters.

1. window

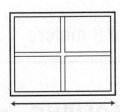

    about _____ meters

2. bookshelf

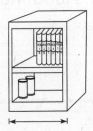

    about _____ meters

1. Which is the best estimate for the width of a real stove?

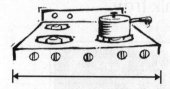

- ○ about 4 meters
- ○ about 2 meters
- ○ about 3 meters
- ○ about 1 meter

2. Which is the best estimate for the length of a real bus?

- ○ about 3 meters
- ○ about 6 meters
- ○ about 4 meters
- ○ about 12 meters

PROBLEM SOLVING

3. Barbara and Luke each placed 2 meter sticks end-to-end along the length of a large table. About how long is the table?

about _____ meters

Name_____

Lesson 76

COMMON CORE STANDARD CC.2.MD.4
Lesson Objective: Measure and then find
the difference in the lengths of two objects.

Measure and Compare Lengths

Which object is longer? How much longer?

1. Measure the leaf.

The leaf is _____*9*_____ centimeters.

2. Measure the stick.

The stick is _____*5*_____ centimeters.

3. Complete the number sentence to find the difference.

_____*9*_____ – _____*5*_____ = _____*4*_____
centimeters   centimeters   centimeters

The leaf is _____*4*_____ centimeters longer than the stick.

Measure the length of each object. Write a number sentence to find the difference between the lengths.

1.

_____ centimeters

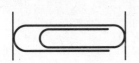

_____ centimeters

_____ – _____ = _____
centimeters   centimeters   centimeters

The string is _____ centimeters longer than the paper clip.

Core Standards for Math, Grade 2

1. Measure the length of each object. How much longer is the celery than the carrot?

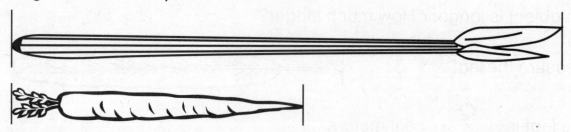

| 1 centimeter | 3 centimeters | 4 centimeters | 7 centimeters |
| ○ | ○ | ○ | ○ |

2. Which number sentence can be used to find how much longer the ribbon is than the paper clip?

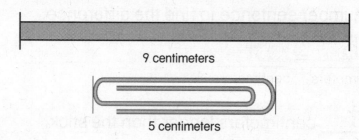

9 centimeters

5 centimeters

○ $9 + 5 = 14$ ○ $9 - 5 = 4$

○ $9 + 4 = 13$ ○ $5 - 4 = 1$

PROBLEM SOLVING  REAL WORLD

Solve. Write or draw to explain.

3. A string is 11 centimeters long, a ribbon is 24 centimeters long, and a large paper clip is 5 centimeters long. How much longer is the ribbon than the string?

_____ centimeters

Core Standards for Math, Grade 2

Name_____

Lesson 77

COMMON CORE STANDARD CC.2.MD.5
Lesson Objective: Solve addition and
subtraction problems involving the lengths of
objects by using the strategy *draw a diagram*.

Problem Solving • Add and Subtract in Inches

Zack has two strings. One string is 12 inches long and the other string is 5 inches long. How long are Zack's strings altogether?

Unlock the Problem

What do I need to find?

how long Zack's
strings are in all

What information do I need to use?

One string is __12__ inches long.

The other string is __5__ inches long.

Show how to solve the problem.

12 + 5 = ▨   The strings are __17__ inches long in all.

Write a number sentence using a ▨ for the missing number. Solve.

1. Sara has two pieces of yarn. Each piece is 7 inches long. How many inches of yarn does she have in all?

_____   Sara has _____ inches of yarn in all.

1. Mr. Owen has a board that is 17 inches long. Then he cuts 8 inches off the board. How long is the board now?

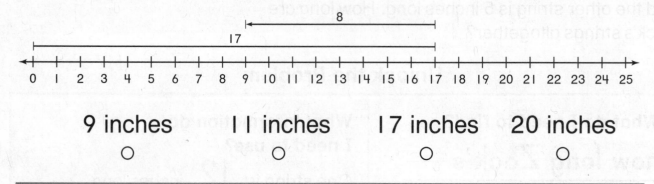

9 inches ○   11 inches ○   17 inches ○   20 inches ○

2. Juan has a cube train that is 13 inches long. He removes 5 inches of the cube train. How long is the cube train now?

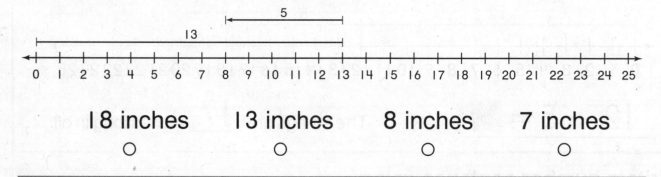

18 inches ○   13 inches ○   8 inches ○   7 inches ○

3. Meg has a ribbon that is 9 inches long and another ribbon that is 12 inches long. How many inches of ribbon does Meg have in all?

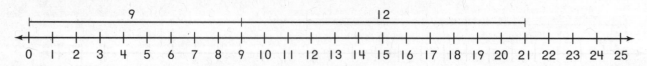

_____ inches

Name _____

Lesson 78

COMMON CORE STANDARD CC.2.MD.6
Lesson Objective: Solve problems involving
adding and subtracting lengths by using the
strategy *draw a diagram*.

Problem Solving • Add and Subtract Lengths

Christy has a ribbon that is 12 centimeters long.
Erin has a ribbon that is 9 centimeters long. How
many centimeters of ribbon do they have altogether?

Unlock the Problem

What do I need to find?	**What information do I need to use?**
how much ribbon	Christy has ___12___ centimeters of ribbon.
they have altogether	Erin has ___9___ centimeters of ribbon.

Show how to solve the problem.

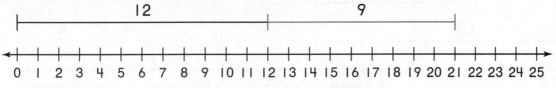

$$12 + 9 = \boxed{}$$

They have ___21___ centimeters of ribbon altogether.

Write a number sentence using a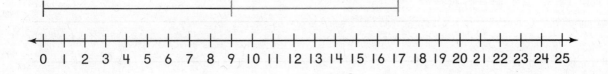
for the missing number. Then solve.

1. Lucas has one string that is 9 centimeters long
   and another string that is 8 centimeters long.
   How many centimeters of string are there in all?

_____   _____ centimeters of string in all

1. Karen has a toy car that is 9 centimeters long. She has a toy truck that is 14 centimeters long. She puts them end-to-end. How long are the car and truck together?

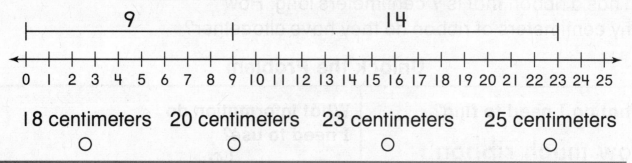

18 centimeters   20 centimeters   23 centimeters   25 centimeters

    ○   ○   ○   ○

2. Matt had a fruit roll that was 13 centimeters long. Then he ate 7 centimeters of the fruit roll. How long is the fruit roll now?

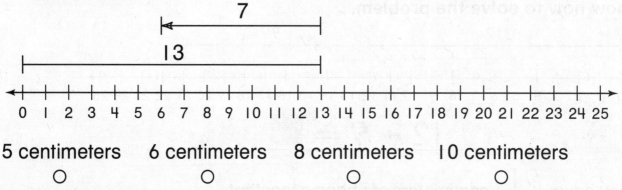

5 centimeters   6 centimeters   8 centimeters   10 centimeters

    ○   ○   ○   ○

3. Amy drew this diagram to show a problem about lengths in centimeters.

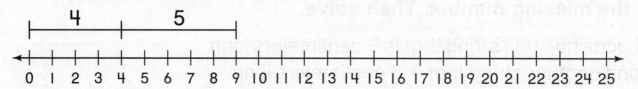

Write a problem that Amy might be trying to solve. Solve the problem.

_____

_____

_____

_____ centimeters

Core Standards for Math, Grade 2

Name_____

Lesson 79

COMMON CORE STANDARD CC.2.MD.7
Lesson Objective: Tell and write time to
the hour and half hour.

Time to the Hour and Half Hour

It is zero minutes after the hour.
Look at how you write this time.

It is 30 minutes after the hour.
Look at how you write this time.

Look at the clock hands. Write the time.

1.

2.

3.

4.

5.

6.

1. Petra's soccer practice starts at 5:00.
   Which clock shows this time?

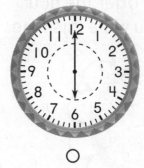   

    ○   ○   ○   ○

2. Lee leaves school at 2:30. Which clock
   shows this time?

    ○   ○   ○   ○

PROBLEM SOLVING REAL WORLD

3. Amy's music lesson begins at 4:00.
   Draw hands on the clock to show
   this time.

Core Standards for Math, Grade 2

Name_____

Lesson 80

COMMON CORE STANDARD CC.2.MD.7
Lesson Objective: Tell and write time to
the nearest five minutes.

Time to 5 Minutes

The minute hand moves from one
number to the next in 5 minutes.

Start at the 12. Count by fives.

Stop at the number the minute
hand points to.

The hour is 8 o'clock.

It is 20 minutes after 8:00.

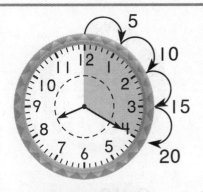

Look at the clock hands. Write the time.

1.

2.

3.

4.

5.

6.

1. What is the time on the clock?

○ 3:40
○ 3:50
○ 4:10
○ 10:20

2. What is the time on the clock?

○ 3:15
○ 3:00
○ 12:10
○ 12:15

PROBLEM SOLVING REAL WORLD

Draw the minute hand to show the time.
Then write the time.

3. My hour hand points between the 4 and the 5.
My minute hand points to the 9. What time do I show?

COMMON CORE STANDARD CC.2.MD.7
Lesson Objective: Practice telling time to
the nearest five minutes.

Practice Telling Time

Use the clock hands to tell time.
First find the hour.

The hour is ___11___.

Now figure out minutes.
When the minute hand points
to the 3 it is quarter past.

It is ___15___ minutes past 11.

The time is ___quarter past 11___.

Draw the minute hand to show the time.
Write the time.

1. quarter past 9

2. 30 minutes after 11

3. half past 10

4. 15 minutes after 6

1. Which clock shows half past 7?

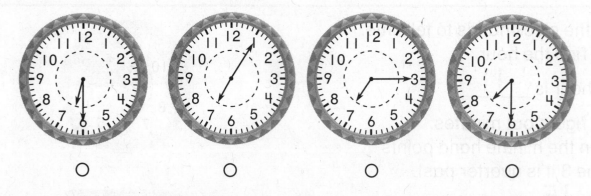

○   ○   ○   ○

2. Which clock shows ten minutes after 2?

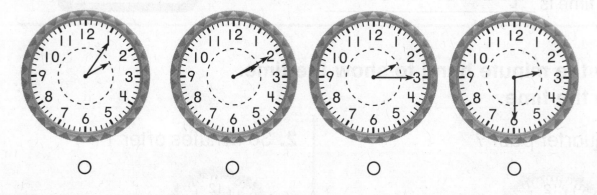

○   ○   ○   ○

PROBLEM SOLVING

Draw hands on the clock to solve.

3. Josh got to school at half past 8.
Show this time on the clock.

Core Standards for Math, Grade 2

Name_____

Lesson 82

COMMON CORE STANDARD CC.2.MD.7
Lesson Objective: Tell and write time using
a.m. and p.m.

A.M. and P.M.

A.M. times *start* after midnight.

A.M. times *end* before noon.

get dressed for school

7:30

P.M. times *start* after noon.

P.M. times *end* before midnight.

tell a bedtime story

7:30

Write the time. Then circle A.M. or P.M.

I. finish homework

A.M.

P.M.

2. go to morning recess

A.M.

P.M.

3. eat breakfast

A.M.

P.M.

4. get ready for bed

A.M.

P.M.

1. Rhonda saw a movie last night. The clock shows when the movie ended.

What time did the movie end?

○ 9:35 P.M.
○ 9:45 P.M.
○ 9:25 A.M.
○ 9:35 A.M.

2. Keisha has a math test today. The clock shows when the test starts.

What time does the test start?

○ 11:10 P.M.
○ 11:20 P.M.
○ 11:05 A.M.
○ 11:10 A.M.

PROBLEM SOLVING REAL WORLD

Use the list of times. Complete the story.

3. Jess woke up at _____. She got

on the bus at _____ and went to

school. She left school at _____.

3:15 P.M.
8:30 A.M.
7:00 A.M.

Lesson 83

COMMON CORE STANDARD CC.2.MD.8
Lesson Objective: Find the total values of collections of dimes, nickels, and pennies.

Dimes, Nickels, and Pennies

   I dime 10¢

Count dimes by tens.
<u>10¢</u>, <u>20¢</u>, <u>30¢</u>

   I nickel 5¢

Count nickels by fives.
<u>5¢</u>, <u>10¢</u>, <u>15¢</u>

   I penny 1¢

Count pennies by ones.
<u>1¢</u>, <u>2¢</u>, <u>3¢</u>

Count on by tens.   Count on by fives.   Count on by ones.

<u>10¢, 20¢, 25¢, 30¢, 31¢</u>

31¢
total value

Count on to find the total value.

1.

_____

total value

2.

_____

total value

1. What is the total value of these coins?

8¢   24¢   28¢   40¢
○   ○   ○   ○

2. What is the total value of these coins?

50¢   40¢   35¢   25¢
○   ○   ○   ○

3. Sharon has these coins. What is
   the total value of Sharon's coins?

26¢   41¢   46¢   51¢
○   ○   ○   ○

PROBLEM SOLVING REAL WORLD

Solve. Write or draw to explain.

4. Aaron has 5 dimes and 2 nickels.
   How much money does Aaron have?

   _____

Name_____

Lesson 84

COMMON CORE STANDARD CC.2.MD.8
Lesson Objective: Find the total values of collections of quarters, dimes, nickels, and pennies.

Quarters

Count by twenty-fives.

I quarter
25¢

25¢, 50¢, 75¢
_____

Count by twenty-fives. Count by tens. Count by ones.

6l¢
total value

25¢, 50¢, 60¢, 6l¢
_____

Count on to find the total value.

I.

total value

_____

2.

total value

_____

Name_____

1. Fred has these coins in his pocket.

How much money does Fred have in his pocket?

49¢   54¢   59¢   95¢
○   ○   ○   ○

---

2. What is the total value of these coins?

62¢   71¢   72¢   77¢
○   ○   ○   ○

---

3. What is the total value of these coins?

73¢   80¢   83¢   88¢
○   ○   ○   ○

---

4. Draw coins to show 56¢.
   Use as few coins as possible.

COMMON CORE STANDARD CC.2.MD.8
Lesson Objective: Order coins in a collection by value and then find the total value.

Count Collections

Draw the coins in order by value. Start with the coin that has the greatest value.

(25¢) (10¢) (5¢) (1¢)

Start at 25¢. Count on.

25¢, 35¢, 40¢, 41¢   total value ___41¢___

Draw the coins in order. Find the total value.

1.

total value _____

2.

total value _____

3.

total value _____

---

1. What is the total value of these coins?
You can draw and label the coins from
greatest to **least** value.

74¢ ○   79¢ ○   81¢ ○   84¢ ○

2. Mike has these coins in his wallet.

What is the total value of the coins
in Mike's wallet?

21¢ ○   29¢ ○   42¢ ○   47¢ ○

PROBLEM SOLVING  REAL WORLD

Solve. Write or draw to explain.

3. Rebecca has these coins. She
spends 1 quarter. How much
money does she have left?

_____

Lesson 86

COMMON CORE STANDARD CC.2.MD.8
Lesson Objective: Represent money
amounts less than a dollar using two different
combinations of coins.

Show Amounts in Two Ways

You can show the same amount in different ways.

15¢

Count the coins.
5, 10, 15

Trade 2 nickels
for 1 dime.

15¢

Count the coins.
10, 15

Use coins. Show the amount in two ways.
Draw and label the coins.

1.

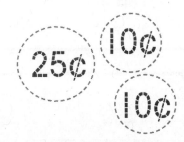

_____

2.

_____

1. Which coin will make the amounts equal?

? _____

○   ○   ○   ○

2. Which coin will make the amounts equal?

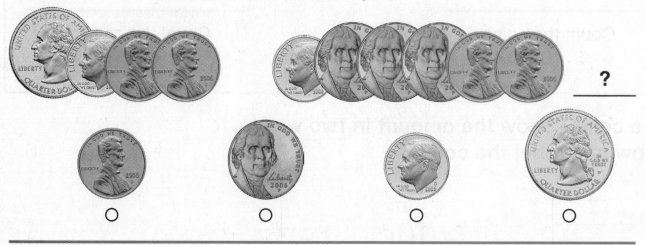

? _____

○   ○   ○   ○

PROBLEM SOLVING REAL WORLD

3. Madeline uses fewer than 5 coins to pay 60¢. Draw coins to show one way she could pay 60¢.

Lesson 87

COMMON CORE STANDARD CC.2.MD.8
Lesson Objective: Show one dollar in a variety of ways.

One Dollar

One dollar has the same value as 100 cents.

You can write one dollar like this: $1.00

Count on to 100¢ to show $1.00.

$1.00
_____
total value

25¢, 50¢, 75¢, 100¢

Draw more coins to show $1.00. Write the total value.

1. dimes

_____

2. nickels

_____

1. Which group of coins has a total value of $1.00?

2. Jessie has these coins.

   Which coin does she need to make $1.00?

3. Lawrence paid $1.00 for a juice drink.
   He paid with only dimes and nickels.
   Draw the coins he could have used.

Amounts Greater Than $1

1. Count on and circle the coins that make one dollar.

2. Count on from 100¢ to find the total value for the whole group of coins.

110¢   120¢

3. 120¢ is the same as 1 dollar and 20 cents.

Write ___$1.20___.

Circle the money that makes $1. Then write the total value of the money shown.

1.

_____

2.

_____

1. What is the total value of this money?

$1.07 $1.15 $1.22 $1.27
○   ○   ○   ○

2. What is the total value of these coins?

$1.46 $1.36 $1.31 $1.26
○   ○   ○   ○

3. What is the total value of this money?

$1.45 $1.50 $1.55 $1.60
○   ○   ○   ○

PROBLEM SOLVING REAL WORLD

Solve. Write or draw to explain.

4. Grace found 3 quarters, 3 dimes, and 1 nickel in her pocket. How much money did she find?

_____

Name_____

Lesson 89

COMMON CORE STANDARD CC.2.MD.8
Lesson Objective: Solve word problems involving money by using the strategy *act it out.*

Problem Solving • Money

Erin used one $1 bill and 3 nickels to buy a marker.
How much money did Erin use to buy the marker?

Unlock the Problem

What do I need to find?	**What information do I need to use?**
how much money Erin used to buy the marker	Erin used one $1 bill and 3 nickels

Show how to solve the problem.

Draw to show the money that Erin used.

$1   5¢   5¢   5¢

Erin used $1.15 to buy the marker.

Use play coins and bills to solve.
Draw to show what you did.

1. Zeke has one $1 bill, 2 dimes, and 1 nickel.
   How much money does Zeke have? _____

1. Molly has 3 quarters, 3 dimes, and
   4 nickels in her coin bank. How much
   money does she have?

   $1.15 $1.20 $1.25 $1.40
     ○   ○   ○   ○

2. Tim spent two $1 bills, 2 quarters,
   1 nickel, and 3 pennies at a fair.
   How much money did he spend?

   $2.30 $2.33 $2.53 $2.58
     ○   ○   ○   ○

3. Chris gave his sister three $1 bills,
   4 quarters, 1 dime, and 2 pennies.
   How much money did he give his sister?

   $3.97 $4.12 $4.17 $4.25
     ○   ○   ○   ○

4. Bill wants to buy a model car that costs
   $3.65. Draw bills and coins to show the
   money he could use to buy the car.

Name_____

Lesson 90

COMMON CORE STANDARD CC.2.MD.9

Lesson Objective: Measure the lengths of objects and use a line plot to display the measurement data.

Display Measurement Data

Each X on the line plot is for the length of one book.

X
X   X   X
X   X   X   X
| | | |
5   6   7   8

Lengths of Books in Inches

One book is 5 inches long.
One book is 6 inches long.
Two books are 7 inches long.
One book is 8 inches long.

1. Use an inch ruler. Measure and record the lengths of 4 pencils in inches.

1st pencil: _____ inches	
2nd pencil: _____ inches	
3rd pencil: _____ inches	
4th pencil: _____ inches	

2. Write the numbers and draw the Xs to complete the line plot.

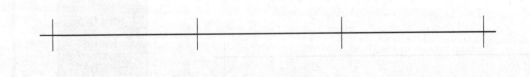

Lengths of Pencils in Inches

Name _____

**Use the line plot
for Questions 1-4.**

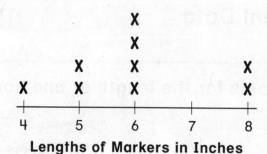

Lengths of Markers in Inches

---

1. How many markers are
4 inches long?

○ 1
○ 4
○ 6
○ 8

3. How many markers are
7 inches long?

○ 7
○ 2
○ 1
○ 0

2. How many markers does the
line plot show?

○ 10
○ 9
○ 8
○ 4

4. How many inches long is the
longest marker?

○ 5
○ 6
○ 8
○ 9

PROBLEM SOLVING  REAL WORLD

5. Jesse measured the lengths of some strings.
Use his list to complete the line plot.

Lengths of Strings
5 inches
7 inches
6 inches
8 inches
5 inches

_____

Name_____

Lesson 91

COMMON CORE STANDARD CC.2.MD.10

Lesson Objective: Collect data in a survey and record that data in a tally chart.

Collect Data

You can take a survey to get information.

Which is your favorite sport?

Each tally mark stands for one person's answer. Count the tally marks.

Favorite Sport

Sport	Tally	Total
soccer	IIII	4
basketball	IIII	5
football	III	3

Elijah asked his classmates to choose their favorite breakfast food. He made this chart.

1. Write numbers to complete the chart.

Favorite Breakfast Food

Food	Tally	Total
cereal	IIII III	8
pancakes	IIII	
toast	III	
eggs	IIII	

2. How many classmates chose pancakes?

_____ classmates

3. Which breakfast food did the fewest classmates choose?

_____

Amber asked her classmates about their favorite flavor of yogurt. Use the tally chart for 1–4.

Favorite Yogurt Flavor	
Yogurt	**Tally**
peach	|||
berry	||||
lime	||
vanilla	|||| ||

1. How many classmates chose berry?

   ○ 2   ○ 5
   ○ 3   ○ 6

2. Which flavor did the **fewest** classmates choose?

   ○ berry   ○ vanilla
   ○ lime   ○ peach

3. Which statement is true?

   ○ More classmates chose lime than peach.
   ○ More classmates chose vanilla than berry.
   ○ Fewer classmates chose vanilla than lime.
   ○ Fewer classmates chose vanilla than peach.

4. What is another question you can ask based on the tally chart? Write your question and then answer it.

   _____

   _____

Name_____

Lesson 92

COMMON CORE STANDARD CC.2.MD.10
Lesson Objective: Interpret data in picture graphs and use that information to solve problems.

Read Picture Graphs

A picture graph uses pictures to show information.

Favorite Color					
red	crayon	crayon	crayon		
blue	crayon	crayon	crayon	crayon	crayon
green	crayon	crayon			

Key: Each crayon **stands for 1 child.**

The row with <u>blue</u> has 5 pictures.

So, <u>5</u> children chose blue.

Use the picture graph to answer the questions.

1. How many children chose red?   _____ children

_____

2. Did more children choose green
   or choose red?   _____

_____

3. Which color was chosen by
   the most children?   _____

_____

4. How many children in all chose
   a favorite color?   _____ children

Name_____

Lesson 92

CC.2.MD.10

Use the picture graph for 1–5.

Favorite Recess Game									
tag	☺	☺							
catch	☺	☺	☺	☺	☺	☺	☺	☺	☺
kickball	☺	☺	☺	☺	☺	☺			
jacks	☺	☺	☺	☺					

Key: Each ☺ stands for 1 child.

1. Which game did the **most** children choose?

   ○ tag
   ○ kickball
   ○ catch
   ○ jacks

3. How many children chose kickball?

   ○ 3
   ○ 6
   ○ 9
   ○ 15

2. How many children in all chose tag or jacks?

   ○ 15
   ○ 9
   ○ 6
   ○ 3

4. How many more children chose catch than kickball?

   ○ 3
   ○ 4
   ○ 5
   ○ 7

5. How many children chose a recess game? Explain how you know.

_____

_____

www.harcourtschoolsupply.com

© Houghton Mifflin Harcourt Publishing Company

184

Core Standards for Math, Grade 2

Lesson 93

COMMON CORE STANDARD CC.2.MD.10
Lesson Objective: Make picture graphs to
represent data.

Make Picture Graphs

This picture graph uses 1 picture for each animal.
Draw a △ for each tally mark.

Animals at the Pet Store	
Animal	**Tally**
fish	IIII
hamster	II
turtle	III

Animals at the Pet Store					
fish	△	△	△	△	
hamster	△	△			
turtle	△	△	△		

Key: Each △ stands for 1 animal.

How many turtles are at the pet store? ___3___ turtles

1. Use the tally chart to complete the picture graph.
   Draw a ☺ for each child.

Favorite Color	
Color	**Tally**
pink	IIII I
yellow	III
blue	IIII II

Favorite Color					
pink	☺	☺	☺	☺	☺
yellow					
blue					

Key: Each ☺ stands for 1 child.

2. Which color did the fewest children choose? _____

3. How many children chose pink? _____ children

4. How many more children chose blue
   than chose yellow? _____ more children

Use the tally chart and picture graph for 1–5.

Favorite Vegetable	
Fruit	**Tally**
carrot	卌
lettuce	|||
tomato	卌	
pepper	||

Favorite Vegetable					
carrot	☺	☺	☺	☺	☺
lettuce					
tomato					
pepper					

Key: Each ☺ stands for 1 child.

---

1. How many ☺ should be in the picture graph next to pepper?

- ○ 2
- ○ 3
- ○ 5
- ○ 6

3. How many ☺ should be in the picture graph next to tomato?

- ○ 7
- ○ 6
- ○ 4
- ○ 3

---

2. How many ☺ should be in the picture graph next to lettuce?

- ○ 1
- ○ 2
- ○ 3
- ○ 6

4. How many fewer children chose pepper than tomato?

- ○ 1
- ○ 2
- ○ 3
- ○ 4

---

5. How is the tally chart like the picture graph?

_____

_____

Name _____

Read Bar Graphs

Look at the number below the right end of each bar.

This number tells how many of each model Max has.

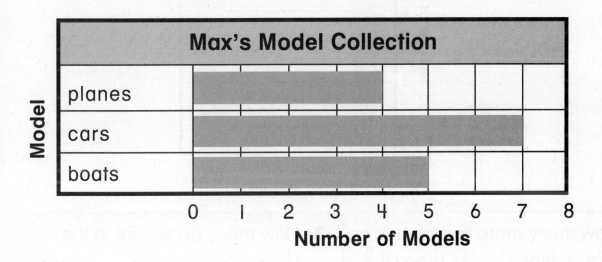

Max's Model Collection

Model	
planes	
cars	
boats	

0   1   2   3   4   5   6   7   8
Number of Models

The bar for model cars ends at 7.

So, Max has ___7___ car models.

Use the bar graph.

1. How many model planes does Max have?   _____ model planes

_____

2. Does Max have more model
boats or model planes?   more model _____

_____

3. How many models does Max have in all?   _____ models

Name_____

Use the bar graph for 1–5.

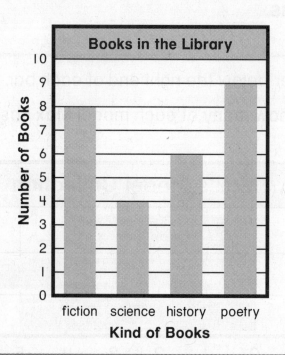

Books in the Library

Number of Books

10
9
8
7
6
5
4
3
2
1
0

fiction   science   history   poetry

Kind of Books

---

1. How many more history books than science books are in the library?

   ○ 10   ○ 4

   ○ 6   ○ 2

3. How many books are in the library in all?

   ○ 27   ○ 23

   ○ 26   ○ 17

---

2. How many fiction books are in the library?

   ○ 4   ○ 8

   ○ 5   ○ 9

4. Which kind of book does the library have the fewest of?

   ○ fiction   ○ history

   ○ science   ○ poetry

---

4. Can you answer question 4 without reading any numbers on the graph? Explain.

_____

_____

Lesson 95

COMMON CORE STANDARD CC.2.MD.10
Lesson Objective: Make bar graphs to represent data.

Make Bar Graphs

These bar graphs show how many games Alex, Sarah, and Tony played.

- Alex played 5 games.
- Sarah played 3 games.
- Tony played 4 games.

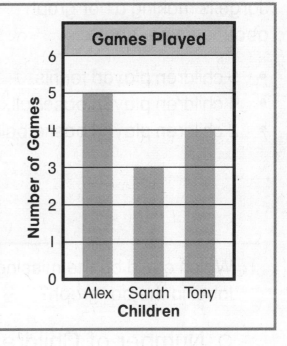

Jim is making a bar graph to show the number of markers his friends have.

- Adam has 4 markers.
- Clint has 3 markers.
- Erin has 2 markers.

1. Write labels for the graph.

_____

2. Draw bars in the graph to show the number of markers that Clint and Erin have.

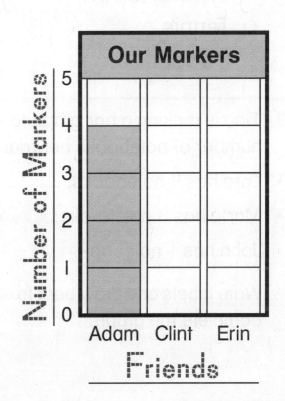

Use the information for 1–2.

Jorge is making a bar graph about summer sports.

- 5 children played tennis.
- 4 children played baseball.
- 2 children played basketball.

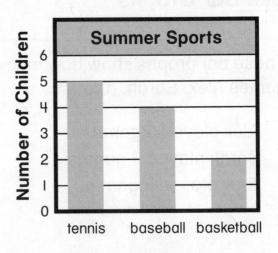

1. Which could be the missing label in the bar graph?

   ○ Number of Children
   ○ Type of Sport
   ○ Tennis
   ○ Soccer

2. How many more children played tennis than played basketball?

   ○ 1   ○ 3
   ○ 2   ○ 4

3. Tina is making a bar graph to show the number of notebooks her friends have.

   - Lara has 4 notebooks.
   - Marta has 3 notebooks.
   - John has 1 notebook.

   Write labels and draw bars to complete the graph.

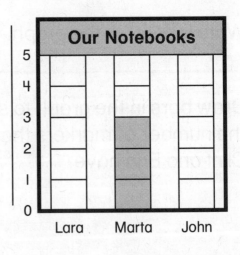

Name_____

Lesson 96

COMMON CORE STANDARD CC.2.MD.10
Lesson Objective: Solve problems involving
data by using the strategy *make a graph.*

Problem Solving • Display Data

The list shows how many hours
Morgan worked on her project.
Describe how the number of hours
changed from Week 1 to Week 4.

Week 1	1 hour
Week 2	2 hours
Week 3	3 hours
Week 4	4 hours

Unlock the Problem

What do I need to find?

how the number of _hours_
changed from Week 1 to Week 4

**What information do
I need to use?**

the number of _hours_ Morgan
worked on her project each week

Show how to solve the problem.

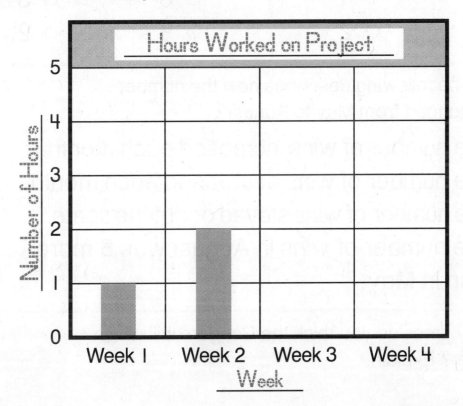

The number of hours _____

_____

Use the bar graph for 1–4.

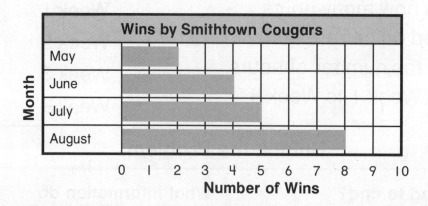

Wins by Smithtown Cougars

Month

May
June
July
August

Number of Wins

1. How many times did the Cougars win in May?

  ○ 8   ○ 4

  ○ 5   ○ 2

2. How many more wins did the Cougars have in August than in July?

  ○ 6   ○ 3

  ○ 4   ○ 2

3. Which of the following describes how the number of wins changed from May to August?

  ○ The number of wins increased each month.

  ○ The number of wins decreased each month.

  ○ The number of wins stayed about the same.

  ○ The number of wins in August was 8 more than in May.

4. How many times do you think the Cougars will win in September? Explain.

_____

_____

_____

Three-Dimensional Shapes

Three-dimensional objects come in different shapes.

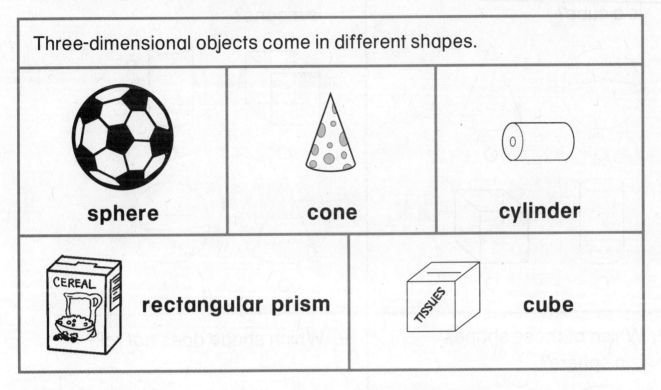

sphere

cone

cylinder

rectangular prism

cube

Circle the objects that match the shape name.

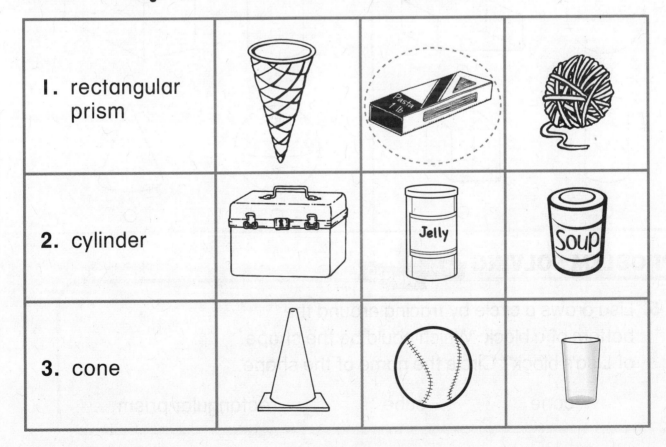

1. rectangular prism

2. cylinder

3. cone

1. Which of these shapes
is a cube?

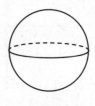 

○ ○

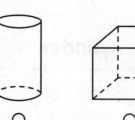

○ ○

2. Which of these shapes
is a sphere?

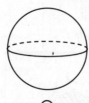 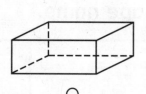

○ ○

 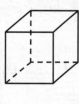

○ ○

3. Which of these shapes
is a cone?

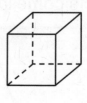

○ ○

 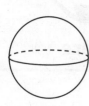

○ ○

4. Which shape does *not* roll?

 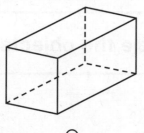

○ ○

○ ○

PROBLEM SOLVING REAL WORLD

5. Lisa draws a circle by tracing around the
bottom of a block. Which could be the shape
of Lisa's block? Circle the name of the shape.

cone   cube   rectangular prism

Core Standards for Math, Grade 2

Name_____

Lesson 98

COMMON CORE STANDARD CC.2.G.1
Lesson Objective: Identify and describe
three-dimensional shapes according to the
number of faces, edges, and vertices.

Attributes of
Three-Dimensional Shapes

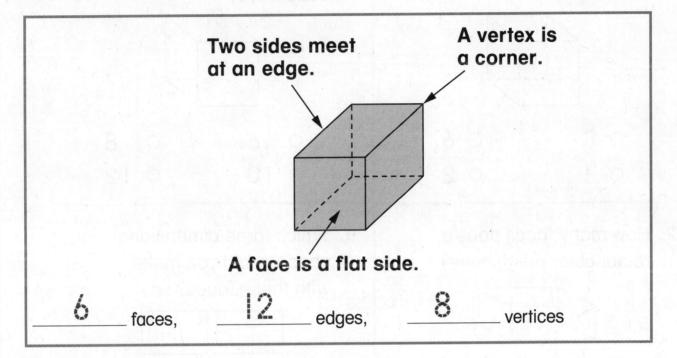

**Two sides meet
at an edge.**

**A vertex is
a corner.**

A face is a flat side.

_____6_____ faces,   _____12_____ edges,   _____8_____ vertices

Write how many for each.

	faces	edges	vertices
1. cube			
2. rectangular prism			

1. How many vertices does a cube have?

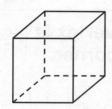

○ 8   ○ 6
○ 4   ○ 2

2. How many faces does a rectangular prism have?

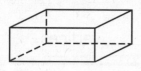

○ 4
○ 6
○ 8
○ 12

3. How many edges does a cube have?

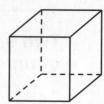

○ 6   ○ 8
○ 10   ○ 12

4. Which three-dimensional shape could you make with these faces?

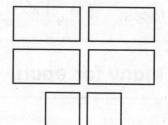

○ cone
○ cube
○ rectangular prism
○ cylinder

PROBLEM SOLVING REAL WORLD

5. Kevin keeps his marbles in a container that has the shape of a cube. He wants to paint each face a different color. How many different paint colors does he need?

_____ different paint colors

Name_____

Lesson 99

COMMON CORE STANDARD CC.2.G.1
Lesson Objective: Name 3-, 4-, 5-, and 6-sided shapes according to the number of sides and vertices.

Two-Dimensional Shapes

Count sides and vertices.
A pentagon has 5 sides.

A hexagon has 6 vertices.

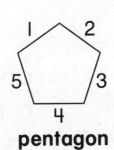

pentagon

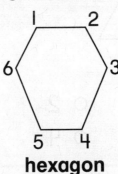

hexagon

Write the number of sides and the number of vertices.

1. triangle

_____ sides
_____ vertices

2. rectangle

_____ sides
_____ vertices

3. quadrilateral

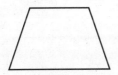

_____ sides
_____ vertices

4. pentagon

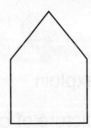

_____ sides
_____ vertices

1. How many vertices does a triangle have?

○ 1   ○ 2
○ 3   ○ 4

2. Which names a shape with 6 sides and 6 vertices?

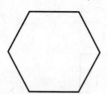

○ hexagon
○ pentagon
○ quadrilateral
○ triangle

3. How many sides does a quadrilateral have?

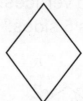

○ 2   ○ 4
○ 5   ○ 8

4. Kay draws a house. What is the shape of Kay's drawing?

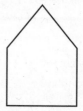

○ triangle
○ quadrilateral
○ pentagon
○ hexagon

PROBLEM SOLVING REAL WORLD

Solve. Draw or write to explain.

5. Oscar is drawing a picture of a house.
He draws a pentagon shape for a window.
How many sides does his window have?

_____ sides

Name_____

Lesson **100**

COMMON CORE STANDARD CC.2.G.1
Lesson Objective: Identify angles in
two-dimensional shapes.

Angles in Two-Dimensional Shapes

Two sides meet and form an angle.

There are ___4___ angles in a square.

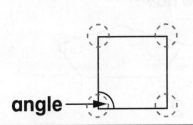

angle ➜

Circle the angles in each shape.
Write how many.

1.

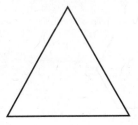

_____ angles

2.

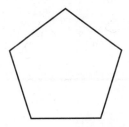

_____ angles

3.

_____ angles

1. How many angles does the shape have?

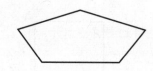

- ○ 2
- ○ 3
- ○ 4
- ○ 5

2. How many angles does the shape have?

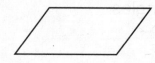

- ○ 4
- ○ 5
- ○ 6
- ○ 8

3. Tom drew a shape with only 3 angles. What kind of shape did he draw?

- ○ hexagon
- ○ quadrilateral
- ○ triangle
- ○ square

4. How many angles does the shape have?

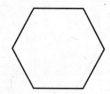

- ○ 12
- ○ 10
- ○ 8
- ○ 6

PROBLEM SOLVING

5. Logan drew 2 two-dimensional shapes that had 8 angles in all. Draw shapes Logan could have drawn.

Lesson 101

COMMON CORE STANDARD CC.2.G.1

Lesson Objective: Sort two-dimensional shapes according to their attributes.

Sort Two-Dimensional Shapes

Circle the shapes with 5 sides.

4 sides   3 sides   5 sides   6 sides

Circle the shapes with fewer than 5 angles.

3 angles   6 angles   4 angles   5 angles

Circle the shapes that match the rule.

1. Shapes with 4 sides

2. Shapes with more than 4 angles

1. Which rule matches the shapes?

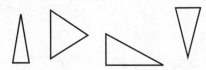

  - ○ shapes with 4 angles
  - ○ shapes with 3 angles
  - ○ shapes with 5 angles
  - ○ shapes with 4 sides

2. Which rule matches the shapes?

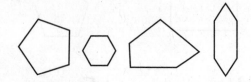

  - ○ shapes with 5 sides
  - ○ shapes with 6 angles
  - ○ shapes with more than 4 sides
  - ○ shapes with fewer than 4 angles

3. Which shape has fewer than 4 sides?

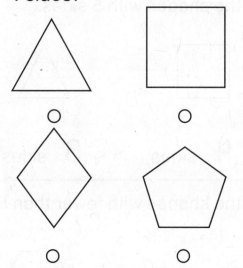

4. Johanna walks home from school each day. She sees that a road sign has the shape of a pentagon. How many angles does the road sign have?

  - ○ 3
  - ○ 4
  - ○ 5
  - ○ 6

5. Draw a shape that has fewer than 4 angles. Name your shape.

_____

COMMON CORE STANDARD CC.2.G.2
Lesson Objective: Partition rectangles into equal-size squares and find the total number of these squares.

Partition Rectangles

How many color tiles cover this rectangle?

Make a row of color tiles on the rectangle. Trace around the square tiles.

How many squares? __3__ squares

Use color tiles to cover the rectangle.
Trace around the square tiles. Write how many.

1.

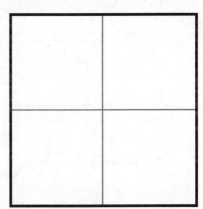

Number of rows: _____

Number of columns: _____

Total: _____ squares

2.

Number of rows: _____

Number of columns: _____

Total: _____ squares

1. Rick covered a rectangle with square tiles. He made 2 rows. He made 4 columns. How many square tiles did he use?

    ○ 5
    ○ 6
    ○ 7
    ○ 8

2. Linda covered a rectangle with square tiles. She made 5 rows. She made 1 column. How many square tiles did she use?

    ○ 10
    ○ 6
    ○ 5
    ○ 4

3. Maria covered a rectangle with square tiles. She made 3 rows. She made 3 columns. How many square tiles did she use?

    ○ 9
    ○ 8
    ○ 6
    ○ 3

4. Jeff covered a rectangle with square tiles. He made 4 rows. He made 3 columns. How many square tiles did he use?

    ○ 7
    ○ 12
    ○ 14
    ○ 16

PROBLEM SOLVING

Solve. Write or draw to explain.

5. Nina wants to put color tiles on a square. 3 color tiles fit across the top of the square. How many rows and columns of of squares will Nina need? How many color tiles will she use in all?

Number of rows: _____

Number of columns: _____

Total: _____ square tiles

_____ tiles

Name_____

Lesson 103

COMMON CORE STANDARD CC.2.G.3
Lesson Objective: Identify and name equal
parts of circles and rectangles as halves,
thirds, or fourths.

Equal Parts

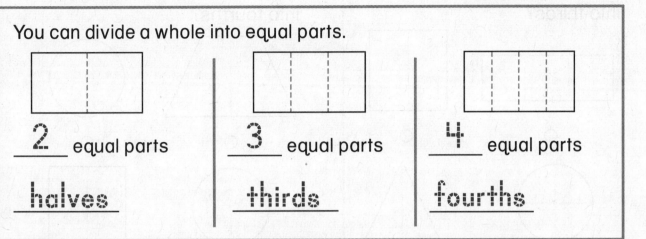

You can divide a whole into equal parts.

_2_ equal parts

halves

_3_ equal parts

thirds

_4_ equal parts

fourths

Write how many equal parts there are in the whole.
Write halves, thirds, or fourths to name the equal parts.

1.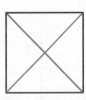

_4_ equal parts

fourths

2.

____ equal parts

_____

3.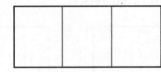

____ equal parts

_____

4.

____ equal parts

_____

5.

____ equal parts

_____

6.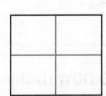

____ equal parts

_____

Core Standards for Math, Grade 2

I. Which whole has been divided into thirds?

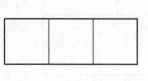

○   ○

○   ○

2. Which whole has been divided into halves?

○   ○

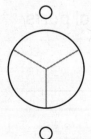 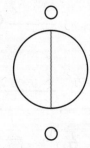

○   ○

3. Which whole has been divided into fourths?

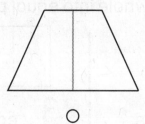 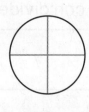

○   ○

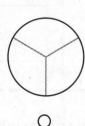 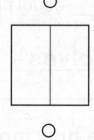

○   ○

4. Which shape is **not** divided into equal parts?

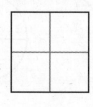

○   ○

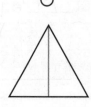 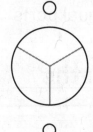

○   ○

5. Write how many equal parts are in the whole. Write **halves**, **thirds**, or **fourths** to name the equal parts.

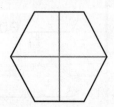 _____ equal parts

_____

Core Standards for Math, Grade 2

Show Equal Parts of a Whole

Trace to show the equal parts.

2 equal parts
2 halves

3 equal parts
3 thirds

4 equal parts
4 fourths

Draw to show equal parts.

1. halves

2. thirds

3. halves

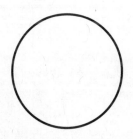

4. fourths

1. Alan divides a circle into thirds. How many equal parts does he show?

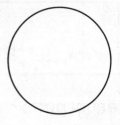

○ I   ○ 2
○ 3   ○ 4

2. Sue divides a rectangle into halves. How many equal parts does she show?

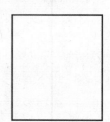

○ 5   ○ 4
○ 3   ○ 2

3. A sandwich is cut into thirds. How many pieces of sandwich are there?

○ 2
○ 3
○ 4
○ 5

4. A cake is cut into fourths. How many pieces of cake are there in all?

○ 4
○ 3
○ 2
○ I

PROBLEM SOLVING

Solve. Write or draw to explain.

5. Joe has one sandwich. He cuts the sandwich into fourths. How many pieces of sandwich does he have?

_____ pieces

Name_____

Lesson 105

COMMON CORE STANDARD CC.2.G.3

Lesson Objective: Identify and describe one equal part as a half of, a third of, or a fourth of a whole.

Describe Equal Parts

One equal part of each shape is shaded.

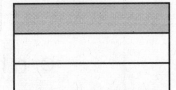

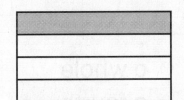

| A half of the shape is shaded. | A third of the shape is shaded. | A fourth of the shape is shaded. |

Draw to show halves.
Color a half of the shape.

1.

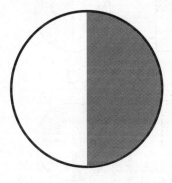

2.

Draw to show fourths.
Color a fourth of the shape.

3.

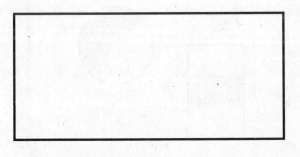

4.

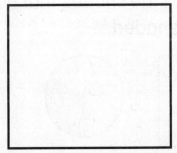

Core Standards for Math, Grade 2

1. How much of the shape is shaded?

- ○ a whole
- ○ a fourth
- ○ a third
- ○ a half

3. How much of the shape is shaded?

- ○ a half
- ○ a third
- ○ a fourth
- ○ a whole

2. Which of these has a half of the shape shaded?

○   ○

○   ○

4. Which of these has a third of the shape shaded?

○   ○

○   ○

PROBLEM SOLVING REAL WORLD

5. Circle all the shapes that have a third of the shape shaded.

 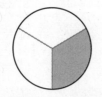 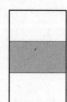 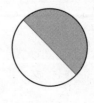

Name_____

COMMON CORE STANDARD CC.2.G.3
Lesson Objective: Solve problems involving wholes divided into equal shares by using the strategy *draw a diagram*.

Problem Solving • Equal Shares

Two gardens are the same size. Each garden is divided into halves, but the gardens are divided differently. How might the gardens be divided?

Unlock the Problem

What do I need to find?	**What information do I need to use?**
<u>how the gardens are</u> <u>divided</u>	There are ___2___ gardens. Each garden is divided into <u>halves</u>.

Show how to solve the problem.

Draw to show your answer.

1. Sophie has two pieces of paper that are the same size. She wants to divide each piece into fourths. What are two different ways she can divide the pieces of paper?

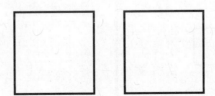

1. Dana divides a square into halves like this.

Which is another way she can divide the square into halves?

○   ○

2. Ben divides a rectangle into fourths like this.

Which is another way he can divide the rectangle into fourths?

○   ○

○   ○

3. Mr. Jones cut a sandwich into fourths. Each piece is a triangle. Which way did he cut the sandwich?

○   ○

○   ○

4. Helen divides her garden into thirds like this.

Show another way she can divide her garden into thirds.

Lesson 1
COMMON CORE STANDARD CC.2.OA.1
Lesson Objective: Use bar models to represent a variety of addition and subtraction situations.

Name _____

Algebra • Use Drawings to Represent Problems

You can use bar models to show problems.
There are 5 girls and 11 boys at the park.
How many more boys than girls are at the park?

How many boys? → | 11 |

How many girls? → | 5 | 6

Write a number sentence. $11 - 5 = 6$

There are __6__ more boys than girls.

Complete the bar model. Then write a number sentence to solve.

1. Nathan had 7 stamps. Then he got 9 more stamps. How many stamps does Nathan have now?

| 7 | 9 |
16

$7 + 9 = 16$ __16__ stamps

Name _____
Lesson 1
CC.2.OA.1

1. Eli has 13 marbles. Amber has 6 marbles. How many more marbles does Eli have than Amber?

| 13 |
| 6 |

- ● 7
- ○ 8
- ○ 10
- ○ 19

3. Julian has 14 grapes. He gives 5 grapes to Lindsay. How many grapes does Julian have left?

| _____ | 5 |
14

- ○ 19
- ○ 11
- ○ 10
- ● 9

2. There were 8 ants on a rock. Some more ants joined them. Then there were 13 ants on the rock. How many ants joined them?

- ○ 4
- ● 5
- ○ 13
- ○ 22

4. Sarah had 6 books. Her grandmother gave her 5 more books. How many books does Sarah have now?

- ○ 1
- ○ 10
- ● 11
- ○ 13

5. Jared has 15 red cubes. He has 7 blue cubes. How many more red cubes than blue cubes does he have? Complete the bar model.

__8__ more red cubes

| 15 |
| 7 | 8 |

Name _____
Lesson 2
COMMON CORE STANDARD CC.2.OA.1
Lesson Objective: Write equations to represent and solve a variety of addition and subtraction situations.

Algebra • Use Equations to Represent Problems

Some red fish and 9 green fish are in a tank.
The tank has 14 fish. How many red fish are there?

| 9 | ? |
14

Write a number sentence.
Use a ■ for the missing number.

$14 - 9 = ■$

__5__ red fish in the tank.

Write a number sentence for the problem.
Use a ■ for the missing number. Then solve.

Possible number sentence is given.

1. There are 13 trees in a park. 8 are pine trees. The rest are oak trees. How many oak trees are there?

So there are $13 - 8 = ■$

__5__ oak trees.

| 8 | ? |
13

Name _____
Lesson 2
CC.2.OA.1

1. There are 14 bees in an apple tree. There are 9 bees in a pear tree. How many more bees are in the apple tree than in the pear tree?

Which number sentence could you use to solve the problem?

- ○ $9 + 14 = ■$
- ● $■ + 9 = 14$
- ○ $9 = ■ + 14$
- ○ $14 = 9 - ■$

3. Lenny had 16 toy cars. He gave some cars to his sister. Now he has 9 cars. Which number sentence shows how many cars he gave to his sister?

- ● $16 - 9 = 7$
- ○ $9 - 2 = 7$
- ○ $16 - 6 = 10$
- ○ $16 + 2 = 18$

2. There are 11 children at the park. Then 5 children go home. Which number sentence shows how many children are still at the park?

- ○ $8 - 4 = 4$
- ● $11 - 5 = 6$
- ○ $11 + 5 = 16$
- ○ $11 + 6 = 17$

PROBLEM SOLVING REAL WORLD

Write or draw to show how you solved the problem.

4. Tony has 7 blue cubes and 6 red cubes. How many cubes does he have in all?

__13__ cubes

Answer Key

Problem Solving • Addition

Lesson Objective: Solve problems involving 2-digit addition by using the strategy *draw a diagram.*

Hannah has 14 pencils. Juan has 13 pencils.
How many pencils do they have in all?

Unlock the Problem

What do I need to find?	What information do I need to use?
how many pencils	Hannah has 14 pencils.
they have in all	Juan has 13 pencils.

Show how to solve the problem.

Hannah's 14 pencils	Juan's 13 pencils

_____?_____ pencils in all

$14 + 13 = \blacksquare$ 27 pencils

Solve.   Check children's work.

1. There are 21 peanuts in a bag. 16 more peanuts are put into the bag. How many peanuts are in the bag in all?

21 peanuts	16 peanuts

$21 + 16 = \blacksquare$

____37____ peanuts in all   ____37____ peanuts

---

1. James and Flora have 38 markers in all. Flora has 16 markers. How many markers does James have?
   - ● 22
   - ○ 44
   - ○ 54
   - ○ 62

2. A pet store has two fish tanks. There are 48 fish in one tank and 23 fish in the other tank. How many fish are there in both tanks?
   - ○ 25
   - ○ 26
   - ● 71
   - ○ 72

3. Miles puts 52 stickers in his notebook. Julie puts 29 stickers in her notebook. How many stickers do Miles and Julie put in their notebook in all?
   - ○ 23
   - ○ 71
   - ● 81
   - ○ 94

4. There are 37 pencils in the pencil box. Ms. Marks hands out 18 of the pencils to the class. How many pencils are left in the pencil box?
   - ○ 55
   - ○ 29
   - ○ 25
   - ● 19

5. Label the bar model. Write a number sentence with a $\blacksquare$ for the missing number. Solve.

   Tom has 23 red pens and 38 black pens. How many pens does Tom have?

23	38

   _____61_____

   $23 + 38 = \blacksquare$

   ____61____ pens

Algebra • Write Equations to Represent Addition

Lesson Objective: Represent addition situations with number sentences using a symbol for the unknown number.

Sara took 16 pictures.
Then she took 17 more pictures.
How many pictures did Sara take in all?

Use a bar model to show the problem.

16 pictures	17 pictures

_____?_____ pictures in all

Write a number sentence. Solve.

$16 + 17 = \blacksquare$ ____33____ pictures

Use a bar model to show the problem. Write a number sentence. Use a $\blacksquare$ for the missing number. Then solve.

1. Josh has 18 basketball cards and 14 baseball cards. How many cards does he have altogether?

18 basketball cards	14 baseball cards

_____32_____ cards altogether

$18 + 14 = \blacksquare$ ____32____ cards

---

1. Gina scores 26 points in the game. Eric scores 31 points. Which number sentence can be used to find how many they score in all?
   - ○ $26 + \blacksquare = 31$
   - ○ $31 + \blacksquare = 55$
   - ● $26 + 31 = \blacksquare$
   - ○ $31 + 62 = \blacksquare$

2. On a hike, Sierra sees 42 frogs and 27 turtles. Which number sentence can be used to find how many frogs and turtles Sierra sees in all?
   - ○ $\blacksquare + 24 = 27$
   - ● $42 + 27 = \blacksquare$
   - ○ $42 + 72 = \blacksquare$
   - ○ $27 + \blacksquare = 42$

3. Tim and Liz collect stamps. Tim has 93 stamps. Liz has 32 stamps. How many stamps do Tim and Liz have in all?
   - ● 125
   - ○ 115
   - ○ 120
   - ○ 105

4. Amber collects 49 pebbles at the beach. Meg collects 44 pebbles at the beach. How many pebbles do they collect in all?
   - ○ 103
   - ● 93
   - ○ 83
   - ○ 5

PROBLEM SOLVING 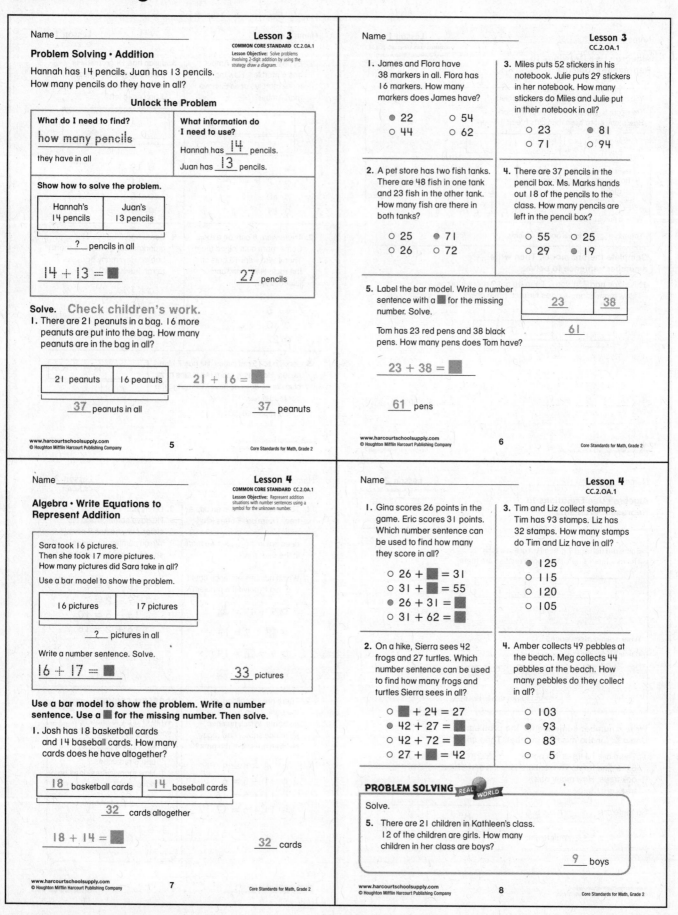 REAL WORLD

Solve.

5. There are 21 children in Kathleen's class. 12 of the children are girls. How many children in her class are boys?

   ____9____ boys

Name_____

Lesson 5
COMMON CORE STANDARD CC.2.OA.1
Lesson Objective: Solve problems involving 2-digit subtraction by using the strategy *draw a diagram.*

Problem Solving • Subtraction

Katie had a box of 42 craft sticks. She used 26 craft sticks to make a sailboat. How many craft sticks were not used?

Unlock the Problem

What do I need to find?	What information do I need to use?
how many craft sticks were not used	Katie had 42 craft sticks She used 26 craft sticks

Show how to solve the problem.

craft sticks used → | 26 | 16 | ← craft sticks not used

42

craft sticks in all

$42 - 26 = $ ■   16 craft sticks

Write a number sentence with a ■ for the missing number. Solve.   Check children's work.

1. Ms. Lee took 35 purses to the fair. She sold 14 purses. How many purses does she have left?

14	?
35	

$35 - 14 = $ ■   21 purses

Name_____

Lesson 5
CC.2.OA.1

1. Mrs. Dobbs has 38 stickers. She gives away 12 stickers. Which number sentence shows how many stickers she has left?

___	___

- ○ $26 - 12 = 14$
- ○ $12 + 26 = 38$
- ● $38 - 12 = 26$
- ○ $12 - 6 = 6$

2. Which bar model shows the number sentence?

$22 - 8 = 14$

○ | 14 | 8 |
14

● | 14 | 8 |
22

○ | 22 | 14 |
8

○ | 22 | 8 |
14

3. Alison makes 54 cookies. She gives away 32 cookies. Which number sentence shows how many cookies she has left?

___	___

- ○ $54 + 32 = 86$
- ○ $32 + 50 = 82$
- ○ $32 - 12 = 20$
- ● $54 - 32 = 22$

4. Larry had 46 carrots. Rabbits ate 27 carrots. How many carrots does he have left? Label the bar model. Write a number sentence with a ■ for the missing number. Solve.

27	19
46	

Possible answer:
$46 - 27 = $ ■

19 carrots

Name_____

Lesson 6
COMMON CORE STANDARD CC.2.OA.1
Lesson Objective: Represent subtraction situations with number sentences using a symbol for the unknown number.

Algebra • Write Equations to Represent Subtraction

37 birds were in the trees.
13 birds flew away.
How many birds are in the trees now?

The bar model shows the problem.

13	?
37	

Use the bar model to write a number sentence.

$37 - 13 = $ ■

Subtract to find the missing part.

So, the answer is 24 birds.

$$\begin{array}{r} 37 \\ -13 \\ \hline 24 \end{array}$$

Write a number sentence for the problem. Use a ■ for the missing number. Then solve.   Possible number sentence is given.

1. Gina has 23 pens. 15 pens are blue and the rest are red. How many pens are red?

15	?
23	

$23 - 15 = $ ■   8 red pens

Name_____

Lesson 6
CC.2.OA.1

1. There were 27 children in a classroom. Then 18 children went outside. Which number sentence can be used to find how many children are in the classroom now?

- ○ $27 + 18 = $ ■
- ○ $18 - 27 = $ ■
- ○ $45 - 27 = $ ■
- ● $27 - 18 = $ ■

2. Ms. Clark baked some cookies. She gave 25 cookies to her friends. Now she has 7 cookies. Which number sentence can be used to find how many cookies she baked?

- ○ ■ $+ 25 = 7$
- ● ■ $- 25 = 7$
- ○ ■ $+ 7 = 25$
- ○ ■ $- 25 = 32$

3. Tom had 45 marbles. He gave 31 marbles to his sister. Which number sentence can be used to find how many marbles Tom has now?

- ● $45 - 31 = $ ■
- ○ $31 - 45 = $ ■
- ○ $45 + 31 = $ ■
- ○ $76 - 31 = $ ■

4. There were 36 apples on a tree. Some apples fell down. Now there are 11 apples on the tree. Which number sentence can be used to find how many apples fell down?

- ○ $36 + $ ■ $= 11$
- ○ $11 - $ ■ $= 36$
- ● $36 - $ ■ $= 11$
- ○ $25 - $ ■ $= 11$

PROBLEM SOLVING REAL WORLD

Solve. Write or draw to explain.

5. There were 21 children in the library. After 7 children left the library, how many children were still in the library?   14 children

Answer Key

Solve Multistep Problems

Mr. Wright had 34 blue pencils and 25 red pencils. He gave 42 pencils to students. How many pencils does he have now?

The first sentence tells you what Mr. Wright had.

 and

blue pencils   red pencils

$$\begin{array}{r} 34 \\ + 25 \\ \hline 59 \end{array}$$

The second sentence tells you that he gave 42 of the pencils to students.

pencils

$$\begin{array}{r} 59 \\ - 42 \\ \hline 17 \end{array}$$

Mr. Wright has __17__ pencils now.

Solve the problem in steps. Show what you did.

1. Kara had 37 stickers. She gave 11 stickers to Sam and 5 stickers to Jane. How many stickers does Kara have now?

   Check children's work.

   __21__ stickers

---

1. There were 53 people in line at the movies. Then 17 people left the line. Later, 22 more people left. How many people are in line now?
   - ○ 4
   - ● 14
   - ○ 24
   - ○ 58

2. Molly has 39 coins in her collection. Her sister has 26 coins. How many more coins are needed so they will have 85 coins in all?
   - ● 20
   - ○ 21
   - ○ 30
   - ○ 65

3. Jack counted 48 ants on one log and 33 ants on another log. Some ants left. Then there were 54 ants in all. How many ants left?
   - ○ 17
   - ○ 21
   - ● 27
   - ○ 81

4. There were 24 ducks on a pond. Then 27 more ducks came to the pond. Later, 14 ducks flew away. How many ducks are on the pond now?
   - ○ 51
   - ● 37
   - ○ 27
   - ○ 21

PROBLEM SOLVING REAL WORLD

Solve. Write or draw to explain.

5. Ava has 25 books. She gives away 7 books. Then Tom gives her 12 books. How many books does Ava have now?

   __30__ books

Use Doubles Facts

Use doubles facts to help you find sums.

If you know 6 + 6, you can find 6 + 7.

__6__ + __6__ = __12__

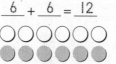

7 is 1 more than 6. So 6 + 7 is 1 more than 6 + 6.

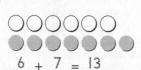

__6__ + __7__ = __13__

Write a doubles fact you can use to find the sum. Write the sum.

Doubles facts may vary. Check children's work.

1. 4 + 5 = __9__   ___ + ___ = ___

2. 5 + 6 = __11__   ___ + ___ = ___

3. 7 + 8 = __15__   ___ + ___ = ___

4. 8 + 9 = __17__   ___ + ___ = ___

---

1. Which doubles fact could you use to find the sum?

   4 + 5 = _____
   - ○ 3 + 3 = 6
   - ○ 4 + 6 = 10
   - ● 5 + 5 = 10
   - ○ 6 + 6 = 12

2. Which doubles fact could you use to find the sum?

   9 + 8 = _____
   - ● 8 + 8 = 16
   - ○ 7 + 7 = 14
   - ○ 9 + 1 = 10
   - ○ 10 + 10 = 20

3. What is the sum?

   7 + 6 = _____
   - ○ 11
   - ○ 12
   - ● 13
   - ○ 14

4. Maggie picked 3 apples. Lisa picked 4 apples. How many apples did they pick in all?
   - ○ 6
   - ● 7
   - ○ 8
   - ○ 9

PROBLEM SOLVING REAL WORLD

Solve. Write or draw to explain.

5. There are 6 ants on a log. Then 7 ants crawl onto the log. How many ants are on the log now?

   __13__ ants

Answer Key

Name _____

Practice Addition Facts

Use what you know to find sums.

☆☆☆ ★★★★★

Add in any order.
$3 + 5 = \underline{8}$

★★★★★ ☆☆☆

If you know 3 + 5, then you know 5 + 3.
$5 + 3 = \underline{8}$

☆☆☆☆☆ ★

Count on to add. To add 1, 2, or 3 to any number, count on from that number.
$5 + 1 = \underline{6}$

Write the sums.

1. $5 + 7 = \underline{12}$
   $7 + 5 = \underline{12}$

2. $\underline{6} = 5 + 1$
   $\underline{7} = 5 + 2$

3. $6 + 2 = \underline{8}$
   $6 + 3 = \underline{9}$

4. $\underline{14} = 9 + 5$
   $\underline{14} = 5 + 9$

5. $7 + 3 = \underline{10}$
   $3 + 7 = \underline{10}$

6. $5 + 2 = \underline{7}$
   $5 + 3 = \underline{8}$

7. $\underline{9} = 3 + 6$
   $\underline{9} = 6 + 3$

8. $4 + 1 = \underline{5}$
   $1 + 4 = \underline{5}$

9. $8 + 2 = \underline{10}$
   $8 + 3 = \underline{11}$

Name _____

1. What is the sum for both number sentences?

   $6 + 1 = \underline{\hphantom{..}}$

   $1 + 6 = \underline{\hphantom{..}}$

   ○ 4
   ○ 5
   ○ 6
   ● 7

2. What is the sum?

   $8 + 7 = \underline{\hphantom{..}}$

   ○ 13
   ○ 14
   ● 15
   ○ 16

3. Which of the following has the same sum?

   $2 + 9 = ?$

   ○ 8 + 2
   ● 9 + 2
   ○ 2 + 10
   ○ 3 + 9

4. Marco had 6 stamps. His mother gave him 3 more stamps. How many stamps does Marco have now?

   ○ 7
   ○ 8
   ● 9
   ○ 10

PROBLEM SOLVING  REAL WORLD

Solve. Write or draw to explain.

5. Jason has 7 puzzles. Quincy has the same number of puzzles as Jason. How many puzzles do they have altogether?

   $\underline{14}$ puzzles

Name _____

Algebra • Make a Ten to Add

$8 + 5 = \underline{?}$

Step 1 Start with the greater addend. Break apart the other addend to make a ten.

8 + 5

Step 2 You need to add 2 to 8 to make a ten. So, break apart 5 as 2 and 3.

$8 + 2 = 10$ 3

Step 3 Add on the rest to the 10. $10 + \underline{3} = \underline{13}$

Step 4 Write the sum. $8 + 5 = \underline{13}$

Show how you can make a ten to find the sum. Write the sum.

1. $7 + 6 = \underline{13}$
   3 3
   $10 + \underline{3} = \underline{13}$

2. $9 + 2 = \underline{11}$
   1 1
   $10 + \underline{1} = \underline{11}$

3. $4 + 8 = \underline{12}$
   2 2
   $10 + \underline{2} = \underline{12}$

4. $5 + 9 = \underline{14}$
   $10 + \underline{4} = \underline{14}$

5. $8 + 6 = \underline{14}$
   $10 + \underline{4} = \underline{14}$

6. $4 + 9 = \underline{13}$
   $10 + \underline{3} = \underline{13}$

Name _____

1. How could you break apart the 7 to make a ten?

   6 + 7

   $6 + \underline{\hphantom{..}} + \underline{\hphantom{..}}$

   ○ 2 + 5
   ● 4 + 3
   ○ 5 + 2
   ○ 1 + 6

2. What is the sum?

   $9 + 5 = \underline{\hphantom{..}}$

   ○ 11
   ○ 12
   ○ 13
   ● 14

3. How could you break apart the 9 to make a ten?

   8 + 9

   $8 + \underline{\hphantom{..}} + \underline{\hphantom{..}}$

   ○ 7 + 2
   ○ 4 + 5
   ● 2 + 7
   ○ 3 + 6

4. What is the sum?

   $4 + 8 = \underline{\hphantom{..}}$

   ○ 2
   ● 12
   ○ 13
   ○ 16

PROBLEM SOLVING  REAL WORLD

Solve. Write or draw to explain.

5. There are 9 children on the bus. Then 8 more children get on the bus. How many children are on the bus now?

   $\underline{17}$ children

Answer Key

Name_____

Lesson 11
COMMON CORE STANDARD CC.2.OA.2
Lesson Objective: Find sums of three addends by applying the Commutative and Associative Properties of Addition.

Algebra • Add 3 Addends

Add numbers in any order.
The sum stays the same.

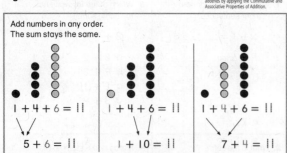

$1 + 4 + 6 = 11$ $1 + 4 + 6 = 11$ $1 + 4 + 6 = 11$

$5 + 6 = 11$ $1 + 10 = 11$ $7 + 4 = 11$

Solve two ways. Circle the two addends you add first.
Circled addends will vary.

1. $2 + 3 + 2 = \underline{7}$ $2 + 3 + 2 = \underline{7}$

2. $7 + 2 + 3 = \underline{12}$ $7 + 2 + 3 = \underline{12}$

3. $1 + 1 + 9 = \underline{11}$ $1 + 1 + 9 = \underline{11}$

4. $6 + 4 + 4 = \underline{14}$ $6 + 4 + 4 = \underline{14}$

Name_____

Lesson 11
CC.2.OA.2

1. What is the sum?

   $2 + 4 + 8 = \underline{}$

   ○ 12
   ● 14
   ○ 15
   ○ 16

2. What is the sum?

   $\begin{array}{r} 4 \\ 3 \\ + 6 \\ \hline \end{array}$

   ● 13
   ○ 10
   ○ 9
   ○ 7

3. What is the sum?

   $\begin{array}{r} 4 \\ 5 \\ + 7 \\ \hline \end{array}$

   ○ 9
   ○ 11
   ● 16
   ○ 17

4. Ava grows 3 red flowers, 4 yellow flowers, and 4 purple flowers in her garden. How many flowers does Ava grow in all?

   ○ 7
   ○ 8
   ○ 10
   ● 11

PROBLEM SOLVING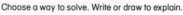

Choose a way to solve. Write or draw to explain.

5. Amber has 2 red crayons, 5 blue crayons, and 4 yellow crayons. How many crayons does she have in all?

   $\underline{11}$ crayons

Name_____

Lesson 12
COMMON CORE STANDARD CC.2.OA.2
Lesson Objective: Use the inverse relationship of addition and subtraction to recall basic facts.

Algebra • Relate Addition and Subtraction

Use addition facts to help you subtract.

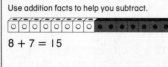

$8 + 7 = 15$

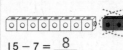

$15 - 7 = \underline{8}$

Think of $8 + 7 = 15$ to find the difference for a related fact:
$15 - 7 = \underline{}$

Write the sum and the difference for the related facts.

1. $6 + 3 = \underline{9}$ 2. $7 + 6 = \underline{13}$
   $9 - 6 = \underline{3}$ $13 - 7 = \underline{6}$

3. $6 + 8 = \underline{14}$ 4. $7 + 4 = \underline{11}$
   $14 - 8 = \underline{6}$ $11 - 7 = \underline{4}$

5. $8 + 4 = \underline{12}$ 6. $8 + 8 = \underline{16}$
   $12 - 4 = \underline{8}$ $16 - 8 = \underline{8}$

7. $9 + 7 = \underline{16}$ 8. $7 + 5 = \underline{12}$
   $16 - 7 = \underline{9}$ $12 - 7 = \underline{5}$

Name_____

Lesson 12
CC.2.OA.2

1. What is the difference for the related subtraction fact?

   $9 + 6 = 15$
   $15 - 9 = \underline{}$

   ○ 3
   ○ 4
   ○ 5
   ● 6

2. What is the sum for the related addition fact?

   $12 - 7 = 5$
   $5 + 7 = \underline{}$

   ○ 11
   ● 12
   ○ 13
   ○ 14

3. Which shows a related addition fact?

   $13 - 6 = 7$

   ● $6 + 7 = 13$
   ○ $7 + 13 = 20$
   ○ $7 - 6 = 1$
   ○ $13 + 6 = 19$

4. There are 11 brown birds and 5 red birds in a tree. How many more brown birds than red birds are there?

   ○ 5
   ● 6
   ○ 7
   ○ 9

PROBLEM SOLVING

Solve. Write or draw to explain.

5. There are 13 children on the bus. Then 5 children get off the bus. How many children are on the bus now?

   $\underline{8}$ children

Name_____ **Lesson 13**
COMMON CORE STANDARD CC.2.OA.2
Practice Subtraction Facts
Lesson Objective: Recall differences for basic facts using mental strategies.

Here are two ways to find differences.

$10 - 3 =$?

Count back 1, 2, or 3.

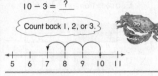

5 6 7 8 9 10 11

$10 - 1 = \underline{9}$
$10 - 2 = \underline{8}$
$10 - 3 = \underline{7}$

Think of a related addition fact.

$3 + 7 = \underline{10}$
So, $10 - 3 = \underline{7}$

Write the difference.

1. $13 - 5 = \underline{8}$ 2. $10 - 4 = \underline{6}$

3. $12 - 3 = \underline{9}$ 4. $11 - 2 = \underline{9}$

5. $9 - 3 = \underline{6}$ 6. $12 - 5 = \underline{7}$

7. $16 - 8 = \underline{8}$ 8. $13 - 7 = \underline{6}$

Name_____ **Lesson 13**
CC.2.OA.2

1. What is the difference?

$15 - 7 = \underline{\quad}$

○ 7
● 8
○ 12
○ 15

2. What is the difference?

$\underline{\quad} = 13 - 9$

● 4
○ 5
○ 6
○ 7

3. What is the difference?

$16 - 7 = \underline{\quad}$

● 9
○ 8
○ 7
○ 6

4. Elena invited 8 friends to her party. 2 of them could not go. How many friends went to Elena's party?

○ 2
○ 4
○ 5
● 6

PROBLEM SOLVING REAL WORLD

Solve. Write or draw to explain.

5. Mr. Li has 16 pencils. He gives 9 pencils to some students. How many pencils does Mr. Li have now?

$\underline{7}$ pencils

Name_____ **Lesson 14**
COMMON CORE STANDARD CC.2.OA.2
Use Ten to Subtract
Lesson Objective: Find differences on a number line to develop the mental strategy of decomposing to simplify facts.

You can get to ten to help find differences.

$13 - 7 =$?

Step ① Start with the first number.

Step ② Subtract ones to get to 10.

$13 - 3 = 10$

Step ③ Subtract the rest from the 10.

Think: I had 13. I subtracted 3 to get to 10.
Now I subtract the 4 I have left. $10 - \underline{4} = \underline{6}$

Step ④ Write the difference. $13 - 7 = \underline{6}$

Show the tens fact you used. Write the difference.

1. $15 - 8 = \underline{7}$
5   3
$10 - \underline{3} = \underline{7}$

2. $12 - 4 = \underline{8}$
2   2
$10 - \underline{2} = \underline{8}$

3. $11 - 7 = \underline{4}$
$10 - \underline{6} = \underline{4}$

4. $13 - 5 = \underline{8}$
$10 - \underline{2} = \underline{8}$

Name_____ **Lesson 14**
CC.2.OA.2

1. Which tens fact could you use to find the difference?

$11 - 4 = \underline{\quad}$
⋀
?   ?

○ $10 - 5 = 5$
○ $10 - 4 = 6$
● $10 - 3 = 7$
○ $10 - 2 = 8$

2. Which tens fact could you use to find the difference?

$16 - 7 = \underline{\quad}$
⋀
?   ?

○ $10 - 4 = 6$
○ $10 - 3 = 7$
○ $10 - 2 = 8$
● $10 - 1 = 9$

3. Mr. Brown picked 12 plums. He gave 8 plums away. How many plums did he have left?

○ 3
● 4
○ 5
○ 6

4. Which number makes the number sentence true?

$13 - 5 = 8$
$10 - \underline{\quad} = 8$

● 2
○ 3
○ 4
○ 6

PROBLEM SOLVING REAL WORLD

Solve. Write or draw to explain.

5. Carl read 15 pages on Monday night and 9 pages on Tuesday night. How many more pages did he read on Monday night than on Tuesday night?

$\underline{6}$ more pages

Answer Key

COMMON CORE STANDARD CC.2.OA.3

Lesson Objective: Classify numbers up to 20 as even or odd.

Algebra · Even and Odd Numbers

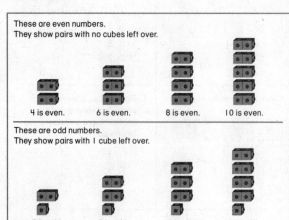

These are even numbers.
They show pairs with no cubes left over.

4 is even. 6 is even. 8 is even. 10 is even.

These are odd numbers.
They show pairs with 1 cube left over.

3 is odd. 5 is odd. 7 is odd. 9 is odd.

Count out the number of cubes.
Make pairs. Then write even or odd.

1. 15 __odd__		2. 11 __odd__	
3. 12 __even__		4. 13 __odd__	
5. 16 __even__		6. 14 __even__	

---

1. The Morris family has an even number of dogs and an odd number of cats. Which could be the number of pets in the Morris family?

○ 1 dog and 2 cats
○ 1 dog and 3 cats
○ 2 dogs and 2 cats
● 2 dogs and 1 cat

2. Elsa shades a pair of ten frames to show an even number. Which could be Elsa's ten frames?

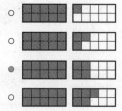

PROBLEM SOLVING REAL WORLD

3. Mr. Dell has an odd number of sheep and an even number of cows on his farm. Circle the choice that could tell about his farm.

(9 sheep and 10 cows)
10 sheep and 11 cows
8 sheep and 12 cows

Lesson Objective: Write equations with equal addends to represent even numbers.

Algebra · Represent Even Numbers

An even number of cubes will make two equal groups.

Count 8 cubes. Put the cubes into two equal groups. Do the two groups have equal numbers of cubes? To check, match one to one.

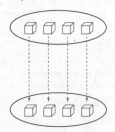

8 = __4__ + __4__

How many cubes are there in all? Complete the addition sentence to show the equal groups.

1. __4__ = __2__ + __2__

2. __6__ = __3__ + __3__

3. __8__ = __4__ + __4__

4. __10__ = __5__ + __5__

---

1. The frames show two groups for 8. Which addition sentence shows the groups?

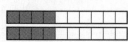

○ 1 + 7 = 8
○ 2 + 6 = 8
○ 3 + 5 = 8
● 4 + 4 = 8

2. Mary and Ana each have the same number of stickers. They have 10 stickers altogether. Which addition sentence shows the number of stickers Mary and Ana each have?

○ 4 + 6 = 10
● 5 + 5 = 10
○ 3 + 7 = 10
○ 2 + 8 = 10

PROBLEM SOLVING REAL WORLD

Solve. Write or draw to explain.

3. The seats in a van are in pairs. There are 16 seats. How many pairs of seats are there?

__8__ pairs of seats

Answer Key

Name_____   **Lesson 17**
COMMON CORE STANDARD CC.2.OA.4

Problem Solving • Equal Groups
Lesson Objective: Solve problems involving equal groups by using the strategy *act it out.*

Clarence puts grapes in 4 rows.
He puts 5 grapes in each row.
How many grapes does Clarence have?

Unlock the Problem

What do I need to find?	**What information do I need to use?**
how many grapes	Clarence has __4__ rows of grapes.
Clarence has	He puts __5__ grapes in each row.

Show how to solve the problem.

○○○○○
○○○○○
○○○○○
○○○○○

Clarence has __20__ grapes.

Draw to show what you did.

1. Rachel puts her markers in 3 rows.
   Each row has 3 markers.
   How many markers does Rachel have?

   Check children's drawings.

   Rachel has __9__ markers.

www.harcourtschoolsupply.com
© Houghton Mifflin Harcourt Publishing Company
33
Core Standards for Math, Grade 2

Name_____   **Lesson 17**
CC.2.OA.4

1. Ms. Green put 4 stamps on each card. How many stamps will she put on 5 cards?
   - ● 20
   - ○ 16
   - ○ 9
   - ○ 8

2. Gina has 4 mice cages. There are 4 mice in each cage. How many mice does Gina have?
   - ○ 8
   - ○ 10
   - ○ 12
   - ● 16

3. Eric puts his dimes in 5 rows. He puts 3 dimes in each row. How many dimes does he have in all?
   - ○ 5
   - ○ 8
   - ○ 12
   - ● 15

4. Rachel puts 4 pencils in each box. How many pencils will she put in 3 boxes?
   - ○ 16
   - ● 12
   - ○ 7
   - ○ 4

5. Rob puts 3 counters in each row. How many counters in all does he put in 4 rows? Draw to show your work.

   Check children's work.

   __12__ counters

www.harcourtschoolsupply.com
© Houghton Mifflin Harcourt Publishing Company
34
Core Standards for Math, Grade 2

Name_____   **Lesson 18**
COMMON CORE STANDARD CC.2.OA.4

Algebra • Repeated Addition
Lesson Objective: Write equations using repeated addition to find the total number of objects in arrays.

Find the total number of cats.
- Circle each row.
- Count how many rows.
  __3__ equal rows
- Count how many in one row.
  __4__ cats in one row
- Write an addition sentence. Add the number of cats in each row.

$$\underline{4} + \underline{4} + \underline{4} = \underline{12}$$

Find the number of shapes in each row.
Complete the addition sentence to find the total.

1. ●●●●●
   ●●●●●
   ●●●●●
   3 rows of __5__
   $$\underline{5} + \underline{5} + \underline{5} = \underline{15}$$

2. ✗✗✗✗
   ✗✗✗✗
   ✗✗✗✗
   ✗✗✗✗
   4 rows of __4__
   $$\underline{4} + \underline{4} + \underline{4} + \underline{4} = \underline{16}$$

www.harcourtschoolsupply.com
© Houghton Mifflin Harcourt Publishing Company
35
Core Standards for Math, Grade 2

Name_____   **Lesson 18**
CC.2.OA.4

1. Which could you use to find the number of squares?

   ▪▪▪▪▪
   ▪▪▪▪▪
   ▪▪▪▪▪
   ▪▪▪▪▪
   ▪▪▪▪▪

   - ● 5 + 5 + 5 + 5 = ___
   - ○ 5 + 5 + 5 = ___
   - ○ 4 + 4 + 4 = ___
   - ○ 4 + 4 + 4 + 4 = ___

2. Some children sat in 2 rows. There were 3 children in each row. How many children were there in all?
   - ○ 1
   - ○ 2
   - ○ 5
   - ● 6

3. Which could you use to find the number of circles?

   ●●●●●
   ●●●●●
   ●●●●●

   - ○ 3 + 3 + 3 = ___
   - ○ 3 + 3 + 3 + 3 = ___
   - ● 5 + 5 + 5 = ___
   - ○ 5 + 5 + 5 + 5 = ___

4. Mr. Henry has 4 rows of trees. There are 2 trees in each row. How many trees does he have in all?
   - ○ 10
   - ● 8
   - ○ 6
   - ○ 2

PROBLEM SOLVING REAL WORLD

Solve. Write or draw to explain.

5. A classroom has 3 rows of desks. There are 5 desks in each row. How many desks are there altogether?

   __15__ desks

www.harcourtschoolsupply.com
© Houghton Mifflin Harcourt Publishing Company
36
Core Standards for Math, Grade 2

Answer Key

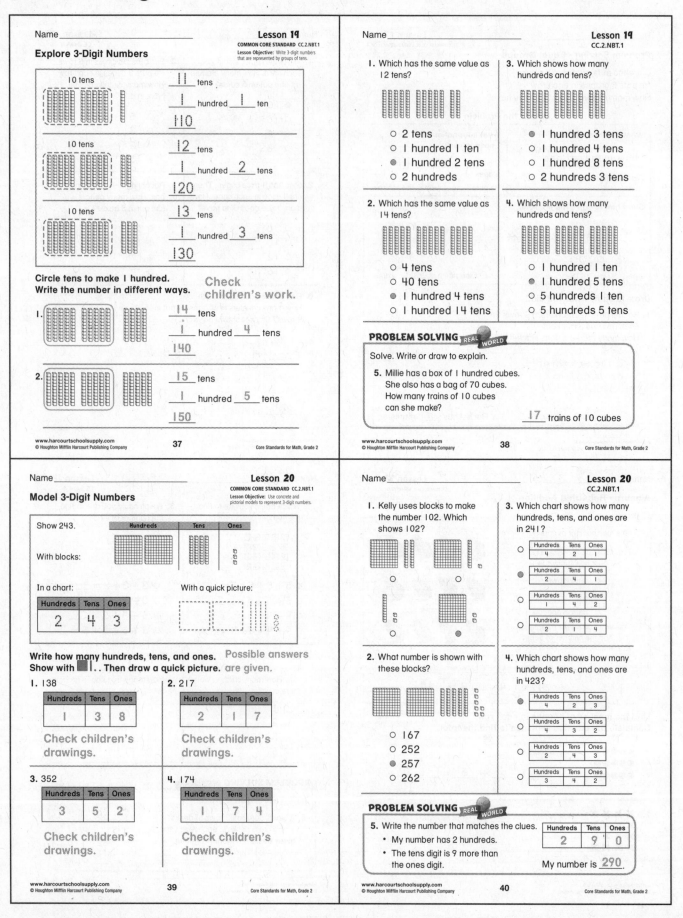

Lesson 19
Explore 3-Digit Numbers
COMMON CORE STANDARD CC.2.NBT.1
Lesson Objective: Write 3-digit numbers that are represented by groups of tens.

10 tens
__11__ tens
__1__ hundred __1__ ten
__110__

10 tens
__12__ tens
__1__ hundred __2__ tens
__120__

10 tens
__13__ tens
__1__ hundred __3__ tens
__130__

Circle tens to make 1 hundred.
Write the number in different ways.

Check children's work.

1. __14__ tens
__1__ hundred __4__ tens
__140__

2. __15__ tens
__1__ hundred __5__ tens
__150__

Lesson 19
CC.2.NBT.1

1. Which has the same value as 12 tens?

- ○ 2 tens
- ● 1 hundred 2 tens
- ○ 1 hundred 1 ten
- ○ 2 hundreds

2. Which has the same value as 14 tens?

- ○ 4 tens
- ○ 40 tens
- ● 1 hundred 4 tens
- ○ 1 hundred 14 tens

3. Which shows how many hundreds and tens?

- ● 1 hundred 3 tens
- ○ 1 hundred 4 tens
- ○ 1 hundred 8 tens
- ○ 2 hundreds 3 tens

4. Which shows how many hundreds and tens?

- ○ 1 hundred 1 ten
- ● 1 hundred 5 tens
- ○ 5 hundreds 1 ten
- ○ 5 hundreds 5 tens

PROBLEM SOLVING REAL WORLD

Solve. Write or draw to explain.

5. Millie has a box of 1 hundred cubes. She also has a bag of 70 cubes. How many trains of 10 cubes can she make?

__17__ trains of 10 cubes

Lesson 20
Model 3-Digit Numbers
COMMON CORE STANDARD CC.2.NBT.1
Lesson Objective: Use concrete and pictorial models to represent 3-digit numbers.

Show 243.

With blocks:

Hundreds	Tens	Ones

In a chart:

Hundreds	Tens	Ones
2	4	3

With a quick picture:

Write how many hundreds, tens, and ones. Show with ▮|.. Then draw a quick picture.

Possible answers are given.

1. 138

Hundreds	Tens	Ones
1	3	8

Check children's drawings.

2. 217

Hundreds	Tens	Ones
2	1	7

Check children's drawings.

3. 352

Hundreds	Tens	Ones
3	5	2

Check children's drawings.

4. 174

Hundreds	Tens	Ones
1	7	4

Check children's drawings.

Lesson 20
CC.2.NBT.1

1. Kelly uses blocks to make the number 102. Which shows 102?

2. What number is shown with these blocks?

- ○ 167
- ○ 252
- ● 257
- ○ 262

3. Which chart shows how many hundreds, tens, and ones are in 241?

○
Hundreds	Tens	Ones
4	2	1

●
Hundreds	Tens	Ones
2	4	1

○
Hundreds	Tens	Ones
1	4	2

○
Hundreds	Tens	Ones
2	1	4

4. Which chart shows how many hundreds, tens, and ones are in 423?

●
Hundreds	Tens	Ones
4	2	3

○
Hundreds	Tens	Ones
4	3	2

○
Hundreds	Tens	Ones
2	4	3

○
Hundreds	Tens	Ones
3	4	2

PROBLEM SOLVING REAL WORLD

5. Write the number that matches the clues.
- My number has 2 hundreds.
- The tens digit is 9 more than the ones digit.

Hundreds	Tens	Ones
2	9	0

My number is __290__

Lesson 21
COMMON CORE STANDARD CC.2.NBT.1
Lesson Objective: Apply place value concepts to write 3-digit numbers that are represented by pictorial models.

Name_____

Hundreds, Tens, and Ones

How many are there in all?

Hundreds	Tens	Ones

__3__ hundreds __2__ tens __5__ ones

Write how many in the chart.

Hundreds	Tens	Ones
3	2	5

Write the number as hundreds plus tens plus ones.

__300__ + __20__ + __5__

3 hundreds 2 tens 5 ones is the same as __325__.

Write how many hundreds, tens, and ones are in the model. Write the number in two ways.

1.

Hundreds	Tens	Ones
2	1	3

213

__200__ + __10__ + __3__

2.

Hundreds	Tens	Ones
1	2	6

126

__100__ + __20__ + __6__

Name_____

Lesson 21
CC.2.NBT.1

1. Count the hundreds, tens, and ones. Which number does the picture show?

○ 441   ○ 141
○ 414   ● 114

2. Which is a way to write the number shown with these blocks?

○ 200 + 20 + 5
● 200 + 30 + 5
○ 300 + 20 + 5
○ 500 + 30 + 2

3. Liz has 248 beads. How many hundreds are in this number?

● 2 hundreds
○ 4 hundreds
○ 6 hundreds
○ 8 hundreds

4. Ray sold 362 tickets to the show. Which is another way to write the number 362?

○ 6 hundreds 3 tens 2 ones
○ 3 hundreds 6 tens 3 ones
● 3 hundreds 6 tens 2 ones
○ 2 hundreds 6 tens 3 ones

PROBLEM SOLVING REAL WORLD

5. Write the number that answers the riddle. Use the chart.
A model for my number has 6 ones blocks, 2 hundreds blocks, and 3 tens blocks. What number am I?

Hundreds	Tens	Ones
2	3	6

__236__

Name_____

Lesson 22
COMMON CORE STANDARD CC.2.NBT.1
Lesson Objective: Use place value to describe the values of digits in numbers to 1,000.

Place Value to 1,000

The value of each digit in 426 is shown by its place in the number.

4 hundreds | 2 tens | 6 ones

400   20   6

426

Circle the value or the meaning of the underlined digit.

1. 7<u>8</u>2	800	(80)	8
2. <u>3</u>52	(3 hundreds)	3 tens	3 ones
3. 7<u>4</u>2	4	(40)	400
4. 41<u>9</u>	9 hundreds	9 tens	(9 ones)
5. <u>5</u>84	(500)	50	5

Name_____

Lesson 22
CC.2.NBT.1

1. A classroom has 537 books. What is the value of the digit 5 in 537?

○ 5
○ 50
● 500
○ 537

2. There are 203 birds. What is the value of the digit 3 in the number 203?

● 3
○ 30
○ 200
○ 300

3. Miss Brown drove 280 miles during summer vacation. What digit is in the tens place in the number 280?

● 8
○ 6
○ 2
○ 0

4. Which number has the digit 6 in the hundreds place?

○ 68
○ 196
○ 362
● 610

PROBLEM SOLVING REAL WORLD

5. Write the 3-digit number that answers the riddle.
• I have the same hundreds digit as ones digit.
• The value of my tens digit is 50.
• The value of my ones digit is 4.   The number is __454__.

Answer Key

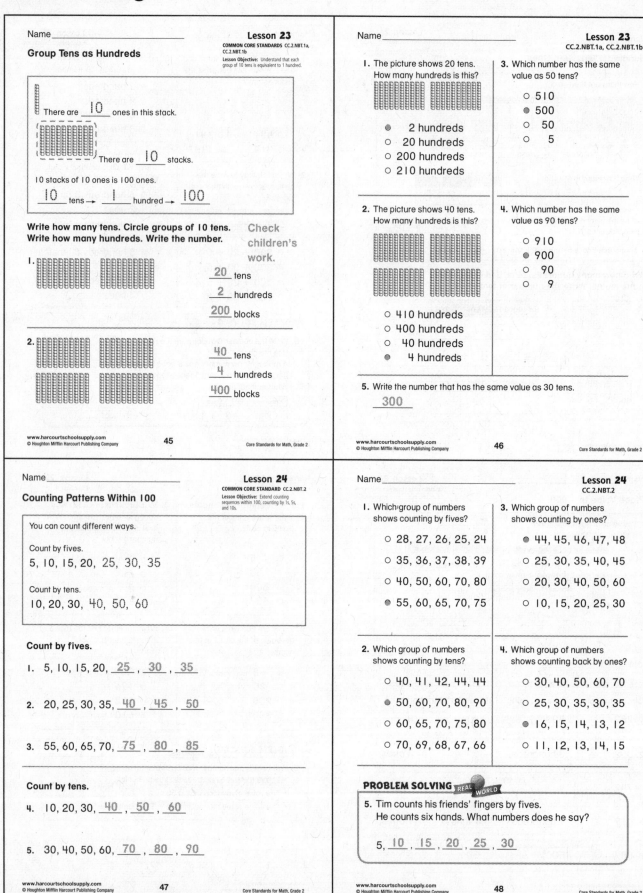

Lesson 23

Group Tens as Hundreds

COMMON CORE STANDARDS CC.2.NBT.1a, CC.2.NBT.1b
Lesson Objective: Understand that each group of 10 tens is equivalent to 1 hundred.

There are __10__ ones in this stack.

There are __10__ stacks.

10 stacks of 10 ones is 100 ones.

__10__ tens → __1__ hundred → __100__

Write how many tens. Circle groups of 10 tens.
Write how many hundreds. Write the number.

Check children's work.

1. __20__ tens
   __2__ hundreds
   __200__ blocks

2. __40__ tens
   __4__ hundreds
   __400__ blocks

45

Lesson 23
CC.2.NBT.1a, CC.2.NBT.1b

1. The picture shows 20 tens. How many hundreds is this?
   - ● 2 hundreds
   - ○ 20 hundreds
   - ○ 200 hundreds
   - ○ 210 hundreds

2. The picture shows 40 tens. How many hundreds is this?
   - ○ 410 hundreds
   - ○ 400 hundreds
   - ○ 40 hundreds
   - ● 4 hundreds

3. Which number has the same value as 50 tens?
   - ○ 510
   - ● 500
   - ○ 50
   - ○ 5

4. Which number has the same value as 90 tens?
   - ○ 910
   - ● 900
   - ○ 90
   - ○ 9

5. Write the number that has the same value as 30 tens.
   __300__

46

Lesson 24

Counting Patterns Within 100

COMMON CORE STANDARD CC.2.NBT.2
Lesson Objective: Extend counting sequences within 100, counting by 1s, 5s, and 10s.

You can count different ways.

Count by fives.
5, 10, 15, 20, 25, 30, 35

Count by tens.
10, 20, 30, 40, 50, 60

Count by fives.

1. 5, 10, 15, 20, __25__, __30__, __35__

2. 20, 25, 30, 35, __40__, __45__, __50__

3. 55, 60, 65, 70, __75__, __80__, __85__

Count by tens.

4. 10, 20, 30, __40__, __50__, __60__

5. 30, 40, 50, 60, __70__, __80__, __90__

47

Lesson 24
CC.2.NBT.2

1. Which group of numbers shows counting by fives?
   - ○ 28, 27, 26, 25, 24
   - ○ 35, 36, 37, 38, 39
   - ○ 40, 50, 60, 70, 80
   - ● 55, 60, 65, 70, 75

2. Which group of numbers shows counting by tens?
   - ○ 40, 41, 42, 44, 44
   - ● 50, 60, 70, 80, 90
   - ○ 60, 65, 70, 75, 80
   - ○ 70, 69, 68, 67, 66

3. Which group of numbers shows counting by ones?
   - ● 44, 45, 46, 47, 48
   - ○ 25, 30, 35, 40, 45
   - ○ 20, 30, 40, 50, 60
   - ○ 10, 15, 20, 25, 30

4. Which group of numbers shows counting back by ones?
   - ○ 30, 40, 50, 60, 70
   - ○ 25, 30, 35, 30, 35
   - ● 16, 15, 14, 13, 12
   - ○ 11, 12, 13, 14, 15

PROBLEM SOLVING REAL WORLD

5. Tim counts his friends' fingers by fives. He counts six hands. What numbers does he say?

   5, __10__, __15__, __20__, __25__, __30__

48

Answer Key

Name_____

**Counting Patterns
Within 1,000**

Lesson 25
COMMON CORE STANDARD CC.2.NBT.2
Lesson Objective: Extend counting
sequences within 1,000, counting by 1s, 5s,
10s, and 100s.

> You can count in different ways.
> Look for a pattern to use.
>
> Count by tens.
>
> 500, 510, 520, 530, 540, 550
>
> Count by hundreds.
>
> 300, 400, 500, 600, 700, 800

Count by tens.

1. 410, 420, 430, 440, 450

2. 730, 740, 750, 760, 770

3. 250, 260, 270, 280, 290

Count by hundreds.

4. 100, 200, 300, 400, 500

5. 500, 600, 700, 800, 900

Name_____

Lesson 25
CC.2.NBT.2

1. Which group of numbers shows counting by tens?
   - ○ 610, 611, 612
   - ● 630, 640, 650
   - ○ 635, 640, 645
   - ○ 692, 691, 690

3. Which group of numbers shows counting by hundreds?
   - ○ 500, 510, 520
   - ○ 505, 510, 515
   - ○ 400, 401, 402
   - ● 400, 500, 600

2. Which group of numbers shows counting by fives?
   - ● 340, 345, 350
   - ○ 360, 361, 362
   - ○ 430, 440, 450
   - ○ 500, 600, 700

4. Which group of numbers shows counting back by ones?
   - ○ 256, 257, 258
   - ○ 225, 230, 235
   - ● 218, 217, 216
   - ○ 190, 200, 210

PROBLEM SOLVING REAL WORLD

5. Lee has a jar of 100 pennies.
   She adds groups of 10 pennies to the jar.
   She adds 5 groups. What numbers does she say?

   110, 120, 130, 140, 150

Name_____

Understand Place Value

Lesson 26
COMMON CORE STANDARD CC.2.NBT.3
Lesson Objective: Use place value to
describe the values of digits in 2-digit numbers.

> 0, 1, 2, 3, 4, 5, 6, 7, 8, and 9 are digits.
> A digit's place in a number shows
> the value of the digit.
>
> 52 has two digits.
>
> **52**
>
> The digit 5 is in the tens place.
> The digit 5 shows 5 tens.
> Its value is 50.
>
> The digit 2 is in the ones place.
> The digit 2 shows 2 ones.
> Its value is 2.

Circle the value of the underlined digit.

1. 27 — (20) 2

2. 18 — 1 (10)

3. 56 — 60 (6)

4. 30 — (30) 3

5. 75 — (5) 50

6. 41 — 4 (40)

Name_____

Lesson 26
CC.2.NBT.3

1. What is the value of the underlined digit?

   27
   - ○ 2
   - ○ 7
   - ● 20
   - ○ 70

3. What is the value of the underlined digit?

   48
   - ● 8
   - ○ 12
   - ○ 40
   - ○ 80

2. Lucas has 53 toy cars. What is the value of the digit 3 in the number 53?
   - ○ 0   ○ 10
   - ● 3   ○ 30

4. Ben has 62 crackers. What is the value of the 6 in this number?
   - ○ 6
   - ○ 8
   - ○ 20
   - ● 60

PROBLEM SOLVING REAL WORLD

Write the 2-digit number that matches the clues.

5. My number has a tens digit that is 8 more than the ones digit. Zero is not one of my digits.

   My number is 91.

Answer Key

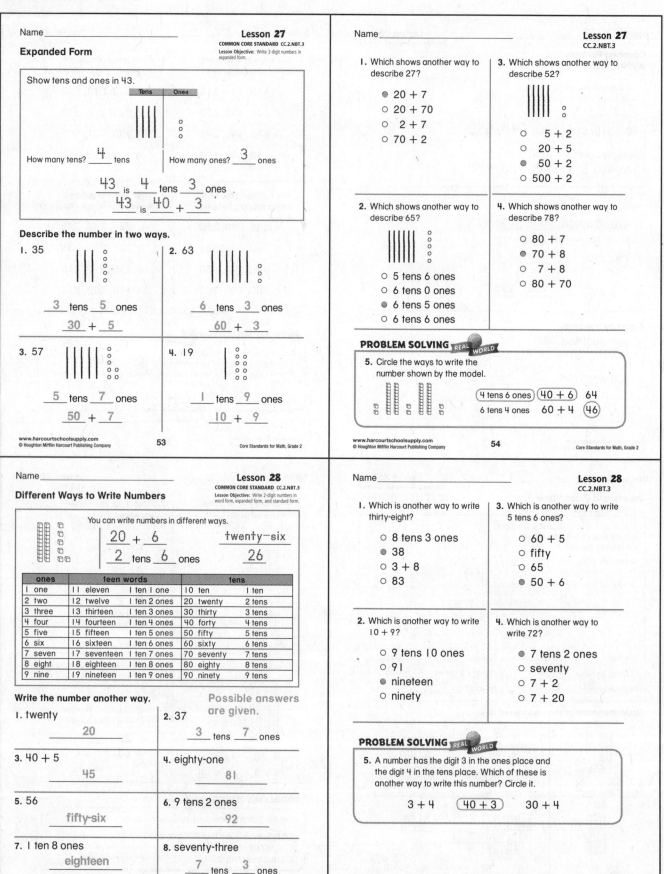

Name_____

**Algebra • Different Names
for Numbers**

Lesson 29
COMMON CORE STANDARD CC.2.NBT.3
Lesson Objective: Apply place value concepts to find equivalent representations of numbers.

Here are some ways to show 28.

Describe the tens and ones with words and addition.	Describe the tens and ones with words and addition.	Describe the tens and ones with words and addition.
_2_ tens _8_ ones	_1_ ten _18_ ones	_0_ tens _28_ ones
_20_ + _8_	_10_ + _18_	_0_ + _28_

Describe the blocks in two ways.

1. 32

_1_ ten _22_ ones	_3_ tens _2_ ones	_2_ tens _12_ ones
_10_ + _22_	_30_ + _2_	_20_ + _12_

2. 47

_3_ tens _17_ ones	_4_ tens _7_ ones	_2_ tens _27_ ones
_30_ + _17_	_40_ + _7_	_20_ + _27_

Name_____

Lesson 29
CC.2.NBT.3

1. The blocks show 29. How many tens and ones are there?

○ 2 tens 3 ones
● 1 ten 19 ones
○ 1 ten 14 ones
○ 1 ten 9 ones

3. The blocks show 30. How many tens and ones are there?

○ 1 ten 5 ones
○ 1 ten 10 ones
○ 2 tens 5 ones
● 2 tens 10 ones

2. The blocks show 33. There are 2 tens and 13 ones. Which shows the number as tens plus ones?

○ 20 + 3   ○ 30 + 13
● 20 + 13 ○ 40 + 3

4. The blocks show 47. There are 3 tens and 17 ones. Which shows the number as tens plus ones?

○ 20 + 17 ● 30 + 17
○ 30 + 7   ○ 40 + 17

PROBLEM SOLVING REAL WORLD

5. Toni has these blocks. Circle the blocks that she could use to show 34.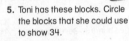

Check children's work.

Name_____

Problem Solving • Tens and Ones

Lesson 30
COMMON CORE STANDARD CC.2.NBT.3
Lesson Objective: Solve problems by finding different combinations of tens and ones to represent 2-digit numbers using the strategy *find a pattern.*

Anya has 25 toys. She can put them away in boxes of 10 toys or as single toys. What are the different ways Anya can put away the toys?

Unlock the Problem

What do I need to find?	**What information do I need to use?**
the different ways	She can put them away in
Anya can put away the toys	boxes of 10 toys or as single toys.

Look for a pattern.

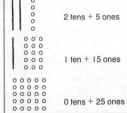

	Boxes of 10 toys	Single toys
2 tens + 5 ones	2	5
1 ten + 15 ones	1	15
0 tens + 25 ones	0	25

Find a pattern to solve.

1. Mr. Moore is buying 29 apples. He can buy them in packs of 10 apples or as single apples. What are the different ways Mr. Moore can buy the apples?

Packs of 10 apples	Single apples
2	9
1	19
0	29

Name_____

Lesson 30
CC.2.NBT.3

1. Jon wants to buy 21 apples. What choice is missing from the list?

Bags of 10 apples	Single apples
2	1
1	11

● 0 bags, 21 apples
○ 0 bags, 11 apples
○ 1 bag, 21 apples
○ 2 bags, 2 apples

3. Ann needs 12 folders for school. What choice is missing from the list?

Packs of 10 folders	Single folders
0	12

○ 2 packs, 0 folders
○ 2 packs, 1 folder
○ 1 pack, 12 folders
● 1 pack, 2 folders

2. Ms. Brice can buy markers in packs of 10 or as single markers. Which of these is a way she can buy 47 markers?

○ 4 packs, 17 markers
● 3 packs, 17 markers
○ 2 packs, 7 markers
○ 1 pack, 27 markers

4. Jeff can carry his pears in bags of 10 pears or as single pears. Which of these is a way he can carry his 36 pears?

○ 2 bags, 26 pears
○ 6 bags, 3 pears
● 3 bags, 6 pears
○ 1 bag, 16 pears

5. Stamps are sold in packs of 10 stamps or as single stamps. Leah wants to buy 26 stamps. What are all of the different ways she can buy the stamps?

Packs of 10 stamps	Single stamps
2	6
1	16
0	26

Answer Key

Name_____ **Lesson 31**
COMMON CORE STANDARD CC.2.NBT.3

Number Names
Lesson Objective: Read and write 3-digit numbers in word form.

You can write a number using words.

257

What is shown with the hundreds blocks?

two hundred

What is shown with the tens and ones blocks?

fifty-seven

So you write 257 as __two hundred fifty-seven__

Write the number using words.

1. 163

one hundred sixty-three

2. 427

four hundred twenty-seven

Write the number.

3. two hundred nine

209

4. five hundred seventy-nine

579

Name_____ **Lesson 31**
CC.2.NBT.3

1. There are five hundred twenty-three children at the school. Which shows this number?

○ 520
● 523
○ 530
○ 532

3. Which is another way to write the number 275?

● two hundred seventy-five
○ two hundred seventy
○ two hundred fifty-seven
○ two hundred five

2. Vin has three hundred forty pieces in his puzzle. Which shows this number?

○ 304
○ 314
● 340
○ 341

4. Which is another way to write the number 618?

○ six hundred eight
● six hundred eighteen
○ six hundred eighty-one
○ eight hundred sixteen

5. Write the number 454 using words.

four hundred fifty-four

Name_____ **Lesson 32**
COMMON CORE STANDARD CC.2.NBT.3

Different Forms of Numbers
Lesson Objective: Write 3-digit numbers in expanded form and in standard form.

There is more than one way to show and write a number.

three hundred sixty-two

__3__ hundreds __6__ tens __2__ ones

$$300 + 60 + 2$$
$$362$$

Read the number and draw a quick picture. Then write the number in different ways.

1. four hundred thirty-two

__4__ hundreds __3__ tens __2__ ones

$$400 + 30 + 2$$
$$432$$

2. two hundred seventy-five

__2__ hundreds __7__ tens __5__ ones

$$200 + 70 + 5$$
$$275$$

Name_____ **Lesson 32**
CC.2.NBT.3

1. Look at the picture.

Which shows how many hundreds, tens, and ones?

○ 2 hundreds 4 tens 3 ones
○ 3 hundreds 3 tens 4 ones
○ 3 hundreds 2 tens 4 ones
● 2 hundreds 3 tens 4 ones

2. Claudia has four hundred sixty-five stickers in her collection. Which is another way to write the number?

● 400 + 60 + 5
○ 400 + 600 + 5
○ 40 + 60 + 5
○ 4 + 6 + 5

PROBLEM SOLVING REAL WORLD

Write the number another way.

3. 200 + 30 + 7

237

4. 895

800 + 90 + 5

Answers will vary. Possible answers are given.

Lesson 33 — page 65

COMMON CORE STANDARD CC.2.NBT.3
Lesson Objective: Apply place value concepts to find equivalent representations of numbers.

Algebra · Different Ways to Show Numbers

These two models can both be used to show the number 124.

Hundreds	Tens	Ones
1	2	4

I ten has the same value as 10 ones.

Hundreds	Tens	Ones
1	1	14

Write how many hundreds, tens, and ones are in the model.

1. 132

Hundreds	Tens	Ones
1	3	2

Hundreds	Tens	Ones
1	2	12

2. 246

Hundreds	Tens	Ones
2	4	6

Hundreds	Tens	Ones
2	3	16

Lesson 33 — page 66

CC.2.NBT.3

1. Which shows how many hundreds, tens, and ones are in 328?

Hundreds	Tens	Ones
2	8	3

● | Hundreds | Tens | Ones |
|---|---|---|
| 3 | 2 | 8 |

Hundreds	Tens	Ones
3	8	2

Hundreds	Tens	Ones
8	2	3

2. What number is shown with these blocks?

○ 413
○ 143
● 134
○ 84

PROBLEM SOLVING REAL WORLD

Markers are sold in boxes, packs, or as single markers. Each box has 10 packs. Each pack has 10 markers.

3. Draw pictures to show two ways to buy 276 markers.

Check children's work.

Lesson 34 — page 67

COMMON CORE STANDARD CC.2.NBT.4
Lesson Objective: Solve problems involving number comparisons by using the strategy make a model.

Problem Solving · Compare Numbers

At the zoo, there are 137 birds and 142 reptiles. Are there more birds or more reptiles at the zoo?

Unlock the Problem

What do I need to find?

I need to find if there are more __birds__ or __reptiles__.

What information do I need to use?

There are __137__ birds.
There are __142__ reptiles.

Show how to solve the problem.

Birds   Reptiles

The number of hundreds is the same. There are more tens in the number of reptiles.

There are more __reptiles__ at the zoo.

Draw quick pictures to model the numbers.

1. There are 153 birds and 149 fish at the nature center. Are there more birds or more fish?

Check children's drawings.

There are more __birds__.

Lesson 34 — page 68

CC.2.NBT.4

1. There are 174 markers in a bin. Which number is greater than 174?
○ 138
○ 154
○ 147
● 179

2. There are 213 books in the classroom. Which number is less than 213?
○ 231
● 205
○ 276
○ 250

3. There are 332 puzzle pieces in a box. Which number is greater than 332?
○ 286
○ 241
● 391
○ 323

4. There are 409 pennies in a jar. Which number is less than 409?
● 390
○ 419
○ 437
○ 526

5. Tim has 128 paper clips. Draw a quick picture to show a number that is greater than the number of paper clips.

Possible answer:

Answer Key

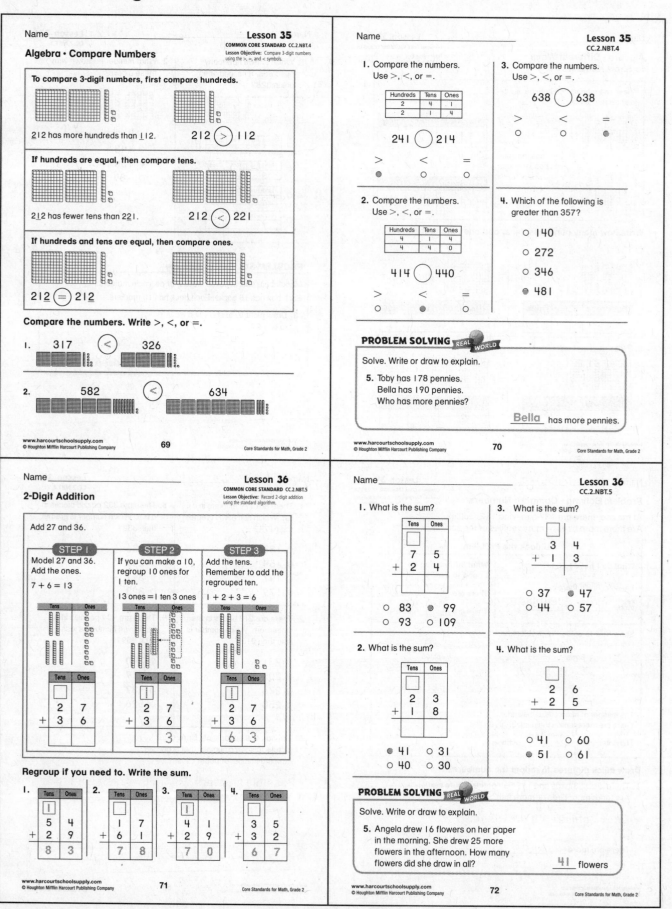

Lesson 35
COMMON CORE STANDARD CC.2.NBT.4
Lesson Objective: Compare 3-digit numbers using the >, =, and < symbols.

Name_____

Algebra • Compare Numbers

To compare 3-digit numbers, first compare hundreds.

2̲12 has more hundreds than 1̲12.   212 (>) 112

If hundreds are equal, then compare tens.

21̲2 has fewer tens than 22̲1.   212 (<) 221

If hundreds and tens are equal, then compare ones.

21̲2 (=) 21̲2

Compare the numbers. Write >, <, or =.

1. 317 (<) 326

2. 582 (<) 634

Lesson 35
CC.2.NBT.4

Name_____

1. Compare the numbers.
   Use >, <, or =.

Hundreds	Tens	Ones
2	4	1
2	1	4

   241 ( ) 214

   \>   <   =
   ●   ○   ○

2. Compare the numbers.
   Use >, <, or =.

Hundreds	Tens	Ones
4	1	4
4	4	0

   414 ( ) 440

   \>   <   =
   ○   ●   ○

3. Compare the numbers.
   Use >, <, or =.

   638 ( ) 638

   \>   <   =
   ○   ○   ●

4. Which of the following is greater than 357?

   ○ 140
   ○ 272
   ○ 346
   ● 481

PROBLEM SOLVING REAL WORLD

Solve. Write or draw to explain.

5. Toby has 178 pennies.
   Bella has 190 pennies.
   Who has more pennies?

   Bella has more pennies.

Lesson 36
COMMON CORE STANDARD CC.2.NBT.5
Lesson Objective: Record 2-digit addition using the standard algorithm.

Name_____

2-Digit Addition

Add 27 and 36.

STEP 1
Model 27 and 36.
Add the ones.

$7 + 6 = 13$

Tens	Ones
2	7
+ 3	6

STEP 2
If you can make a 10, regroup 10 ones for 1 ten.

13 ones = 1 ten 3 ones

Tens	Ones
1	
2	7
+ 3	6
	3

STEP 3
Add the tens.
Remember to add the regrouped ten.

$1 + 2 + 3 = 6$

Tens	Ones
1	
2	7
+ 3	6
6	3

Regroup if you need to. Write the sum.

1.
Tens	Ones
1	
5	4
+ 2	9
8	3

2.
Tens	Ones
1	7
+ 6	1
7	8

3.
Tens	Ones
1	
4	1
+ 2	9
7	0

4.
Tens	Ones
3	5
+ 3	2
6	7

Lesson 36
CC.2.NBT.5

Name_____

1. What is the sum?

Tens	Ones
7	5
+ 2	4

   ○ 83   ● 99
   ○ 93   ○ 109

2. What is the sum?

Tens	Ones
2	3
+ 1	8

   ● 41   ○ 31
   ○ 40   ○ 30

3. What is the sum?

3	4
+ 1	3

   ○ 37   ● 47
   ○ 44   ○ 57

4. What is the sum?

2	6
+ 2	5

   ○ 41   ○ 60
   ● 51   ○ 61

PROBLEM SOLVING REAL WORLD

Solve. Write or draw to explain.

5. Angela drew 16 flowers on her paper in the morning. She drew 25 more flowers in the afternoon. How many flowers did she draw in all?

   _41_ flowers

Answer Key

Name_____   **Lesson 37**
COMMON CORE STANDARD CC.2.NBT.5

Practice 2-Digit Addition   Lesson Objective: Practice 2-digit addition with and without regrouping.

Eliza sold 47 pencils in one week.
She sold 65 pencils the next week.
How many pencils did she sell in both weeks?

Add 47 and 65. Add the ones. $7 + 5 = 12$	Regroup. 12 ones = 1 ten and 2 ones	Add the tens. $1 + 4 + 6 = 11$
4 7 + 6 5	[1] 4 7 + 6 5 2	[1] 4 7 + 6 5 11 2

Write the sum.

1. [1] 43 + 69 = 112
2. [1] 76 + 58 = 134
3. [1] 38 + 42 = 80
4. [1] 85 + 68 = 153

5. 82 + 47 = 129
6. 81 + 17 = 98
7. [1] 27 + 86 = 113
8. 51 + 38 = 89

Name_____   **Lesson 37**
CC.2.NBT.5

1. What is the sum?

58
+ 44

○ 92
○ 98
● 102
○ 112

2. Elizabeth collected 72 markers. Tori collected 52 markers. How many markers did they collect in all?

72
+ 52

○ 114
● 124
○ 130
○ 136

3. Tony found 31 shells on the beach. Andy found 27 shells. How many shells did they find in all?

31
+ 27

○ 46
○ 48
○ 54
● 58

4. What is the sum?

88
+ 39

○ 117
● 127
○ 131
○ 139

PROBLEM SOLVING REAL WORLD

Solve. Write or draw to explain.

5. There are 45 books on the shelf. There are 37 books on the table. How many books in all are on the shelf and the table?

__82__ books

Name_____   **Lesson 38**
COMMON CORE STANDARD CC.2.NBT.5

Rewrite 2-Digit Addition   Lesson Objective: Rewrite horizontal addition problems vertically in the standard algorithm format.

Add. $43 + 19 = ?$

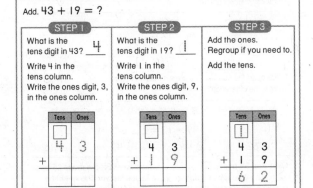

STEP 1	STEP 2	STEP 3
What is the tens digit in 43? **4** Write 4 in the tens column. Write the ones digit, 3, in the ones column.	What is the tens digit in 19? **1** Write 1 in the tens column. Write the ones digit, 9, in the ones column.	Add the ones. Regroup if you need to. Add the tens.

Rewrite the numbers. Then add.

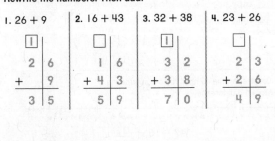

1. $26 + 9$ [1] 26 + 9 = 35
2. $16 + 43$ 16 + 43 = 59
3. $32 + 38$ [1] 32 + 38 = 70
4. $23 + 26$ 23 + 26 = 49

Name_____   **Lesson 38**
CC.2.NBT.5

1. What is the sum of $34 + 56$?

○ 100
● 90
○ 80
○ 74

2. What is the sum of $39 + 32$?

● 71
○ 68
○ 61
○ 51

3. What is the sum of $18 + 64$?

○ 92
○ 84
● 82
○ 72

4. What is the sum of $40 + 56$?

○ 97
● 96
○ 90
○ 86

PROBLEM SOLVING REAL WORLD

Use the table. Show how you solved the problem.

5. How many pages in all did Sasha and Kara read?

Check children's work.

__91__ pages

Pages Read This Week	
Child	Number of Pages
Sasha	62
Kara	29
Juan	50

Answer Key

Name _____

**Algebra · Break Apart
Ones to Subtract**

To subtract a one-digit number, break it apart.

Break apart ones in 7.

• Use 4 because 44 has a 4 in the ones place.
• The other part is 3.

$44 - 7 = \underline{?}$

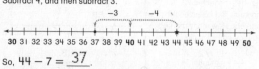

Start at 44.
Subtract 4, and then subtract 3.

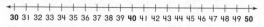

So, $44 - 7 = \underline{37}$.

Break apart ones to subtract. Write the difference.

1. $42 - 8 = \underline{34}$ 2. $47 - 8 = \underline{39}$

3. $43 - 5 = \underline{38}$ 4. $41 - 8 = \underline{33}$

Name _____

1. Break apart ones to subtract. What is the difference?

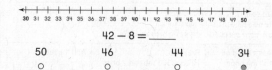

$42 - 8 = \underline{}$

50	46	44	34
○	○	○	●

2. Break apart ones to subtract. What is the difference?

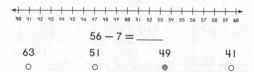

$56 - 7 = \underline{}$

63	51	49	41
○	○	●	○

3. Harrison had 61 cars. He gave 6 cars to his brother. How many cars does Harrison have now?

○ 67
○ 57
● 55
○ 54

4. Tracy had 33 stamps. She gave 5 stamps to her friend. How many stamps does Tracy have now?

○ 30
● 28
○ 25
○ 18

5. Sam wants to subtract 9 from 47. How should he break apart the 9? Explain.

Possible answer: He should break the 9 into 7 and 2.

Then he can subtract 7 to get 40, and 2 more to get 38.

Name _____

**Algebra · Break Apart
Numbers to Subtract**

To subtract a two-digit number, break it apart.

First break apart 16 into tens and ones.

Now break apart ones in 6.

• Use 4 because 54 has a 4 in the ones place.
• The other part is 2.

$54 - 16 = \underline{?}$

Use the number line to subtract the three parts.

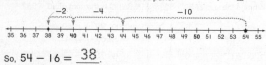

So, $54 - 16 = \underline{38}$.

**Break apart the number you are subtracting.
Write the difference.**

1. $51 - 16 = \underline{35}$ 2. $57 - 18 = \underline{39}$

3. $54 - 17 = \underline{37}$ 4. $52 - 18 = \underline{34}$

Name _____

1. Break apart the number you are subtracting. What is the difference?

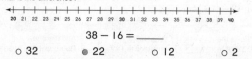

$38 - 16 = \underline{}$

| ○ 32 | ● 22 | ○ 12 | ○ 2 |

2. Break apart the number you are subtracting. What is the difference?

$49 - 13 = \underline{}$

| ○ 62 | ○ 46 | ○ 42 | ● 36 |

3. Miles had 54 baseball cards. He gave 18 baseball cards to Greyson. How many baseball cards does Miles have now?

○ 44
○ 40
○ 38
● 36

4. Last week Brooke made 28 bags for the festival. This week she made 14 bags. How many more bags did Brooke make last week than this week?

○ 52
○ 44
● 14
○ 4

5. Break apart the number you are subtracting. Write the difference.

$47 - 15 = \underline{32}$

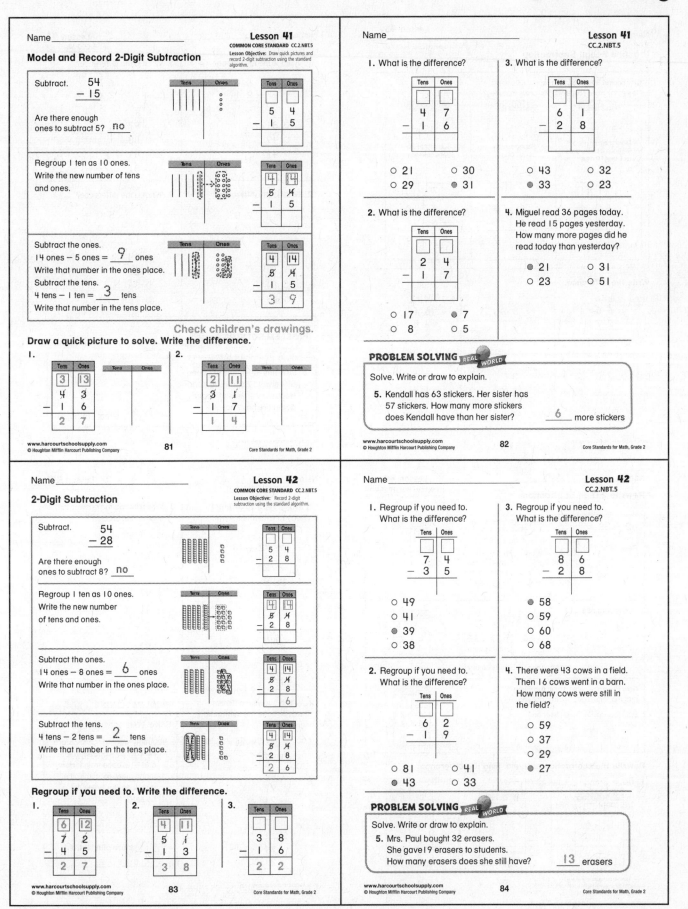

Answer Key

COMMON CORE STANDARD CC.2.NBT.5
Lesson Objective: Practice 2-digit
subtraction with and without regrouping.

Practice 2-Digit Subtraction

Clay scored 80 points. Meg scored 61 points.
How many more points did Clay score than Meg?

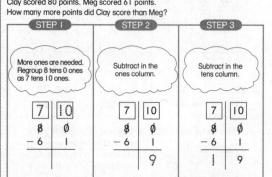

STEP 1 — More ones are needed. Regroup 8 tens 0 ones as 7 tens 10 ones.

STEP 2 — Subtract in the ones column.

STEP 3 — Subtract in the tens column.

```
 7 |10       7 |10       7 |10
 8   0       8   0       8   0
-6   1      -6   1      -6   1
                 9       1   9
```

Write the difference.

1.
```
 5 10
 6  0
-2  7
 3  3
```

2.
```
 3  7
-2  2
 1  5
```

3.
```
 5 11
 6  1
-4  8
 1  3
```

4.
```
 6 10
 7  0
-2  6
 4  4
```

5.
```
 2  17
 3  7
-1  9
 1  8
```

6.
```
 5  5
-1  4
 4  1
```

---

1. What is the difference?
```
 6 0
-2 1
```
○ 81
○ 49
○ 41
● 39

3. What is the difference?
```
 6 7
-2 6
```
○ 97
○ 83
● 41
○ 31

2. What is the difference?
```
 2 8
-1 5
```
○ 12
● 13
○ 14
○ 15

4. What is the difference?
```
 5 0
-2 6
```
● 24
○ 25
○ 36
○ 76

PROBLEM SOLVING REAL WORLD

Solve. Write or draw to explain.

5. Julie has 42 sheets of paper.
She gives 17 sheets to Kari.
How many sheets of paper
does Julie have now?

_25_ sheets of paper

COMMON CORE STANDARD CC.2.NBT.5
Lesson Objective: Rewrite horizontal
subtraction problems vertically in the
standard algorithm format.

Rewrite 2-Digit Subtraction

$62 - 38 = ?$

Rewrite 62 first. | 62 |
The 6 is in the tens place. Write it in the tens column.
The 2 is in the ones place. Write it in the ones column.

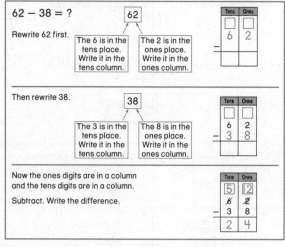

Tens	Ones
6	2

Then rewrite 38. | 38 |
The 3 is in the tens place. Write it in the tens column.
The 8 is in the ones place. Write it in the ones column.

Tens	Ones
6	2
3	8

Now the ones digits are in a column
and the tens digits are in a column.

Subtract. Write the difference.

Tens	Ones
5	12
6	2
3	8
2	4

Rewrite the subtraction problem. Find the difference.

1. $56 - 24$

Tens	Ones
5	6
2	4
3	2

2. $74 - 37$

Tens	Ones
6	14
7	4
3	7
3	7

3. $43 - 15$

Tens	Ones
3	13
4	3
1	5
2	8

---

1. Which shows a different way to write the subtraction problem?

$72 - 43$

●
```
 72
-43
```
○
```
 72
-34
```
○
```
 27
-43
```
○
```
 27
-34
```

3. Which shows the answer to the subtraction problem?

$59 - 12$

○ 71
○ 57
● 47
○ 41

2. Which shows a different way to write the subtraction problem?

$97 - 21$

○
```
 97
-12
```
●
```
 97
-21
```
○
```
 79
-12
```
○
```
 79
-21
```

PROBLEM SOLVING REAL WORLD

Solve. Write or draw to explain.

4. Jimmy went to the toy store.
He saw 23 wooden trains
and 41 plastic trains. How
many more plastic trains
than wooden trains did
he see?

_18_ more plastic trains

Page 89 (Lesson 45)

Name_____

Lesson 45
COMMON CORE STANDARD CC.2.NBT.5
Lesson Objective: Use addition to find differences.

Add to Find Differences

Count up to solve. 34 − 27 = ?
Start at 27. Count up 3 to 30.

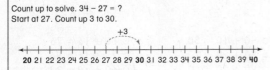

+3
20 21 22 23 24 25 26 27 28 29 **30** 31 32 33 34 35 36 37 38 39 **40**

To get to 34 from 30, count up 4 more.

+3   +4
20 21 22 23 24 25 26 27 28 29 **30** 31 32 33 34 35 36 37 38 39 **40**

So, 34 − 27 = ___7___.

 7 was added to get to 34.

Count up to find the difference.

1. 41 − 37 = __4__

30 31 32 33 34 35 36 37 38 39 **40** 41 42 43 44 45 46 47 48 49 **50**

2. 43 − 38 = __5__

30 31 32 33 34 35 36 37 38 39 **40** 41 42 43 44 45 46 47 48 49 **50**

Page 90 (Lesson 45)

Name_____

Lesson 45
CC.2.NBT.5

1. Use the number line. Count up to find the difference.
What is the difference?

$$84 − 75 = \_\_\_\_$$

70 71 72 73 74 **75** 76 77 78 79 **80** 81 82 83 84 85 86 87 88 89 **90**

○ 4   ○ 5   ◉ 9   ○ 19

2. Use the number line. Count up to find the difference.
What is the difference?

$$43 − 37 = \_\_\_\_$$

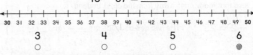
30 31 32 33 34 35 36 37 38 39 **40** 41 42 43 44 45 46 47 48 49 **50**

○ 3   ○ 4   ○ 5   ◉ 6

3. Use the number line. Count up to find the difference.
What is the difference?

$$66 − 58 = \_\_\_\_$$

50 51 52 53 54 55 56 57 58 59 **60** 61 62 63 64 65 66 67 68 69 **70**

○ 6   ○ 7   ◉ 8   ○ 9

4. Amy needs to subtract 49 from 58. Explain how
she can solve the problem by counting up.

Possible answer: Amy can start at 49 on the number

line and count up 1 to 50. Then she can count up 8 to

58. 8 + 1 = 9, so 58 − 49 = 9.

Page 91 (Lesson 46)

Name_____

Lesson 46
COMMON CORE STANDARD CC.2.NBT.6
Lesson Objective: Find a sum by breaking apart a 1-digit addend to make a 2-digit addend a multiple of 10.

Break Apart Ones to Add

Sometimes when you are adding, you can
break apart ones to make a ten.

37 + 8 = __?__

Look at the two-digit addend, 37. What digit

is in the ones place? __7__

Decide how many you need to add to
the ones digit to make 10.

7 + __3__ = 10, and 37 + __3__ = 40

Break apart that number from the one-digit addend, 8.

8 − 3 = 5

Finally, write the new number sentence. 40 + 5 = __45__

Break apart ones to make a ten. Check children's work.
Then add and write the sum.

1. 28 + 6 = __34__   2. 34 + 7 = __41__

Page 92 (Lesson 46)

Name_____

Lesson 46
CC.2.NBT.6

1. Break apart ones to make
a ten. What is the sum?

17 + 8 = _____

○ 13
○ 15
○ 24
◉ 25

2. Break apart ones to make a
ten. What is the sum?

57 + 4 = _____

○ 31
○ 41
○ 51
◉ 61

3. Break apart ones to make
a ten. What is the sum?

89 + 5 = _____

○ 104
◉ 94
○ 84
○ 83

4. Break apart ones to make
a ten. What is the sum?

32 + 9 = _____

◉ 41
○ 40
○ 31
○ 30

PROBLEM SOLVING REAL WORLD

Solve. Write or draw to explain.

5. Jimmy had 18 toy airplanes. His mother
bought him 7 more toy airplanes. How many
toy airplanes does he have now?

__25__ toy airplanes

Answer Key

Use Compensation

This is a way to add 2-digit numbers.
Take ones from one addend to make the other addend a tens number.

$27 + 38 = $ _?_

First, find the addend with the greater ones digit. _38_

How many ones would you need to add to make it a tens number?

$38 + $ ____ $= 40$ Add _2_ to make _40_.

Next, take that many ones away from the other addend.

$27 - 2 = 25$ The two new addends are _25_ and _40_.

Write the new addition sentence to find the sum.

_25_ $+$ _40_ $=$ _65_

Show how to make one addend the next tens number.
Complete the new addition sentence.

Check children's work.

1. $28 + 16 = ?$

   _30_ $+$ _14_ $=$ _44_

2. $37 + 24 = ?$

   _40_ $+$ _21_ $=$ _61_

---

1. Which shows a way to find the sum?

   $41 + 29$

   - ○ $40 + 10 = 50$
   - ● $50 + 20 = 70$
   - ○ $40 + 20 = 60$
   - ○ $50 + 30 = 80$

3. Which shows a way to find the sum?

   $66 + 16$

   - ○ $60 + 16 = 76$
   - ○ $70 + 16 = 86$
   - ○ $60 + 12 = 72$
   - ● $70 + 12 = 82$

2. Which shows a way to find the sum?

   $38 + 18$

   - ○ $30 + 16 = 46$
   - ○ $30 + 18 = 48$
   - ● $40 + 16 = 56$
   - ○ $40 + 18 = 58$

4. Which shows a way to find the sum?

   $17 + 23$

   - ○ $10 + 20 = 30$
   - ○ $10 + 23 = 33$
   - ○ $17 + 20 = 37$
   - ● $10 + 30 = 40$

PROBLEM SOLVING REAL WORLD

Solve. Write or draw to explain.

5. The oak tree at the school was 34 feet tall.
   Then it grew 18 feet taller.
   How tall is the oak tree now?

   _52_ feet tall

Break Apart Addends as Tens and Ones

$25 + 46 = ?$

Break apart 25 into tens and ones.   Break apart 46 into tens and ones.

25 $+$ 46

(20 + 5) $+$ (40 + 6)

Then, add the tens from the two addends.   _20_ $+$ _40_ $=$ _60_

Add the ones from the two addends.   _5_ $+$ _6_ $=$ _11_

Add the two sums.   _60_ $+$ _11_ $=$ _71_

So, $25 + 46 = $ _71_.

Break apart the addends to find the sum.

1. $12 + 48 = ?$

   _10_ $+$ _2_ $+$ _40_ $+$ _8_

   Add the tens.   _10_ $+$ _40_ $=$ _50_

   Add the ones.   _2_ $+$ _8_ $=$ _10_

   How many in all?   _50_ $+$ _10_ $=$ _60_

   So, $12 + 48 = $ _60_.

---

1. Which shows how to break apart the addends to find the sum?

   $57 + 37$

   - ● $50 + 30 + 7 + 7$
   - ○ $50 + 20 + 7$
   - ○ $20 + 14 + 7$
   - ○ $30 + 7 + 7$

3. Which shows how to break apart the addends to find the sum?

   $45 + 18$

   - ○ $40 + 10 + 5$
   - ○ $50 + 10 + 8 + 5$
   - ● $40 + 10 + 5 + 8$
   - ○ $40 + 5 + 8$

2. Which shows how to break apart the addends to find the sum?

   $25 + 17$

   - ○ $20 + 10 + 7$
   - ● $20 + 10 + 5 + 7$
   - ○ $30 + 10 + 5$
   - ○ $20 + 7 + 5$

4. Which shows how to break apart the addends to find the sum?

   $49 + 23$

   - ● $40 + 20 + 9 + 3$
   - ○ $40 + 20 + 9$
   - ○ $40 + 20 + 10$
   - ○ $40 + 9 + 3$

5. Break apart the addends to find the sum.

   $67 \longrightarrow$ _60_ $+$ _7_
   $+ 28 \longrightarrow$ _20_ $+$ _8_
   _80_ $+$ _15_ $=$ _95_

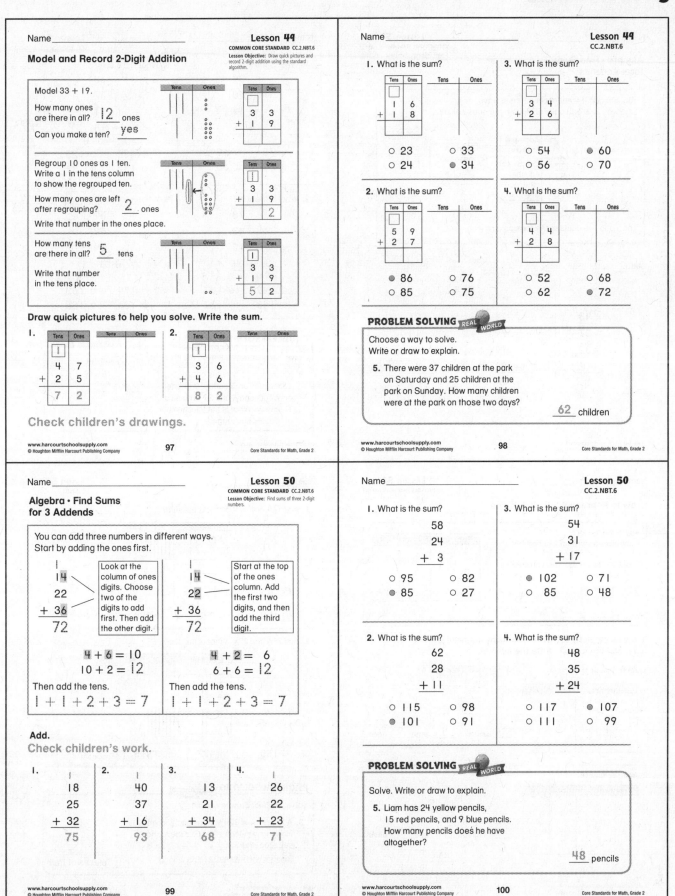

Lesson 49 (page 97)

COMMON CORE STANDARD CC.2.NBT.6
Lesson Objective: Draw quick pictures and record 2-digit addition using the standard algorithm.

Name_____

Model and Record 2-Digit Addition

Model 33 + 19.

How many ones are there in all? **12** ones

Can you make a ten? **yes**

	Tens	Ones
	3	3
+	1	9

Regroup 10 ones as 1 ten. Write a 1 in the tens column to show the regrouped ten.

How many ones are left after regrouping? **2** ones

Write that number in the ones place.

	Tens	Ones
	3	3
+	1	9
		2

How many tens are there in all? **5** tens

Write that number in the tens place.

	Tens	Ones
	3	3
+	1	9
	5	2

Draw quick pictures to help you solve. Write the sum.

1.
	Tens	Ones
	4	7
+	2	5
	7	2

2.
	Tens	Ones
	3	6
+	4	6
	8	2

Check children's drawings.

Lesson 49 (page 98)

CC.2.NBT.6

Name_____

1. What is the sum?

	Tens	Ones
	1	6
+	1	8

○ 23 ○ 33
○ 24 ● 34

2. What is the sum?

	Tens	Ones
	5	9
+	2	7

● 86 ○ 76
○ 85 ○ 75

3. What is the sum?

	Tens	Ones
	3	4
+	2	6

○ 54 ● 60
○ 56 ○ 70

4. What is the sum?

	Tens	Ones
	4	4
+	2	8

○ 52 ○ 68
○ 62 ● 72

PROBLEM SOLVING REAL WORLD

Choose a way to solve. Write or draw to explain.

5. There were 37 children at the park on Saturday and 25 children at the park on Sunday. How many children were at the park on those two days?

62 children

Lesson 50 (page 99)

COMMON CORE STANDARD CC.2.NBT.6
Lesson Objective: Find sums of three 2-digit numbers.

Name_____

Algebra • Find Sums for 3 Addends

You can add three numbers in different ways. Start by adding the ones first.

14
22
+ 36
72

Look at the column of ones digits. Choose two of the digits to add first. Then add the other digit.

14
22
+ 36
72

Start at the top of the ones column. Add the first two digits, and then add the third digit.

$4 + 6 = 10$
$10 + 2 = 12$

$4 + 2 = 6$
$6 + 6 = 12$

Then add the tens.

$1 + 1 + 2 + 3 = 7$

Then add the tens.

$1 + 1 + 2 + 3 = 7$

Add.
Check children's work.

1.
18
25
+ 32
75

2.
40
37
+ 16
93

3.
13
21
+ 34
68

4.
26
22
+ 23
71

Lesson 50 (page 100)

CC.2.NBT.6

Name_____

1. What is the sum?

58
24
+ 3

○ 95 ○ 82
● 85 ○ 27

2. What is the sum?

62
28
+ 11

○ 115 ○ 98
● 101 ○ 91

3. What is the sum?

54
31
+ 17

● 102 ○ 71
○ 85 ○ 48

4. What is the sum?

48
35
+ 24

○ 117 ● 107
○ 111 ○ 99

PROBLEM SOLVING REAL WORLD

Solve. Write or draw to explain.

5. Liam has 24 yellow pencils, 15 red pencils, and 9 blue pencils. How many pencils does he have altogether?

48 pencils

Answer Key

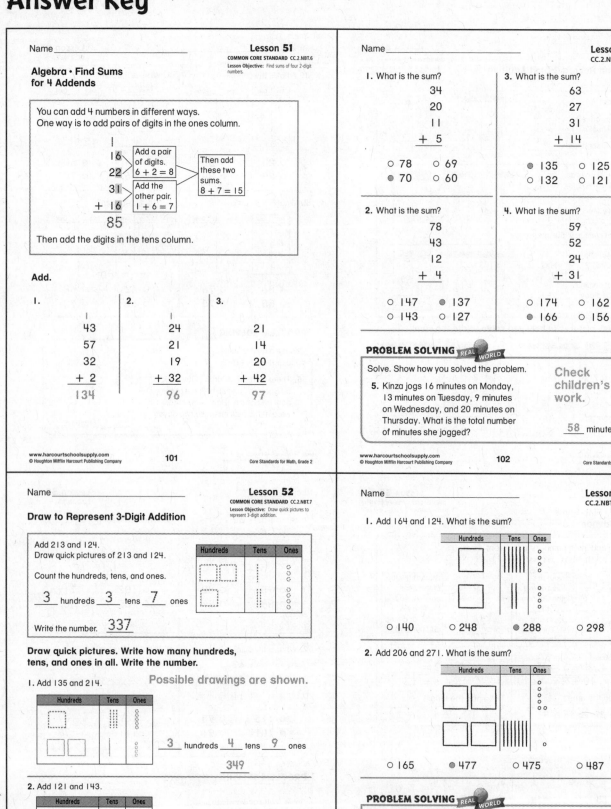

Lesson 51

COMMON CORE STANDARD CC.2.NBT.6
Lesson Objective: Find sums of four 2-digit numbers.

Name_____

**Algebra • Find Sums
for 4 Addends**

You can add 4 numbers in different ways.
One way is to add pairs of digits in the ones column.

```
  1
  16     Add a pair
  22     of digits.        Then add
  31     6 + 2 = 8         these two
+ 16     Add the          sums.
  85     other pair.      8 + 7 = 15
         1 + 6 = 7
```

Then add the digits in the tens column.

Add.

1.
```
  1
  43
  57
  32
+  2
 134
```

2.
```
  1
  24
  21
  19
+ 32
  96
```

3.
```
  21
  14
  20
+ 42
  97
```

Lesson 51
CC.2.NBT.6

Name_____

1. What is the sum?
```
  34
  20
  11
+  5
```
   ○ 78   ○ 69
   ● 70   ○ 60

2. What is the sum?
```
  78
  43
  12
+  4
```
   ○ 147   ● 137
   ○ 143   ○ 127

3. What is the sum?
```
  63
  27
  31
+ 14
```
   ● 135   ○ 125
   ○ 132   ○ 121

4. What is the sum?
```
  59
  52
  24
+ 31
```
   ○ 174   ○ 162
   ● 166   ○ 156

PROBLEM SOLVING REAL WORLD

Solve. Show how you solved the problem.

5. Kinza jogs 16 minutes on Monday, 13 minutes on Tuesday, 9 minutes on Wednesday, and 20 minutes on Thursday. What is the total number of minutes she jogged?

Check children's work.

____58____ minutes

Lesson 52
COMMON CORE STANDARD CC.2.NBT.7
Lesson Objective: Draw quick pictures to represent 3-digit addition.

Name_____

Draw to Represent 3-Digit Addition

Add 213 and 124.
Draw quick pictures of 213 and 124.

Count the hundreds, tens, and ones.

____3____ hundreds ____3____ tens ____7____ ones

Hundreds	Tens	Ones

Write the number. ____337____

Draw quick pictures. Write how many hundreds, tens, and ones in all. Write the number.

Possible drawings are shown.

1. Add 135 and 214.

Hundreds	Tens	Ones

____3____ hundreds ____4____ tens ____9____ ones

349

2. Add 121 and 143.

Hundreds	Tens	Ones

____2____ hundreds ____6____ tens ____4____ ones

264

Lesson 52
CC.2.NBT.7

Name_____

1. Add 164 and 124. What is the sum?

Hundreds	Tens	Ones

   ○ 140   ○ 248   ● 288   ○ 298

2. Add 206 and 271. What is the sum?

Hundreds	Tens	Ones

   ○ 165   ● 477   ○ 475   ○ 487

PROBLEM SOLVING REAL WORLD

Solve. Write or draw to explain.

3. A farmer sold 324 lemons and 255 limes. How many pieces of fruit did the farmer sell altogether?

Check children's drawings.   ____579____ pieces of fruit

Lesson 53 (page 105)

Name_____

Break Apart 3-Digit Addends

COMMON CORE STANDARD CC.2.NBT.7
Lesson Objective: Apply place value concepts when using a break apart strategy for 3-digit addition.

$$743 \\ +124$$

Break apart each addend.
Write the value of each digit.

$743 = \underline{700} + \underline{40} + \underline{3}$

$124 = \underline{100} + \underline{20} + \underline{4}$

Add the hundreds, tens, and ones.
Then add these sums together.

Hundreds	Tens	Ones

$743 \longrightarrow \underline{700} + \underline{40} + \underline{3}$

$+124 \longrightarrow \underline{100} + \underline{20} + \underline{4}$

$\underline{800} + \underline{60} + \underline{7} = \underline{867}$

Break apart the addends to find the sum.

Possible answers are given.

Hundreds	Tens	Ones

1. $253 \longrightarrow \underline{200} + \underline{50} + \underline{3}$

$+536 \longrightarrow \underline{500} + \underline{30} + \underline{6}$

$\underline{700} + \underline{80} + \underline{9} = \underline{789}$

Lesson 53 (page 106)

Name_____

CC.2.NBT.7

1. Which shows 681 broken apart into hundreds, tens, and ones?

   ○ $500 + 10 + 8$
   ○ $500 + 80 + 1$
   ○ $600 + 10 + 8$
   ● $600 + 80 + 1$

2. Break apart the addends into hundreds, tens, and ones. What is the sum?

   $$371 \\ +148$$

   ○ 223 ○ 419 ● 519 ○ 529

PROBLEM SOLVING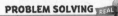

Solve. Write or draw to explain.

3. There are 126 crayons in a bucket. A teacher puts 144 more crayons in the bucket. How many crayons are in the bucket now?

   $\underline{270}$ crayons

Lesson 54 (page 107)

Name_____

3-Digit Addition: Regroup Ones

COMMON CORE STANDARD CC.2.NBT.7
Lesson Objective: Record 3-digit addition using the standard algorithm with possible regrouping of ones.

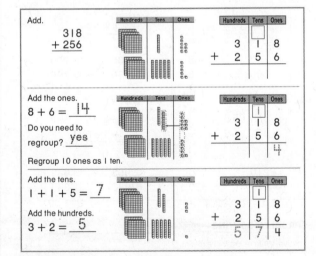

Add.

$$318 \\ +256$$

Add the ones.
$8 + 6 = \underline{14}$
Do you need to regroup? $\underline{yes}$
Regroup 10 ones as 1 ten.

Add the tens.
$1 + 1 + 5 = \underline{7}$

Add the hundreds.
$3 + 2 = \underline{5}$

Write the sum.

1.
Hundreds	Tens	Ones
5	2	6
+ 1	4	2
6	6	8

2.
Hundreds	Tens	Ones
	1	
4	5	7
+ 3	3	5
7	9	2

Lesson 54 (page 108)

Name_____

CC.2.NBT.7

1. What is the sum?

Hundreds	Tens	Ones
3	7	5
+ 2	1	6

   ○ 691 ○ 581
   ● 591 ○ 159

2. What is the sum?

Hundreds	Tens	Ones
1	4	9
+ 1	2	8

   ○ 267 ○ 278
   ● 277 ○ 377

3. What is the sum?

Hundreds	Tens	Ones
3	6	7
+ 1	2	8

   ○ 239 ● 495
   ○ 485 ○ 595

4. What is the sum?

Hundreds	Tens	Ones
4	5	5
+ 2	3	5

   ○ 600 ○ 650
   ○ 610 ● 690

PROBLEM SOLVING

Solve. Write or draw to explain.

5. In the garden, there are 258 yellow daisies and 135 white daisies. How many daisies are in the garden altogether?

   $\underline{393}$ daisies

Answer Key

COMMON CORE STANDARD CC.2.NBT.7
Lesson Objective: Record 3-digit addition using the standard algorithm with possible regrouping of tens.

3-Digit Addition: Regroup Tens

Add. 271
    + 158

Add the ones.

$1 + 8 = \underline{9}$

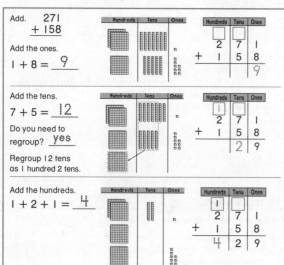

Add the tens.

$7 + 5 = \underline{12}$

Do you need to regroup? __yes__

Regroup 12 tens as 1 hundred 2 tens.

Add the hundreds.

$1 + 2 + 1 = \underline{4}$

Write the sum.

1.
Hundreds	Tens	Ones
2	6	4
+ 1	4	5
4	0	9

2.
Hundreds	Tens	Ones
2	3	2
+ 6	0	6
8	3	8

---

1. What is the sum?

Hundreds	Tens	Ones
1	9	2
+ 3	5	6

○ 448   ○ 544
○ 458   ● 548

2. What is the sum?

Hundreds	Tens	Ones
3	9	1
+ 2	9	6

○ 697   ○ 685
● 687   ○ 587

3. What is the sum?

Hundreds	Tens	Ones
1	8	3
+ 2	5	6

● 439   ○ 349
○ 433   ○ 339

4. What is the sum?

363
+ 254

○ 671   ● 617
○ 651   ○ 607

PROBLEM SOLVING

Solve. Write or draw to explain.

5. There are 142 blue toy cars and 293 red toy cars at the toy store. How many toy cars are there in all?

__435__ toy cars

COMMON CORE STANDARD CC.2.NBT.7
Lesson Objective: Record 3-digit addition using the standard algorithm with possible regrouping of both ones and tens.

Addition: Regroup Ones and Tens

Sometimes, you may need to regroup more than once.

189
+ 623

Step 1 Add the ones. There are 12 ones in all. Regroup 12 ones as 1 ten 2 ones.

1 8 9
+ 6 2 3
_____ 2

Step 2 Add the tens. There are 11 tens in all. Regroup 11 tens as 1 hundred 1 ten.

1 8 9
+ 6 2 3
_____ 1 2

Step 3 Add the hundreds. There are 8 hundreds in all.

1 8 9
+ 6 2 3
_____ 8 1 2

Write the sum.

1.
2 7 8
+ 4 6 5
7 4 3

2.
1 5 7
+ 7 7 1
9 2 8

3.
3 6 4
+ 4 1 9
7 8 3

---

1. What is the sum?

139
+ 379

● 518   ○ 508
○ 500   ○ 418

2. What is the sum?

158
+ 162

○ 210   ○ 310
○ 220   ● 320

3. What is the sum?

243
+ 457

○ 600   ● 700
○ 690   ○ 790

4. What is the sum?

275
+ 168

○ 453   ○ 433
● 443   ○ 343

PROBLEM SOLVING

Solve. Write or draw to explain.

5. Saul and Luisa each scored 167 points on a computer game. How many points did they score in all?

__334__ points

Answer Key

Lesson 57

Name_____

Lesson 57
COMMON CORE STANDARD CC.2.NBT.7
Lesson Objective: Solve problems involving 3-digit subtraction by using the strategy *make a model*.

Problem Solving · 3-Digit Subtraction

There were 237 books on the shelves.
Mr. Davies took 126 books off the shelves.
How many books were still on the shelves?

Unlock the Problem

What do I need to find?	What information do I need to use?
how many books	There were __237__ books on the shelves.
were still on the shelves	Mr. Davies took __126__ books off the shelves.

Show how to solve the problem.

There were __111__ books still on the shelves.

Make a model to solve. Then draw a quick picture of your model.

Check children's work.

1. Mr. Cho has 256 pencils.
   Then he sells 132 pencils.
   How many pencils does he have now?

   __124__ pencils

Name_____

Lesson 57
CC.2.NBT.7

1. There were 487 cars in a parking lot.
   Then 156 cars left. How many cars are in the parking lot now?

   ○ 231   ○ 321   ● 331   ○ 336

2. Helen counted 381 leaves on her porch.
   There were 129 red leaves. How many leaves were not red?

   ○ 262   ● 252   ○ 250   ○ 249

3. There were 614 boxes at a post office.
   Then people took 280 boxes home. How many boxes are still at the post office?

   ○ 434   ○ 420   ○ 344   ● 334

4. Michael collected 525 bottle caps. His sister collected 413 bottle caps. How many more bottle caps did Michael collect than his sister? Draw a quick picture to help you solve the problem. Then write your answer.

   Possible drawing:

   __112__ more bottle caps

Lesson 58

Name_____

Lesson 58
COMMON CORE STANDARD CC.2.NBT.7
Lesson Objective: Record 3-digit subtraction using the standard algorithm with possible regrouping of tens.

3-Digit Subtraction: Regroup Tens

Subtract.

$$\begin{array}{r} 463 \\ -317 \end{array}$$

Are there enough ones to subtract 7? __no__

Regroup 1 ten as 10 ones.

There are __13__ ones and __5__ tens.

Subtract the ones.
$13 - 7 = $ __6__

Subtract the tens.
$5 - 1 = $ __4__

Subtract the hundreds.
$4 - 3 = $ __1__

Solve. Write the difference.

1.

Hundreds	Tens	Ones
	5	12
8	6	2
− 3	2	8
5	3	4

2.

Hundreds	Tens	Ones
6	7	8
− 2	4	5
4	3	3

Name_____

Lesson 58
CC.2.NBT.7

1. What is the difference?

Hundreds	Tens	Ones
7	9	5
− 5	3	7

   ○ 257   ○ 267
   ● 258   ○ 268

2. What is the difference?

Hundreds	Tens	Ones
5	5	7
− 4	1	9

   ● 138   ○ 148
   ○ 142   ○ 156

PROBLEM SOLVING REAL WORLD

Solve. Write or draw to explain.

3. There were 985 pencils. Some pencils were sold. Then there were 559 pencils left. How many pencils were sold?

   __426__ pencils

Answer Key

3-Digit Subtraction: Regroup Hundreds

COMMON CORE STANDARD CC.2.NBT.7
Lesson Objective: Record 3-digit subtraction using the standard algorithm with possible regrouping of hundreds.

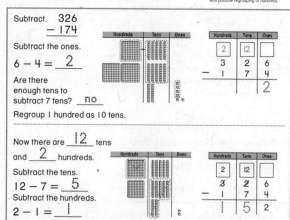

Subtract. 326
        − 174

Subtract the ones.

6 − 4 = __2__

Are there enough tens to subtract 7 tens? __no__

Regroup 1 hundred as 10 tens.

Now there are __12__ tens

and __2__ hundreds.

Subtract the tens.

12 − 7 = __5__

Subtract the hundreds.

2 − 1 = __1__

Solve. Write the difference.

1.
Hundreds	Tens	Ones
6	7	9
− 2	6	1
4	1	8

2.
Hundreds	Tens	Ones
	4	12
5	2̶	5̶
− 2	9	3
2	3	2

---

1. What is the difference?

847
− 392

○ 559   ○ 539
○ 555   ● 455

3. What is the difference?

548
− 276

○ 262   ○ 372
● 272   ○ 374

2. What is the difference?

413
− 152

● 261   ○ 345
○ 341   ○ 565

4. What is the difference?

924
− 460

○ 584   ● 464
○ 544   ○ 440

PROBLEM SOLVING REAL WORLD

Solve. Write or draw to explain.

5. There were 537 people in the parade. 254 of these people were playing an instrument. How many people were not playing an instrument?

__283__ people

Subtraction: Regroup Hundreds and Tens

COMMON CORE STANDARD CC.2.NBT.7
Lesson Objective: Record 3-digit subtraction using the standard algorithm with possible regrouping of both hundreds and tens.

You may need to regroup more than once.

282
− 198

Regroup 1 ten as 10 ones. Subtract the ones.	Regroup 1 hundred as 10 tens. Subtract the tens.	Subtract the hundreds.
7 12 2 8̶ 2̶ − 1 9 8 4	17 1 7̶ 12 2̶ 8̶ 2̶ − 1 9 8 8 4	17 1 7̶ 12 2̶ 8̶ 2̶ − 1 9 8 8 4

Solve. Write the difference.

1. 7 11
4 8̶ 1̶
− 1 7 6
3 0 5

2. 3 16
7 4̶ 6̶
− 2 8
7 1 8

3. 12
2 2̶ 11
3̶ 3̶ 1̶
− 1 4 8
1 8 3

4. 3 9 5
− 1 3 1
2 6 4

5. 4 11
4̶ 1̶ 14
5 2̶ 4̶
− 2 6 5
2 5 9

6. 7 4 8
− 6 0 3
1 4 5

---

1. What is the difference?

725
− 284

● 441   ○ 541
○ 449   ○ 545

3. What is the difference?

852
− 676

○ 276   ● 176
○ 186   ○ 174

2. What is the difference?

561
− 193

○ 358   ○ 458
● 368   ○ 468

4. What is the difference?

637
− 458

○ 175   ○ 189
● 179   ○ 271

PROBLEM SOLVING REAL WORLD

Solve.

5. Mia's coloring book has 432 pages. She has already colored 178 pages. How many pages in the book are left to color?

__254__ pages

Lesson 61

Name_____

Regrouping with Zeros

COMMON CORE STANDARD CC.2.NBT.7
Lesson Objective: Record subtraction using the standard algorithm when there are zeros in the minuend.

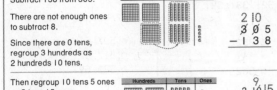

Subtract 138 from 305.

There are not enough ones to subtract 8.

Since there are 0 tens, regroup 3 hundreds as 2 hundreds 10 tens.

$$\begin{array}{r} 2\ 10 \\ \cancel{3}\ \cancel{0}\ 5 \\ -1\ 3\ 8 \end{array}$$

Then regroup 10 tens 5 ones as 9 tens 15 ones.

Subtract the ones.

$15 - 8 = 7$

$$\begin{array}{r} 9 \\ 2\ 10\ 15 \\ \cancel{3}\ \cancel{0}\ \cancel{5} \\ -1\ 3\ 8 \\ \hline 7 \end{array}$$

Subtract the tens.

$9 - 3 = 6$

Subtract the hundreds.

$2 - 1 = 1$

$$\begin{array}{r} 9 \\ 2\ 10\ 15 \\ \cancel{3}\ \cancel{0}\ \cancel{5} \\ -1\ 3\ 8 \\ \hline 1\ 6\ 7 \end{array}$$

So, $305 - 138 = \underline{167}$.

Solve. Write the difference.

1.
$$\begin{array}{r} 9 \\ 7\ 10\ 11 \\ 8\ \cancel{0}\ \cancel{1} \\ -3\ 7\ 5 \\ \hline 4\ 2\ 6 \end{array}$$

2.
$$\begin{array}{r} 6\ 9\ 3 \\ -2\ 4\ 1 \\ \hline 4\ 5\ 2 \end{array}$$

3.
$$\begin{array}{r} 8\ 10 \\ 9\ \cancel{0}\ 7 \\ -6\ 2\ 4 \\ \hline 2\ 8\ 3 \end{array}$$

Lesson 61

Name_____

CC.2.NBT.7

1. What is the difference?

$$\begin{array}{r} 3\ 0\ 6 \\ -1\ 2\ 7 \end{array}$$

○ 289   ● 179
○ 189   ○ 171

3. What is the difference?

$$\begin{array}{r} 4\ 4\ 8 \\ -2\ 6\ 3 \end{array}$$

● 185   ○ 285
○ 195   ○ 291

2. What is the difference?

$$\begin{array}{r} 9\ 0\ 2 \\ -5\ 3\ 8 \end{array}$$

○ 464   ● 374
○ 382   ● 364

4. What is the difference?

$$\begin{array}{r} 7\ 0\ 4 \\ -3\ 5\ 5 \end{array}$$

○ 459   ● 349
○ 449   ○ 341

PROBLEM SOLVING REAL WORLD

Solve.

5. There are 303 students. There are 147 girls. How many boys are there?

$\underline{156}$ boys

Lesson 62

Name_____

Count On and Count Back by 10 and 100

COMMON CORE STANDARD CC.2.NBT.8
Lesson Objective: Identify 10 more, 10 less, 100 more, or 100 less than a given number.

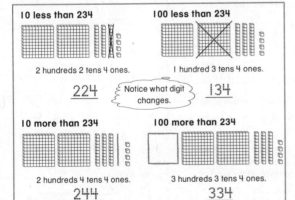

10 less than 234

2 hundreds 2 tens 4 ones.

$\underline{224}$

Notice what digit changes.

100 less than 234

1 hundred 3 tens 4 ones.

$\underline{134}$

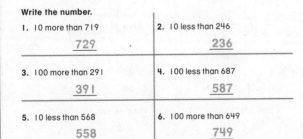

10 more than 234

2 hundreds 4 tens 4 ones.

$\underline{244}$

100 more than 234

3 hundreds 3 tens 4 ones.

$\underline{334}$

Write the number.

1. 10 more than 719
$\underline{729}$

2. 10 less than 246
$\underline{236}$

3. 100 more than 291
$\underline{391}$

4. 100 less than 687
$\underline{587}$

5. 10 less than 568
$\underline{558}$

6. 100 more than 649
$\underline{749}$

Lesson 62

Name_____

CC.2.NBT.8

1. Which number is 10 more than 837?

○ 827
● 847
○ 937
○ 947

3. Which number is 100 more than 326?

○ 226
○ 336
● 426
○ 436

2. Which number is 10 less than 619?

○ 629
○ 610
● 609
○ 519

4. Which number is 100 less than 541?

○ 641
○ 531
○ 451
● 441

PROBLEM SOLVING REAL WORLD

Solve. Write or draw to explain.

5. Sarah has 128 stickers. Alex has 10 fewer stickers than Sarah. How many stickers does Alex have?

$\underline{118}$ stickers

Answer Key

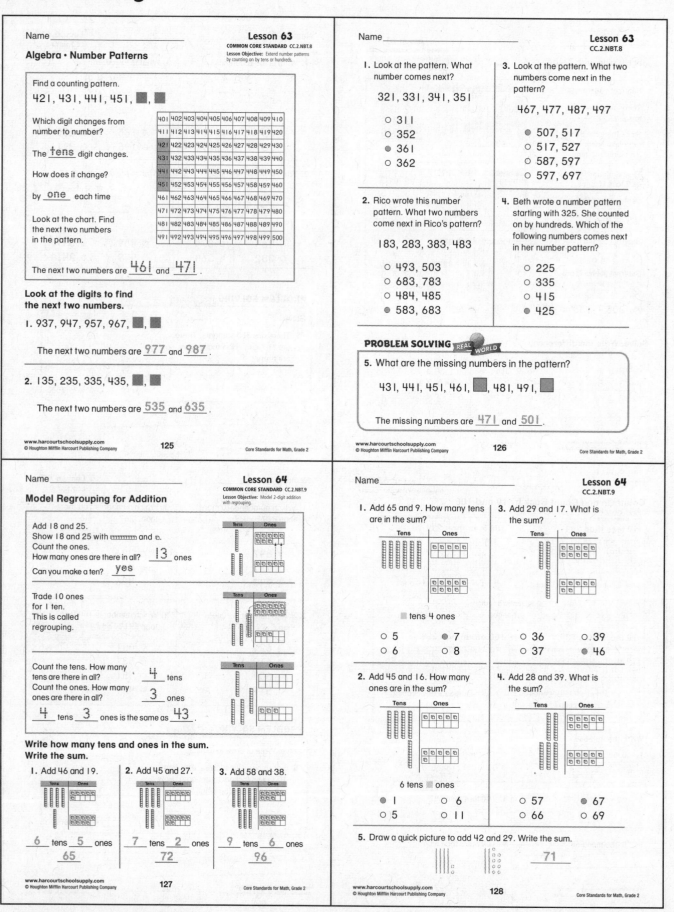

Name _____

Lesson 63

COMMON CORE STANDARD CC.2.NBT.8
Lesson Objective: Extend number patterns by counting on by tens or hundreds.

Algebra • Number Patterns

Find a counting pattern.

421, 431, 441, 451, ▨, ▨

Which digit changes from number to number?

The _tens_ digit changes.

How does it change?

by _one_ each time

Look at the chart. Find the next two numbers in the pattern.

The next two numbers are _461_ and _471_.

401	402	403	404	405	406	407	408	409	410
411	412	413	414	415	416	417	418	419	420
421	422	423	424	425	426	427	428	429	430
431	432	433	434	435	436	437	438	439	440
441	442	443	444	445	446	447	448	449	450
451	452	453	454	455	456	457	458	459	460
461	462	463	464	465	466	467	468	469	470
471	472	473	474	475	476	477	478	479	480
481	482	483	484	485	486	487	488	489	490
491	492	493	494	495	496	497	498	499	500

Look at the digits to find the next two numbers.

1. 937, 947, 957, 967, ▨, ▨

The next two numbers are _977_ and _987_.

2. 135, 235, 335, 435, ▨, ▨

The next two numbers are _535_ and _635_.

125

Name _____

Lesson 63

CC.2.NBT.8

1. Look at the pattern. What number comes next?

321, 331, 341, 351

- ○ 311
- ○ 352
- ● 361
- ○ 362

2. Rico wrote this number pattern. What two numbers come next in Rico's pattern?

183, 283, 383, 483

- ○ 493, 503
- ○ 683, 783
- ○ 484, 485
- ● 583, 683

3. Look at the pattern. What two numbers come next in the pattern?

467, 477, 487, 497

- ● 507, 517
- ○ 517, 527
- ○ 587, 597
- ○ 597, 697

4. Beth wrote a number pattern starting with 325. She counted on by hundreds. Which of the following numbers comes next in her number pattern?

- ○ 225
- ○ 335
- ○ 415
- ● 425

PROBLEM SOLVING REAL WORLD

5. What are the missing numbers in the pattern?

431, 441, 451, 461, ▨, 481, 491, ▨

The missing numbers are _471_ and _501_.

126

Name _____

Lesson 64

COMMON CORE STANDARD CC.2.NBT.9
Lesson Objective: Model 2-digit addition with regrouping.

Model Regrouping for Addition

Add 18 and 25.
Show 18 and 25 with ▭▭▭▭ and ▫.
Count the ones.
How many ones are there in all? _13_ ones
Can you make a ten? _yes_

Trade 10 ones for 1 ten. This is called regrouping.

Count the tens. How many tens are there in all? _4_ tens
Count the ones. How many ones are there in all? _3_ ones

_4_ tens _3_ ones is the same as _43_.

Write how many tens and ones in the sum. Write the sum.

1. Add 46 and 19.

_6_ tens _5_ ones
_65_

2. Add 45 and 27.

_7_ tens _2_ ones
_72_

3. Add 58 and 38.

_9_ tens _6_ ones
_96_

127

Name _____

Lesson 64

CC.2.NBT.9

1. Add 65 and 9. How many tens are in the sum?

▨ tens 4 ones

- ○ 5
- ● 7
- ○ 6
- ○ 8

2. Add 45 and 16. How many ones are in the sum?

6 tens ▨ ones

- ● 1
- ○ 6
- ○ 5
- ○ 11

3. Add 29 and 17. What is the sum?

- ○ 36
- ○ 39
- ○ 37
- ● 46

4. Add 28 and 39. What is the sum?

- ○ 57
- ● 67
- ○ 66
- ○ 69

5. Draw a quick picture to add 42 and 29. Write the sum.

_71_

128

Page 129 (Lesson 65)

Name _____

Lesson 65
COMMON CORE STANDARD CC.2.NBT.9
Lesson Objective: Model 2-digit subtraction with regrouping.

Model Regrouping for Subtraction

Subtract 37 from 65.

Are there enough ones to subtract 7? __no__
So, you will need to regroup.

Trade 1 ten for 10 ones.

Subtract the ones. Then subtract the tens.

15 ones − 7 ones = __8__ ones

5 tens − 3 tens = __2__ tens

__2__ tens __8__ ones is the same as __28__.

The difference is __28__.

Draw to show the regrouping. Write the tens and ones that are in the difference. Write the number.

Check children's work.

1. Subtract 18 from 43.

__2__ tens __5__ ones
__25__

2. Subtract 19 from 55.

__3__ tens __6__ ones
__36__

Page 130 (Lesson 65)

Name _____

Lesson 65
CC.2.NBT.9

1. Subtract 16 from 52. What is the difference?

○ 69 ● 36
○ 44 ○ 34

2. Subtract 14 from 43. Which shows the tens and ones in the difference?

● 2 tens 9 ones
○ 3 tens 1 one
○ 5 tens 7 ones
○ 8 tens 7 ones

3. Subtract 27 from 43. What is the difference?

○ 70 ● 16
○ 24 ○ 14

PROBLEM SOLVING REAL WORLD

Choose a way to solve. Write or draw to explain.

4. Mr. Ortega made 51 cookies. He gave 14 cookies away. How many cookies does he have now?

__37__ cookies

Page 131 (Lesson 66)

Name _____

Lesson 66
COMMON CORE STANDARD CC.2.MD.1
Lesson Objective: Make an inch ruler and use it to measure the lengths of objects.

Make and Use a Ruler

Use a paper strip. Mark the sides of a color tile. Mark 6 tiles. Color each part.

Each part is about __1 inch__ long.

Line up the left edge of the bracelet with the first mark. Count the inches.

The bracelet is about __5__ inches long.

Measure the length with your ruler. Count the inches.

1.

about __4__ inches

2.

about __3__ inches

Page 132 (Lesson 66)

Name _____

Lesson 66
CC.2.MD.1

1. Each square tile is about 1 inch long. How long is the ribbon?

○ about 1 inch   ● about 3 inches
○ about 2 inches   ○ about 4 inches

2. Each square tile is about 1 inch long. How long is the string?

○ about 3 inches   ● about 5 inches
○ about 4 inches   ○ about 6 inches

PROBLEM SOLVING REAL WORLD

3. Use your ruler. Measure the width of this page in inches.

Check children's work.

about __8__ inches

Answer Key

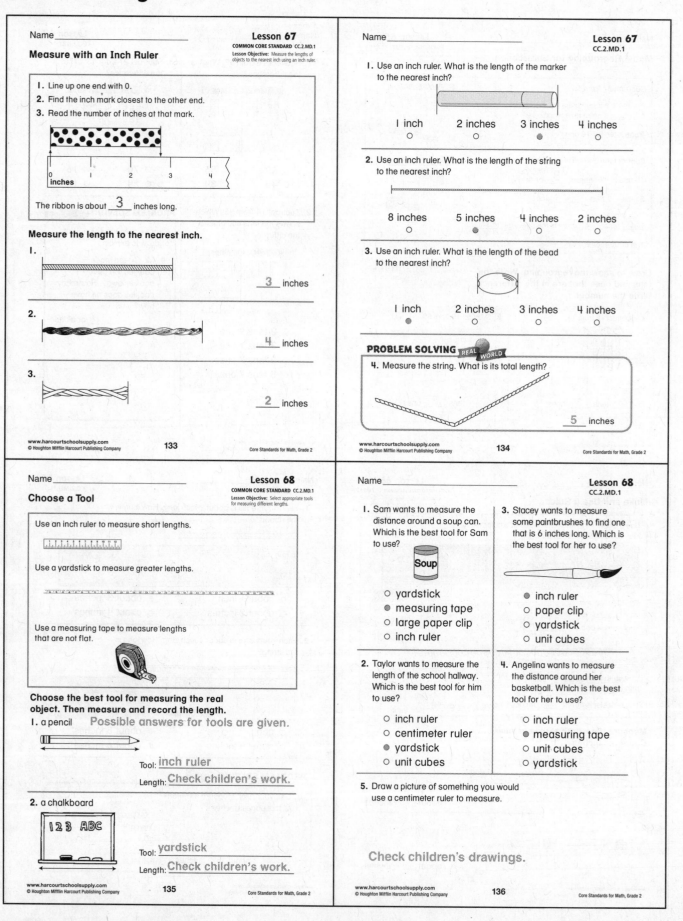

Lesson 67
COMMON CORE STANDARD CC.2.MD.1
Lesson Objective: Measure the lengths of objects to the nearest inch using an inch ruler.

Name_____

Measure with an Inch Ruler

1. Line up one end with 0.
2. Find the inch mark closest to the other end.
3. Read the number of inches at that mark.

The ribbon is about ___3___ inches long.

Measure the length to the nearest inch.

1. _____3_____ inches

2. _____4_____ inches

3. _____2_____ inches

www.harcourtschoolsupply.com
© Houghton Mifflin Harcourt Publishing Company
133
Core Standards for Math, Grade 2

Name_____

Lesson 67
CC.2.MD.1

1. Use an inch ruler. What is the length of the marker to the nearest inch?

   1 inch ○   2 inches ○   3 inches ●   4 inches ○

2. Use an inch ruler. What is the length of the string to the nearest inch?

   8 inches ○   5 inches ●   4 inches ○   2 inches ○

3. Use an inch ruler. What is the length of the bead to the nearest inch?

   1 inch ●   2 inches ○   3 inches ○   4 inches ○

PROBLEM SOLVING REAL WORLD

4. Measure the string. What is its total length?

   _____5_____ inches

www.harcourtschoolsupply.com
© Houghton Mifflin Harcourt Publishing Company
134
Core Standards for Math, Grade 2

Name_____

Lesson 68
COMMON CORE STANDARD CC.2.MD.1
Lesson Objective: Select appropriate tools for measuring different lengths.

Choose a Tool

Use an inch ruler to measure short lengths.

Use a yardstick to measure greater lengths.

Use a measuring tape to measure lengths that are not flat.

Choose the best tool for measuring the real object. Then measure and record the length.

1. a pencil   Possible answers for tools are given.

   Tool: _inch ruler_
   Length: _Check children's work._

2. a chalkboard

   Tool: _yardstick_
   Length: _Check children's work._

www.harcourtschoolsupply.com
© Houghton Mifflin Harcourt Publishing Company
135
Core Standards for Math, Grade 2

Name_____

Lesson 68
CC.2.MD.1

1. Sam wants to measure the distance around a soup can. Which is the best tool for Sam to use?

   ○ yardstick
   ● measuring tape
   ○ large paper clip
   ○ inch ruler

2. Taylor wants to measure the length of the school hallway. Which is the best tool for him to use?

   ○ inch ruler
   ○ centimeter ruler
   ● yardstick
   ○ unit cubes

3. Stacey wants to measure some paintbrushes to find one that is 6 inches long. Which is the best tool for her to use?

   ● inch ruler
   ○ paper clip
   ○ yardstick
   ○ unit cubes

4. Angelina wants to measure the distance around her basketball. Which is the best tool for her to use?

   ○ inch ruler
   ● measuring tape
   ○ unit cubes
   ○ yardstick

5. Draw a picture of something you would use a centimeter ruler to measure.

   Check children's drawings.

www.harcourtschoolsupply.com
© Houghton Mifflin Harcourt Publishing Company
136
Core Standards for Math, Grade 2

Answer Key

Name_____ **Lesson 69**
COMMON CORE STANDARD CC.2.MD.1
Lesson Objective: Measure lengths of objects to the nearest centimeter using a centimeter ruler.

Measure with a Centimeter Ruler

Line up the left end of the ribbon with the zero mark on the ruler.

Which centimeter mark is closest to the other end of the ribbon?

0 1 2 3 4 5 6 7 8 9 10
centimeters

The ribbon is about ___7___ centimeters long.

Measure the length to the nearest centimeter.

1. _____9_____ centimeters

2. _____4_____ centimeters

3. _____10_____ centimeters

Name_____ **Lesson 69**
CC.2.MD.1

1. Use a centimeter ruler. What is the length of the pen cap to the nearest centimeter?

8 centimeters 7 centimeters 6 centimeters 5 centimeters
○ ○ ○ ●

2. Use a centimeter ruler. What is the length of the fish to the nearest centimeter?

8 centimeters 10 centimeters 12 centimeters 16 centimeters
● ○ ○ ○

3. Use a centimeter ruler. What is the length of the ribbon to the nearest centimeter?

5 centimeters 7 centimeters 8 centimeters 9 centimeters
○ ● ○ ○

PROBLEM SOLVING REAL WORLD

4. Draw a string that is about 8 centimeters long. Then use a centimeter ruler to check the length.

Check children's work.

Name_____ **Lesson 70**
COMMON CORE STANDARD CC.2.MD.2
Lesson Objective: Measure the lengths of objects in both inches and feet to explore the inverse relationship between size and number of units.

Measure in Inches and Feet

The real folder is about 12 inches wide.
The real folder is also about 1 foot wide.

12 inches is the same as 1 foot.

Check children's work.

**Measure to the nearest inch.
Then measure to the nearest foot.**

Find the real object.	Measure.
desk 1.	_____ inches _____ feet
rug 2.	_____ inches _____ feet
map 3.	_____ inches _____ feet

Name_____ **Lesson 70**
CC.2.MD.2

1. Which of the following makes the sentence correct?

1 foot is _____ 1 inch.

○ the same as
○ shorter than
● longer than

3. Lee has a string that is 3 inches long. Pat has a string that is 3 feet long. Which of the following is correct?

○ Lee's string is longer.
● Pat's string is longer.
○ Both strings are the same length.

2. Mia measures the length of a book to the nearest inch. It is about 12 inches long. How long is the book?

● 1 foot
○ 2 feet
○ 6 feet
○ 12 feet

PROBLEM SOLVING REAL WORLD

4. Jake has a piece of yarn that is 4 feet long. Blair has a piece of yarn that is 4 inches long. Who has the longer piece of yarn? Explain.

Jake; possible answer:
Feet are longer than
inches, so 4 feet is
longer than 4 inches.

Answer Key

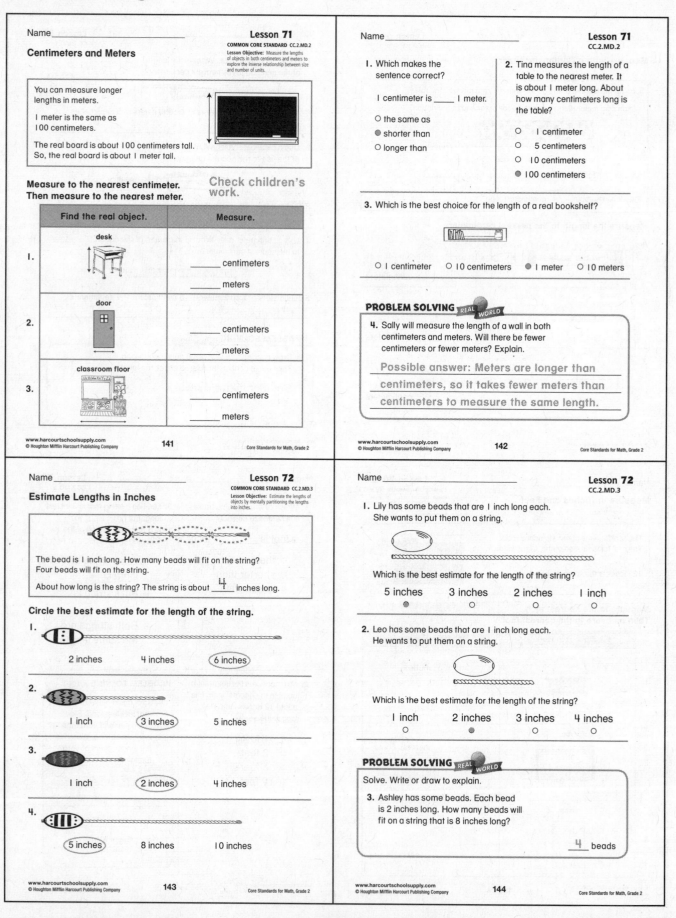

248

Core Standards for Math, Grade 2

Answer Key

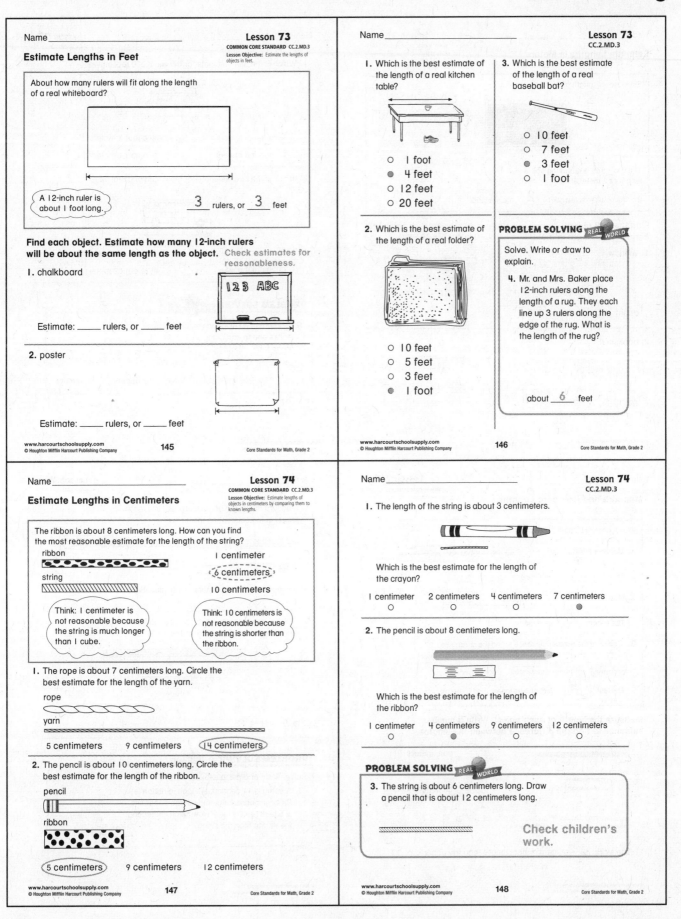

Name_____   **Lesson 73**
COMMON CORE STANDARD CC.2.MD.3
Estimate Lengths in Feet   Lesson Objective: Estimate the lengths of objects in feet.

About how many rulers will fit along the length of a real whiteboard?

A 12-inch ruler is about 1 foot long.   __3__ rulers, or __3__ feet

Find each object. Estimate how many 12-inch rulers will be about the same length as the object. Check estimates for reasonableness.

1. chalkboard

123 ABC

Estimate: _____ rulers, or _____ feet

2. poster

Estimate: _____ rulers, or _____ feet

www.harcourtschoolsupply.com   **145**   Core Standards for Math, Grade 2
© Houghton Mifflin Harcourt Publishing Company

Name_____   **Lesson 73**
CC.2.MD.3

1. Which is the best estimate of the length of a real kitchen table?
   - ○ 1 foot
   - ● 4 feet
   - ○ 12 feet
   - ○ 20 feet

3. Which is the best estimate of the length of a real baseball bat?
   - ○ 10 feet
   - ○ 7 feet
   - ● 3 feet
   - ○ 1 foot

2. Which is the best estimate of the length of a real folder?
   - ○ 10 feet
   - ○ 5 feet
   - ○ 3 feet
   - ● 1 foot

PROBLEM SOLVING REAL WORLD

Solve. Write or draw to explain.

4. Mr. and Mrs. Baker place 12-inch rulers along the length of a rug. They each line up 3 rulers along the edge of the rug. What is the length of the rug?

about __6__ feet

www.harcourtschoolsupply.com   **146**   Core Standards for Math, Grade 2
© Houghton Mifflin Harcourt Publishing Company

Name_____   **Lesson 74**
COMMON CORE STANDARD CC.2.MD.3
Estimate Lengths in Centimeters   Lesson Objective: Estimate lengths of objects in centimeters by comparing them to known lengths.

The ribbon is about 8 centimeters long. How can you find the most reasonable estimate for the length of the string?

ribbon   1 centimeter

string   6 centimeters

                                10 centimeters

Think: 1 centimeter is not reasonable because the string is much longer than 1 cube.

Think: 10 centimeters is not reasonable because the string is shorter than the ribbon.

1. The rope is about 7 centimeters long. Circle the best estimate for the length of the yarn.

rope

yarn

5 centimeters   9 centimeters   4 centimeters

2. The pencil is about 10 centimeters long. Circle the best estimate for the length of the ribbon.

pencil

ribbon

5 centimeters   9 centimeters   12 centimeters

www.harcourtschoolsupply.com   **147**   Core Standards for Math, Grade 2
© Houghton Mifflin Harcourt Publishing Company

Name_____   **Lesson 74**
CC.2.MD.3

1. The length of the string is about 3 centimeters.

Which is the best estimate for the length of the crayon?

1 centimeter   2 centimeters   4 centimeters   7 centimeters
   ○   ○   ○   ●

2. The pencil is about 8 centimeters long.

Which is the best estimate for the length of the ribbon?

1 centimeter   4 centimeters   9 centimeters   12 centimeters
   ○   ●   ○   ○

PROBLEM SOLVING REAL WORLD

3. The string is about 6 centimeters long. Draw a pencil that is about 12 centimeters long.

Check children's work.

www.harcourtschoolsupply.com   **148**   Core Standards for Math, Grade 2
© Houghton Mifflin Harcourt Publishing Company

Answer Key

Name_____ **Lesson 75**

COMMON CORE STANDARD CC.2.MD.3
Lesson Objective: Estimate the lengths of objects in meters.

Estimate Lengths in Meters

Estimate the length of the chalk tray.

The chalk tray is about the same length as 2 meter sticks.

So, the chalk tray is about __2__ meters long.

Find the real object.
Estimate its length in meters.

Check children's estimates for reasonableness.

1. window

about _____ meters

2. bookshelf

about _____ meters

Name_____ **Lesson 75**
CC.2.MD.3

1. Which is the best estimate for the width of a real stove?

○ about 4 meters   ○ about 2 meters
○ about 3 meters   ◉ about 1 meter

2. Which is the best estimate for the length of a real bus?

○ about 3 meters   ○ about 6 meters
○ about 4 meters   ◉ about 12 meters

PROBLEM SOLVING REAL WORLD

3. Barbara and Luke each placed 2 meter sticks end-to-end along the length of a large table. About how long is the table?

about __4__ meters

Name_____ **Lesson 76**

COMMON CORE STANDARD CC.2.MD.4
Lesson Objective: Measure and then find the difference in the lengths of two objects.

Measure and Compare Lengths

Which object is longer? How much longer?

1. Measure the leaf.

The leaf is __9__ centimeters.

2. Measure the stick.

The stick is __5__ centimeters.

3. Complete the number sentence to find the difference.

$$\underset{\text{centimeters}}{9} - \underset{\text{centimeters}}{5} = \underset{\text{centimeters}}{4}$$

The leaf is __4__ centimeters longer than the stick.

Measure the length of each object. Write a number sentence to find the difference between the lengths.

1.

__6__ centimeters

__3__ centimeters

$$\underset{\text{centimeters}}{6} - \underset{\text{centimeters}}{3} = \underset{\text{centimeters}}{3}$$

The string is __3__ centimeters longer than the paper clip.

Name_____ **Lesson 76**
CC.2.MD.4

1. Measure the length of each object. How much longer is the celery than the carrot?

1 centimeter   3 centimeters   4 centimeters   7 centimeters
○   ○   ○   ◉

2. Which number sentence can be used to find how much longer the ribbon is than the paper clip?

9 centimeters

5 centimeters

○ 9 + 5 = 14   ◉ 9 − 5 = 4
○ 9 + 4 = 13   ○ 5 − 4 = 1

PROBLEM SOLVING REAL WORLD

Solve. Write or draw to explain.

3. A string is 11 centimeters long, a ribbon is 24 centimeters long, and a large paper clip is 5 centimeters long. How much longer is the ribbon than the string?

__13__ centimeters

Answer Key

Name

Lesson 77
COMMON CORE STANDARD CC.2.MD.5
Lesson Objective: Solve addition and subtraction problems involving the lengths of objects by using the strategy *draw a diagram.*

Problem Solving · Add and Subtract in Inches

Zack has two strings. One string is 12 inches long and the other string is 5 inches long. How long are Zack's strings altogether?

Unlock the Problem

What do I need to find?	What information do I need to use?
how long Zack's strings are in all	One string is 12 inches long. The other string is 5 inches long.

Show how to solve the problem.

12 — 5

0 1 2 3 4 5 6 7 8 9 10 11 12 13 14 15 16 17 18 19 20 21 22 23 24 25

$12 + 5 =$ ▧   The strings are 17 inches long in all.

Write a number sentence using a ▧ for the missing number. Solve.

1. Sara has two pieces of yarn. Each piece is 7 inches long. How many inches of yarn does she have in all?

0 1 2 3 4 5 6 7 8 9 10 11 12 13 14 15 16 17 18 19 20 21 22 23 24 25

$7 + 7 =$ ▧   Sara has 14 inches of yarn in all.

Name

Lesson 77
CC.2.MD.5

1. Mr. Owen has a board that is 17 inches long. Then he cuts 8 inches off the board. How long is the board now?

8

17

0 1 2 3 4 5 6 7 8 9 10 11 12 13 14 15 16 17 18 19 20 21 22 23 24 25

9 inches	11 inches	17 inches	20 inches
●	○	○	○

2. Juan has a cube train that is 13 inches long. He removes 5 inches of the cube train. How long is the cube train now?

5

13

0 1 2 3 4 5 6 7 8 9 10 11 12 13 14 15 16 17 18 19 20 21 22 23 24 25

18 inches	13 inches	8 inches	7 inches
○	○	●	○

3. Meg has a ribbon that is 9 inches long and another ribbon that is 12 inches long. How many inches of ribbon does Meg have in all?

9   12

0 1 2 3 4 5 6 7 8 9 10 11 12 13 14 15 16 17 18 19 20 21 22 23 24 25

21 inches

Name

Lesson 78
COMMON CORE STANDARD CC.2.MD.6
Lesson Objective: Solve problems involving adding and subtracting lengths by using the strategy *draw a diagram.*

Problem Solving · Add and Subtract Lengths

Christy has a ribbon that is 12 centimeters long. Erin has a ribbon that is 9 centimeters long. How many centimeters of ribbon do they have altogether?

Unlock the Problem

What do I need to find?	What information do I need to use?
how much ribbon they have altogether	Christy has 12 centimeters of ribbon. Erin has 9 centimeters of ribbon.

Show how to solve the problem.

12   9

0 1 2 3 4 5 6 7 8 9 10 11 12 13 14 15 16 17 18 19 20 21 22 23 24 25

$12 + 9 =$ ▧

They have 21 centimeters of ribbon altogether.

Write a number sentence using a ▧ for the missing number. Then solve.

1. Lucas has one string that is 9 centimeters long and another string that is 8 centimeters long. How many centimeters of string are there in all?

9   8

0 1 2 3 4 5 6 7 8 9 10 11 12 13 14 15 16 17 18 19 20 21 22 23 24 25

$9 + 8 =$ ▧   17 centimeters of string in all

Name

Lesson 78
CC.2.MD.6

1. Karen has a toy car that is 9 centimeters long. She has a toy truck that is 14 centimeters long. She puts them end-to-end. How long are the car and truck together?

9   14

0 1 2 3 4 5 6 7 8 9 10 11 12 13 14 15 16 17 18 19 20 21 22 23 24 25

18 centimeters	20 centimeters	23 centimeters	25 centimeters
○	○	●	○

2. Matt had a fruit roll that was 13 centimeters long. Then he ate 7 centimeters of the fruit roll. How long is the fruit roll now?

7

13

0 1 2 3 4 5 6 7 8 9 10 11 12 13 14 15 16 17 18 19 20 21 22 23 24 25

5 centimeters	6 centimeters	8 centimeters	10 centimeters
○	●	○	○

3. Amy drew this diagram to show a problem about lengths in centimeters.

4   5

0 1 2 3 4 5 6 7 8 9 10 11 12 13 14 15 16 17 18 19 20 21 22 23 24 25

Write a problem that Amy might be trying to solve. Solve the problem.

Possible answer: Amy has a stamp that is 4 centimeters long and a stamp that is 5 centimeters long. She puts them end-to-end. How long are they together?

9 centimeters

Answer Key

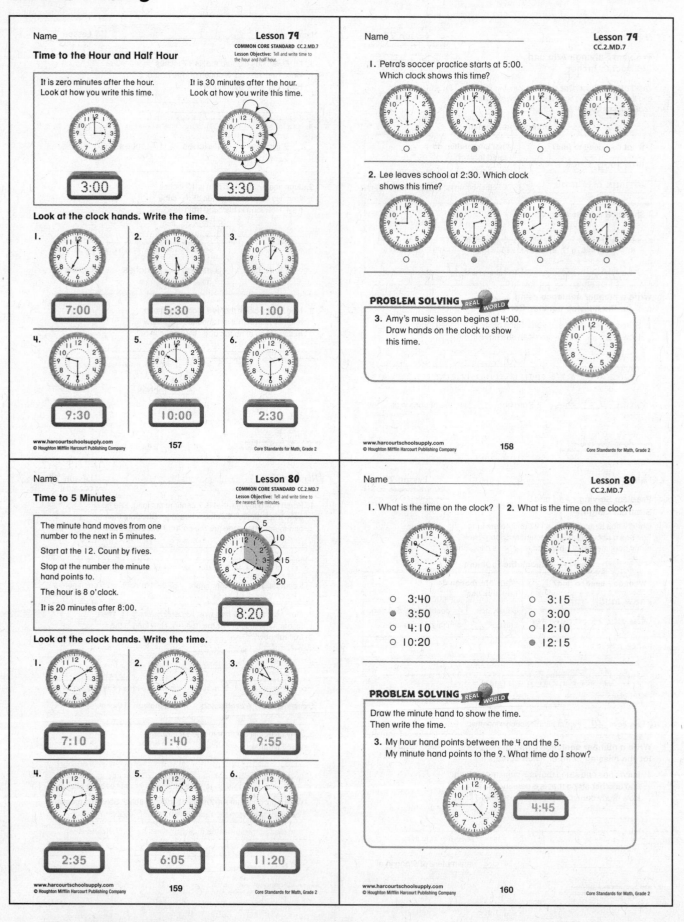

Time to the Hour and Half Hour

COMMON CORE STANDARD CC.2.MD.7
Lesson Objective: Tell and write time to the hour and half hour.

It is zero minutes after the hour. Look at how you write this time.

3:00

It is 30 minutes after the hour. Look at how you write this time.

3:30

Look at the clock hands. Write the time.

1. **7:00**
2. **5:30**
3. **1:00**
4. **9:30**
5. **10:00**
6. **2:30**

1. Petra's soccer practice starts at 5:00. Which clock shows this time?

○   ●   ○   ○

2. Lee leaves school at 2:30. Which clock shows this time?

○   ●   ○

PROBLEM SOLVING REAL WORLD

3. Amy's music lesson begins at 4:00. Draw hands on the clock to show this time.

Time to 5 Minutes

COMMON CORE STANDARD CC.2.MD.7
Lesson Objective: Tell and write time to the nearest five minutes.

The minute hand moves from one number to the next in 5 minutes.

Start at the 12. Count by fives.

Stop at the number the minute hand points to.

The hour is 8 o'clock.

It is 20 minutes after 8:00.

8:20

Look at the clock hands. Write the time.

1. **7:10**
2. **1:40**
3. **9:55**
4. **2:35**
5. **6:05**
6. **11:20**

1. What is the time on the clock?

○ 3:40
● 3:50
○ 4:10
○ 10:20

2. What is the time on the clock?

○ 3:15
○ 3:00
○ 12:10
● 12:15

PROBLEM SOLVING REAL WORLD

Draw the minute hand to show the time. Then write the time.

3. My hour hand points between the 4 and the 5. My minute hand points to the 9. What time do I show?

4:45

Answer Key

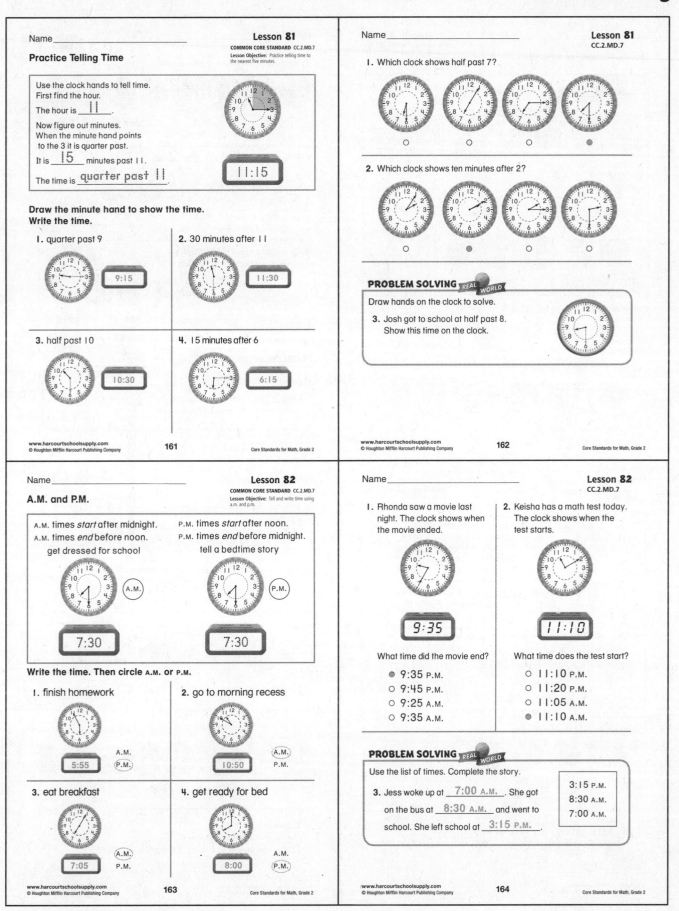

Answer Key

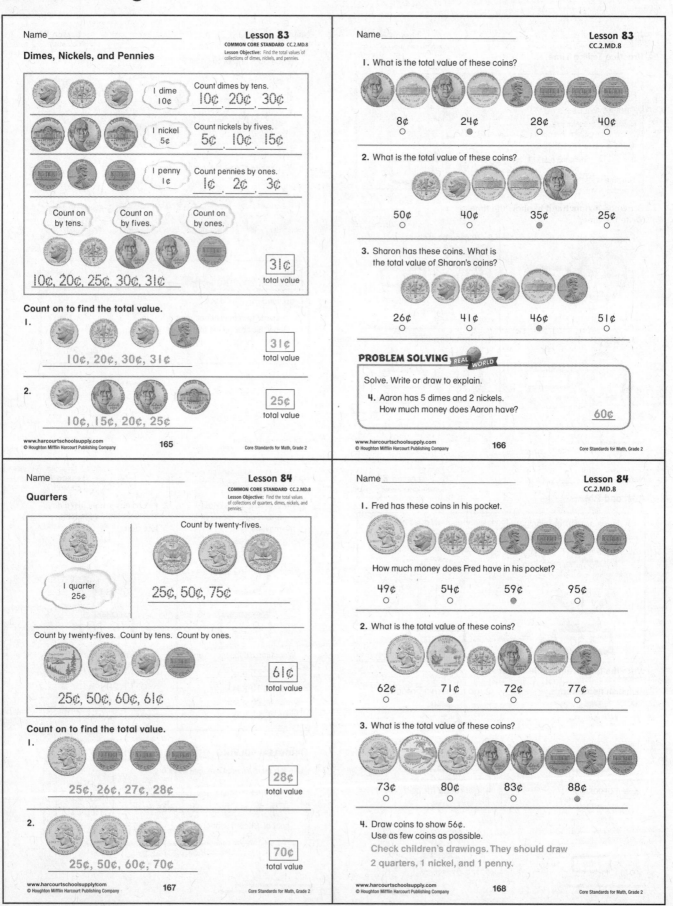

Answer Key

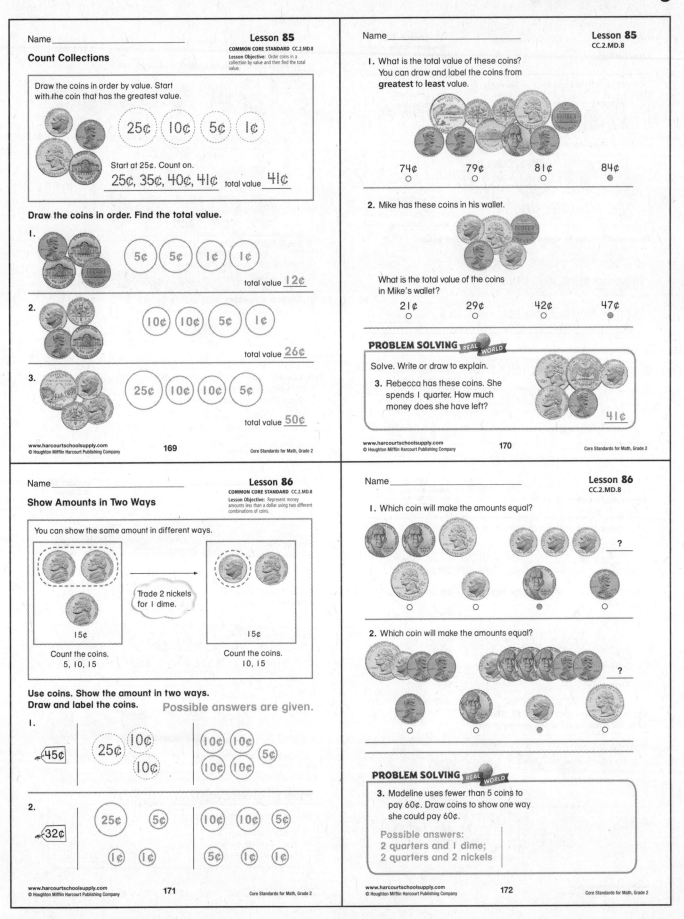

Lesson 85

Count Collections

COMMON CORE STANDARD CC.2.MD.8
Lesson Objective: Order coins in a collection by value and then find the total value.

Draw the coins in order by value. Start with the coin that has the greatest value.

25¢ 10¢ 5¢ 1¢

Start at 25¢. Count on.
25¢, 35¢, 40¢, 41¢ total value __41¢__

Draw the coins in order. Find the total value.

1. 5¢ 5¢ 1¢ 1¢
   total value __12¢__

2. 10¢ 10¢ 5¢ 1¢
   total value __26¢__

3. 25¢ 10¢ 10¢ 5¢
   total value __50¢__

169 Core Standards for Math, Grade 2

Lesson 85
CC.2.MD.8

1. What is the total value of these coins? You can draw and label the coins from **greatest** to **least** value.

   74¢   79¢   81¢   ●84¢

2. Mike has these coins in his wallet.

   What is the total value of the coins in Mike's wallet?

   21¢   29¢   42¢   ●47¢

PROBLEM SOLVING REAL WORLD

Solve. Write or draw to explain.

3. Rebecca has these coins. She spends 1 quarter. How much money does she have left?

   __41¢__

170 Core Standards for Math, Grade 2

Lesson 86

Show Amounts in Two Ways

COMMON CORE STANDARD CC.2.MD.8
Lesson Objective: Represent money amounts less than a dollar using two different combinations of coins.

You can show the same amount in different ways.

Trade 2 nickels for 1 dime.

15¢ → 15¢

Count the coins.   Count the coins.
5, 10, 15   10, 15

Use coins. Show the amount in two ways. Draw and label the coins. Possible answers are given.

1. 45¢   25¢ 10¢ 10¢ | 10¢ 10¢ 10¢ 10¢ 5¢

2. 32¢   25¢ 5¢ 1¢ 1¢ | 10¢ 10¢ 5¢ 5¢ 1¢ 1¢

171 Core Standards for Math, Grade 2

Lesson 86
CC.2.MD.8

1. Which coin will make the amounts equal?

   ○   ○   ●   ○

2. Which coin will make the amounts equal?

   ○   ○   ●   ○

PROBLEM SOLVING REAL WORLD

3. Madeline uses fewer than 5 coins to pay 60¢. Draw coins to show one way she could pay 60¢.

   Possible answers:
   2 quarters and 1 dime;
   2 quarters and 2 nickels

172 Core Standards for Math, Grade 2

Answer Key

Name_____

One Dollar

Lesson **87**
COMMON CORE STANDARD CC.2.MD.8
Lesson Objective: Show one dollar in a variety of ways.

One dollar has the same value as 100 cents.

You can write one dollar like this: $1.00

Count on to 100¢ to show $1.00.

$1.00

total value

25¢, 50¢, 75¢, 100¢

Draw more coins to show $1.00. Write the total value.

1. dimes

10¢ 10¢ 10¢ 10¢ 10¢

10¢ 10¢ 10¢ 10¢ 10¢ $1.00

2. nickels

5¢ 5¢ 5¢ 5¢ 5¢ 5¢ 5¢ 5¢ 5¢ 5¢

5¢ 5¢ 5¢ 5¢ 5¢ 5¢ 5¢ 5¢ 5¢ 5¢ $1.00

Name_____

Lesson **87**
CC.2.MD.8

1. Which group of coins has a total value of $1.00?

2. Jessie has these coins.

Which coin does she need to make $1.00?

3. Lawrence paid $1.00 for a juice drink.
He paid with only dimes and nickels.
Draw the coins he could have used.

Check children's drawings. Possible answers:
9 dimes and 2 nickels; 6 dimes and 8 nickels.

Name_____

Amounts Greater Than $1

Lesson **88**
COMMON CORE STANDARD CC.2.MD.8
Lesson Objective: Find and record the total value for money amounts greater than $1.

1. Count on and circle the coins that make one dollar.

2. Count on from 100¢ to find the total value for the whole group of coins.

3. 120¢ is the same as 1 dollar and 20 cents.   110¢   120¢

Write ___$1.20___.

Circle the money that makes $1. Then write the total value of the money shown.

1.

$1.15

2.

$1.20

Name_____

Lesson **88**
CC.2.MD.8

1. What is the total value of this money?

$1.07 $1.15 $1.22 $1.27

2. What is the total value of these coins?

$1.46 $1.36 $1.31 $1.26

3. What is the total value of this money?

$1.45 $1.50 $1.55 $1.60

PROBLEM SOLVING REAL WORLD

Solve. Write or draw to explain.

4. Grace found 3 quarters, 3 dimes, and 1 nickel in her pocket. How much money did she find? $1.10

Answer Key

Lesson 89

COMMON CORE STANDARD CC.2.MD.8
Lesson Objective: Solve word problems involving money by using the strategy act it out.

Name _____

Problem Solving • Money

Erin used one $1 bill and 3 nickels to buy a marker.
How much money did Erin use to buy the marker?

Unlock the Problem

What do I need to find?	What information do I need to use?
how much money Erin used to buy the marker	Erin used one $1 bill and 3 nickels

Show how to solve the problem.

Draw to show the money that Erin used.

$1   5¢   5¢   5¢

Erin used **$1.15** to buy the marker.

Use play coins and bills to solve.
Draw to show what you did.

1. Zeke has one $1 bill, 2 dimes, and 1 nickel.
   How much money does Zeke have?   **$1.25**

   Check children's drawings.

Name _____

Lesson 89
CC.2.MD.8

1. Molly has 3 quarters, 3 dimes, and 4 nickels in her coin bank. How much money does she have?

   $1.15 ○ $1.20 ○   **$1.25 ●** $1.40 ○

2. Tim spent two $1 bills, 2 quarters, 1 nickel, and 3 pennies at a fair. How much money did he spend?

   $2.30 ○ $2.33 ○ $2.53 ○   **$2.58 ●**

3. Chris gave his sister three $1 bills, 4 quarters, 1 dime, and 2 pennies. How much money did he give his sister?

   $3.97 ○   **$4.12 ●** $4.17 ○ $4.25 ○

4. Bill wants to buy a model car that costs $3.65. Draw bills and coins to show the money he could use to buy the car.

   Check children's drawings.

Name _____

Lesson 90

COMMON CORE STANDARD CC.2.MD.9
Lesson Objective: Measure the lengths of objects and use a line plot to display the measurement data.

Display Measurement Data

Each **X** on the line plot is for the length of one book.

X	X	X	X
5	6	7	8

Lengths of Books in Inches

One book is 5 inches long.
One book is 6 inches long.
Two books are 7 inches long.
One book is 8 inches long.

1. Use an inch ruler. Measure and record the lengths of 4 pencils in inches.

   1st pencil: _____ inches
   2nd pencil: _____ inches
   3rd pencil: _____ inches
   4th pencil: _____ inches

2. Write the numbers and draw the Xs to complete the line plot.

   For Exercises 1–2, answers may vary. Check children's work.

   Lengths of Pencils in Inches

Name _____

Lesson 90
CC.2.MD.9

Use the line plot for Questions 1–4.

Lengths of Markers in Inches

1. How many markers are 4 inches long?
   ● 1
   ○ 4
   ○ 6
   ○ 8

2. How many markers does the line plot show?
   ○ 10
   ● 9
   ○ 8
   ○ 4

3. How many markers are 7 inches long?
   ○ 7
   ○ 2
   ○ 1
   ● 0

4. How many inches long is the longest marker?
   ○ 5
   ○ 6
   ● 8
   ○ 9

PROBLEM SOLVING REAL WORLD

5. Jesse measured the lengths of some strings. Use his list to complete the line plot.

Lengths of Strings
5 inches
7 inches
6 inches
8 inches
5 inches

   Lengths of Strings in Inches

Answer Key

Name_____

Collect Data

You can take a survey to get information.

Which is your favorite sport?

Each tally mark stands for one person's answer. Count the tally marks.

Favorite Sport		
Sport	Tally	Total
soccer	IIII	4
basketball	HH	5
football	III	3

Elijah asked his classmates to choose their favorite breakfast food. He made this chart.

1. Write numbers to complete the chart.

Favorite Breakfast Food		
Food	Tally	Total
cereal	HHt III	8
pancakes	IIII	4
toast	III	3
eggs	HHt	5

2. How many classmates chose pancakes?

_____4_____ classmates

3. Which breakfast food did the fewest classmates choose?

_____toast_____

Name_____

Amber asked her classmates about their favorite flavor of yogurt. Use the tally chart for 1–4.

Favorite Yogurt Flavor	
Yogurt	Tally
peach	III
berry	HHt
lime	II
vanilla	HHt II

1. How many classmates chose berry?

○ 2   ● 5
○ 3   ○ 6

2. Which flavor did the **fewest** classmates choose?

○ berry   ○ vanilla
● lime   ○ peach

3. Which statement is true?

○ More classmates chose lime than peach.

● More classmates chose vanilla than berry.

○ Fewer classmates chose vanilla than lime.

○ Fewer classmates chose vanilla than peach.

4. What is another question you can ask based on the tally chart? Write your question and then answer it.

Possible answer: How many classmates in all voted for their favorite yogurt flavor? 17 classmates

---

Name_____

Read Picture Graphs

A picture graph uses pictures to show information.

Favorite Color	
red	✏ ✏ ✏
blue	✏ ✏ ✏ ✏ ✏
green	✏ ✏

Key: Each ✏ stands for 1 child.

The row with _blue_ has 5 pictures.

So, __5__ children chose blue.

Use the picture graph to answer the questions.

1. How many children chose red?

_____3_____ children

2. Did more children choose green or choose red?

_____red_____

3. Which color was chosen by the most children?

_____blue_____

4. How many children in all chose a favorite color?

_____10_____ children

Name_____

Use the picture graph for 1–5.

Favorite Recess Game	
tag	☺ ☺
catch	☺ ☺ ☺ ☺ ☺ ☺ ☺ ☺
kickball	☺ ☺ ☺ ☺ ☺ ☺
jacks	☺ ☺ ☺ ☺ ☺

Key: Each ☺ stands for 1 child.

1. Which game did the **most** children choose?

○ tag
○ kickball
● catch
○ jacks

2. How many children in all chose tag or jacks?

○ 15
○ 9
● 6
○ 3

3. How many children chose kickball?

○ 3
● 6
○ 9
○ 15

4. How many more children chose catch than kickball?

● 3
○ 4
○ 5
○ 7

5. How many children chose a recess game? Explain how you know.

21; Possible explanation: I counted all the ☺ on the tally chart.

Lesson 93

COMMON CORE STANDARD CC.2.MD.10
Lesson Objective: Make picture graphs to represent data.

Name_____

Make Picture Graphs

This picture graph uses 1 picture for each animal.
Draw a △ for each tally mark.

Animals at the Pet Store	
Animal	Tally
fish	IIII
hamster	II
turtle	III

Animals at the Pet Store				
fish	△	△	△	△
hamster	△	△		
turtle	△	△	△	

Key: Each △ stands for 1 animal.

How many turtles are at the pet store? __3__ turtles

1. Use the tally chart to complete the picture graph.
Draw a ☺ for each child.

Favorite Color	
Color	Tally
pink	HIT
yellow	III
blue	HIT

Favorite Color				
pink	☺	☺	☺	☺	☺
yellow	☺	☺	☺		
blue	☺	☺	☺	☺	☺

Key: Each ☺ stands for 1 child.

2. Which color did the fewest children choose? __yellow__

3. How many children chose pink? __5__ children

4. How many more children chose blue than chose yellow? __2__ more children

Lesson 93

CC.2.MD.10

Name_____

Use the tally chart and picture graph for 1–5.

Favorite Vegetable	
Fruit	Tally
carrot	HIT
lettuce	III
tomato	HIT I
pepper	II

Favorite Vegetable				
carrot	☺	☺	☺	☺	☺
lettuce				
tomato				
pepper				

Key: Each ☺ stands for 1 child.

1. How many ☺ should be in the picture graph next to pepper?
   - ● 2
   - ○ 3
   - ○ 5
   - ○ 6

2. How many ☺ should be in the picture graph next to lettuce?
   - ○ 1
   - ○ 2
   - ● 3
   - ○ 6

3. How many ☺ should be in the picture graph next to tomato?
   - ○ 7
   - ● 6
   - ○ 4
   - ○ 3

4. How many fewer children chose pepper than tomato?
   - ○ 1
   - ○ 2
   - ○ 3
   - ● 4

5. How is the tally chart like the picture graph?

   Possible answer: There is 1 tally mark
   or ☺ for each person in each one.

Lesson 94

COMMON CORE STANDARD CC.2.MD.10
Lesson Objective: Interpret data in bar graphs and use that information to solve problems.

Name_____

Read Bar Graphs

Look at the number below the right end of each bar.
This number tells how many of each model Max has.

Max's Model Collection	
planes	
cars	
boats	

0 1 2 3 4 5 6 7 8
Number of Models

The bar for model cars ends at 7.

So, Max has __7__ car models.

Use the bar graph.

1. How many model planes does Max have? __4__ model planes

2. Does Max have more model boats or model planes? more model __boats__

3. How many models does Max have in all? __16__ models

Lesson 94

CC.2.MD.10

Name_____

Use the bar graph for 1–5.

Books in the Library

Number of Books: 0–10
fiction science history poetry
Kind of Books

1. How many more history books than science books are in the library?
   - ○ 10   ○ 4
   - ○ 6   ● 2

2. How many fiction books are in the library?
   - ○ 4   ● 8
   - ○ 5   ○ 9

3. How many books are in the library in all?
   - ● 27   ○ 23
   - ○ 26   ○ 17

4. Which kind of book does the library have the fewest of?
   - ○ fiction   ○ history
   - ● science   ○ poetry

4. Can you answer question 4 without reading any numbers on the graph? Explain. Possible answer: Yes, I can look at the bars. Since science has the shortest bar, it means that the library has the fewest number of science books.

Answer Key

Name_____

Make Bar Graphs

These bar graphs show how many games Alex, Sarah, and Tony played.

- Alex played 5 games.
- Sarah played 3 games.
- Tony played 4 games.

Games Played

Jim is making a bar graph to show the number of markers his friends have.

- Adam has 4 markers.
- Clint has 3 markers.
- Erin has 2 markers.

1. Write labels for the graph.

2. Draw bars in the graph to show the number of markers that Clint and Erin have.

Our Markers

Number of Markers

Adam Clint Erin

Friends

Name_____

Use the information for 1–2.

Jorge is making a bar graph about summer sports.

- 5 children played tennis.
- 4 children played baseball.
- 2 children played basketball.

Summer Sports

Number of Children

tennis baseball basketball

1. Which could be the missing label in the bar graph?
   - ○ Number of Children
   - ● Type of Sport
   - ○ Tennis
   - ○ Soccer

2. How many more children played tennis than played basketball?
   - ○ 1
   - ○ 2
   - ● 3
   - ○ 4

3. Tina is making a bar graph to show the number of notebooks her friends have.
   - Lara has 4 notebooks.
   - Marta has 3 notebooks.
   - John has 1 notebook.

   Write labels and draw bars to complete the graph.

Our Notebooks

Number of Notebooks

Lara Marta John

Friends

Check children's work.

Name_____

Problem Solving • Display Data

The list shows how many hours Morgan worked on her project. Describe how the number of hours changed from Week 1 to Week 4.

Week 1	1 hour
Week 2	2 hours
Week 3	3 hours
Week 4	4 hours

Unlock the Problem

What do I need to find?	What information do I need to use?
how the number of _hours_ changed from Week 1 to Week 4	the number of _hours_ Morgan worked on her project each week

Show how to solve the problem.

Hours Worked on Project

Number of Hours

Week 1 Week 2 Week 3 Week 4

Week

The number of hours _Answers should include that the number of hours increased each week._

Name_____

Use the bar graph for 1–4.

Wins by Smithtown Cougars

Month

May
June
July
August

0 1 2 3 4 5 6 7 8 9 10

Number of Wins

1. How many times did the Cougars win in May?
   - ○ 8
   - ○ 4
   - ○ 5
   - ● 2

2. How many more wins did the Cougars have in August than in July?
   - ○ 6
   - ● 3
   - ○ 4
   - ○ 2

3. Which of the following describes how the number of wins changed from May to August?
   - ● The number of wins increased each month.
   - ○ The number of wins decreased each month.
   - ○ The number of wins stayed about the same.
   - ○ The number of wins in August was 8 more than in May.

4. How many times do you think the Cougars will win in September? Explain.

   Possible answer: I think they will win at least 9 times in September because the graph shows that they win more games each month, and they won 8 times in August.

Answer Key

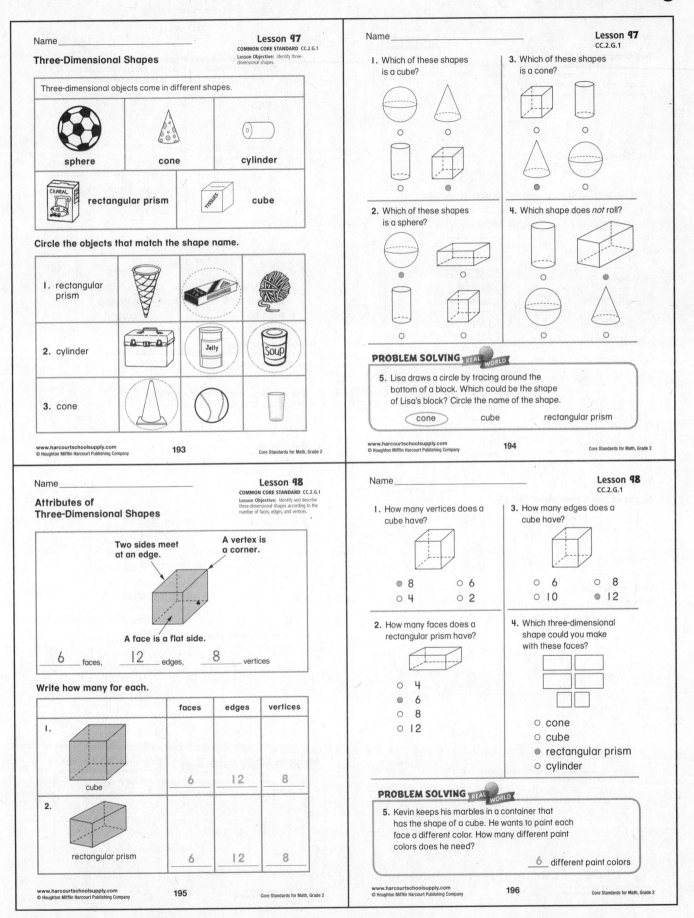

Name _____

Lesson 97
COMMON CORE STANDARD CC.2.G.1
Lesson Objective: Identify three-dimensional shapes.

Three-Dimensional Shapes

Three-dimensional objects come in different shapes.

sphere	cone	cylinder

rectangular prism	cube

Circle the objects that match the shape name.

1. rectangular prism			
2. cylinder			
3. cone			

Name _____

Lesson 97
CC.2.G.1

1. Which of these shapes is a cube?

2. Which of these shapes is a sphere?

3. Which of these shapes is a cone?

4. Which shape does *not* roll?

PROBLEM SOLVING REAL WORLD

5. Lisa draws a circle by tracing around the bottom of a block. Which could be the shape of Lisa's block? Circle the name of the shape.

cone   cube   rectangular prism

Name _____

Lesson 98
COMMON CORE STANDARD CC.2.G.1
Lesson Objective: Identify and describe three-dimensional shapes according to the number of faces, edges, and vertices.

Attributes of Three-Dimensional Shapes

Two sides meet at an edge.

A vertex is a corner.

A face is a flat side.

6 faces, 12 edges, 8 vertices

Write how many for each.

	faces	edges	vertices
1. cube	6	12	8
2. rectangular prism	6	12	8

Name _____

Lesson 98
CC.2.G.1

1. How many vertices does a cube have?
   - ● 8
   - ○ 4
   - ○ 6
   - ○ 2

2. How many faces does a rectangular prism have?
   - ○ 4
   - ● 6
   - ○ 8
   - ○ 12

3. How many edges does a cube have?
   - ○ 6
   - ○ 10
   - ○ 8
   - ● 12

4. Which three-dimensional shape could you make with these faces?
   - ○ cone
   - ○ cube
   - ● rectangular prism
   - ○ cylinder

PROBLEM SOLVING REAL WORLD

5. Kevin keeps his marbles in a container that has the shape of a cube. He wants to paint each face a different color. How many different paint colors does he need?

6 different paint colors

Answer Key

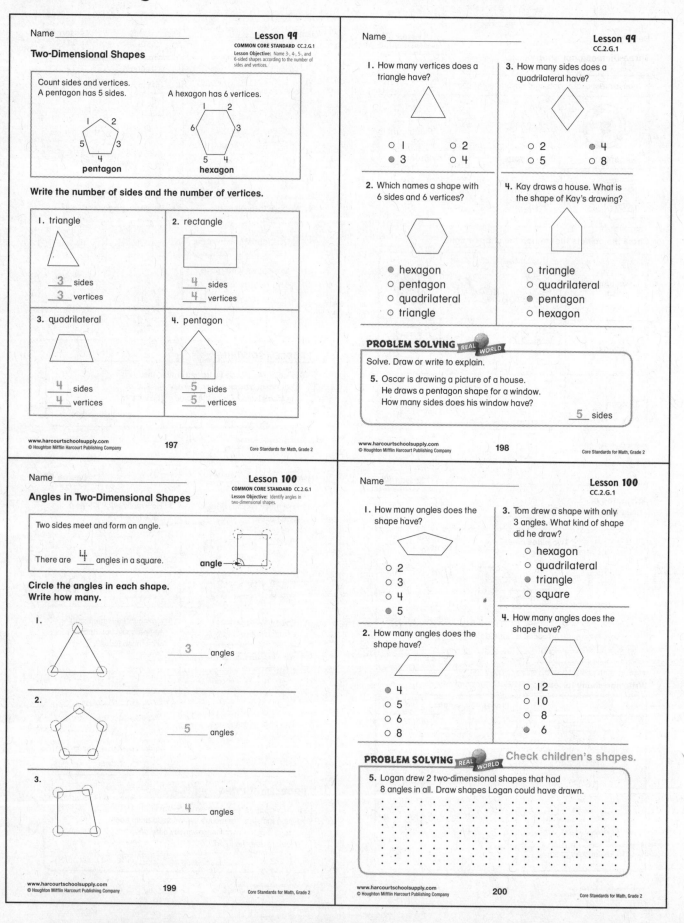

Lesson 99 — Two-Dimensional Shapes

Name _____

COMMON CORE STANDARD CC.2.G.1
Lesson Objective: Name 3-, 4-, 5-, and 6-sided shapes according to the number of sides and vertices.

Count sides and vertices.
A pentagon has 5 sides.

A hexagon has 6 vertices.

pentagon   **hexagon**

Write the number of sides and the number of vertices.

1. triangle

__3__ sides
__3__ vertices

2. rectangle

__4__ sides
__4__ vertices

3. quadrilateral

__4__ sides
__4__ vertices

4. pentagon

__5__ sides
__5__ vertices

Lesson 99

Name _____

CC.2.G.1

1. How many vertices does a triangle have?

○ 1   ○ 2
● 3   ○ 4

2. Which names a shape with 6 sides and 6 vertices?

● hexagon
○ pentagon
○ quadrilateral
○ triangle

3. How many sides does a quadrilateral have?

○ 2   ● 4
○ 5   ○ 8

4. Kay draws a house. What is the shape of Kay's drawing?

○ triangle
○ quadrilateral
● pentagon
○ hexagon

PROBLEM SOLVING REAL WORLD

Solve. Draw or write to explain.

5. Oscar is drawing a picture of a house. He draws a pentagon shape for a window. How many sides does his window have?

__5__ sides

Lesson 100 — Angles in Two-Dimensional Shapes

Name _____

COMMON CORE STANDARD CC.2.G.1
Lesson Objective: Identify angles in two-dimensional shapes.

Two sides meet and form an angle.

There are __4__ angles in a square.   **angle** →

Circle the angles in each shape.
Write how many.

1.

__3__ angles

2.

__5__ angles

3.

__4__ angles

Lesson 100

Name _____

CC.2.G.1

1. How many angles does the shape have?

○ 2
○ 3
○ 4
● 5

2. How many angles does the shape have?

● 4
○ 5
○ 6
○ 8

3. Tom drew a shape with only 3 angles. What kind of shape did he draw?

○ hexagon
○ quadrilateral
● triangle
○ square

4. How many angles does the shape have?

○ 12
○ 10
○ 8
● 6

PROBLEM SOLVING REAL WORLD   Check children's shapes.

5. Logan drew 2 two-dimensional shapes that had 8 angles in all. Draw shapes Logan could have drawn.

Answer Key

Lesson 101

Name_____

COMMON CORE STANDARD CC.2.G.1
Lesson Objective: Sort two-dimensional shapes according to their attributes.

Sort Two-Dimensional Shapes

Circle the shapes with 5 sides.

4 sides   **3** sides   **5** sides   **6** sides

Circle the shapes with fewer than 5 angles.

3 angles   **6** angles   **4** angles   **5** angles

Circle the shapes that match the rule.

1. Shapes with 4 sides

2. Shapes with more than 4 angles

Lesson 101

Name_____

CC.2.G.1

1. Which rule matches the shapes?

   ○ shapes with 4 angles
   ● shapes with 3 angles
   ○ shapes with 5 angles
   ○ shapes with 4 sides

2. Which rule matches the shapes?

   ○ shapes with 5 sides
   ○ shapes with 6 angles
   ● shapes with more than 4 sides
   ○ shapes with fewer than 4 angles

3. Which shape has fewer than 4 sides?

   ●   ○
   ○   ○

4. Johanna walks home from school each day. She sees that a road sign has the shape of a pentagon. How many angles does the road sign have?

   ○ 3
   ○ 4
   ● 5
   ○ 6

5. Draw a shape that has fewer than 4 angles. Name your shape.

   triangle

Check children's drawings.

Lesson 102

Name_____

COMMON CORE STANDARD CC.2.G.2
Lesson Objective: Partition rectangles into equal-size squares and find the total number of these squares.

Partition Rectangles

How many color tiles cover this rectangle?

Make a row of color tiles on the rectangle. Trace around the square tiles.

How many squares? __3__ squares

Use color tiles to cover the rectangle.
Trace around the square tiles. Write how many.

1.

Number of rows: __2__
Number of columns: __2__
Total: __4__ squares

2.

Number of rows: __3__
Number of columns: __1__
Total: __3__ squares

Lesson 102

Name_____

CC.2.G.2

1. Rick covered a rectangle with square tiles. He made 2 rows. He made 4 columns. How many square tiles did he use?

   ○ 5
   ○ 6
   ○ 7
   ● 8

2. Linda covered a rectangle with square tiles. She made 5 rows. She made 1 column. How many square tiles did she use?

   ○ 10
   ○ 6
   ● 5
   ○ 4

3. Maria covered a rectangle with square tiles. She made 3 rows. She made 3 columns. How many square tiles did she use?

   ● 9
   ○ 8
   ○ 6
   ○ 3

4. Jeff covered a rectangle with square tiles. He made 4 rows. He made 3 columns. How many square tiles did he use?

   ○ 7
   ● 12
   ○ 14
   ○ 16

PROBLEM SOLVING REAL WORLD

Solve. Write or draw to explain.

5. Nina wants to put color tiles on a square. 3 color tiles fit across the top of the square. How many rows and columns of of squares will Nina need? How many color tiles will she use in all?

   Number of rows: __3__
   Number of columns: __3__
   Total: __9__ square tiles

   __9__ tiles

Answer Key

www.harcourtschoolsupply.com
© Houghton Mifflin Harcourt Publishing Company

COMMON CORE STANDARD CC.2.G.3
Lesson Objective: Identify and name equal parts of circles and rectangles as halves, thirds, or fourths.

Equal Parts

You can divide a whole into equal parts.

<u>2</u> equal parts
halves

<u>3</u> equal parts
thirds

<u>4</u> equal parts
fourths

Write how many equal parts there are in the whole.
Write halves, thirds, or fourths to name the equal parts.

1.
<u>4</u> equal parts
fourths

2.
<u>2</u> equal parts
halves

3.
<u>3</u> equal parts
thirds

4.
<u>2</u> equal parts
halves

5.
<u>3</u> equal parts
thirds

6.
<u>4</u> equal parts
fourths

---

1. Which whole has been divided into thirds?   ●

3. Which whole has been divided into fourths?   ●

2. Which whole has been divided into halves?   ●

4. Which shape is **not** divided into equal parts?   ●

5. Write how many equal parts are in the whole. Write **halves**, **thirds**, or **fourths** to name the equal parts.

<u>4</u> equal parts
fourths

COMMON CORE STANDARD CC.2.G.3
Lesson Objective: Partition shapes to show halves, thirds, or fourths.

Show Equal Parts of a Whole

Trace to show the equal parts.

2 equal parts
2 halves

3 equal parts
3 thirds

4 equal parts
4 fourths

Draw to show equal parts.

Check children's drawings.

1. halves

2. thirds

3. halves

4. fourths

---

1. Alan divides a circle into thirds. How many equal parts does he show?

○ 1   ○ 2
● 3   ○ 4

3. A sandwich is cut into thirds. How many pieces of sandwich are there?

○ 2
● 3
○ 4
○ 5

2. Sue divides a rectangle into halves. How many equal parts does she show?

○ 5   ○ 4
○ 3   ● 2

4. A cake is cut into fourths. How many pieces of cake are there in all?

● 4
○ 3
○ 2
○ 1

PROBLEM SOLVING REAL WORLD

Solve. Write or draw to explain.

5. Joe has one sandwich. He cuts the sandwich into fourths. How many pieces of sandwich does he have?

<u>4</u> pieces

Lesson 105

COMMON CORE STANDARD CC.2.G.3
Lesson Objective: Identify and describe one equal part as a half of, a third of, or a fourth of a whole.

Name _____

Describe Equal Parts

One equal part of each shape is shaded.

A half of the shape is shaded. A third of the shape is shaded. A fourth of the shape is shaded.

**Draw to show halves.
Color a half of the shape.**

Check children's work.

1.

2.

**Draw to show fourths.
Color a fourth of the shape.**

Check children's work.

3.

4.

Lesson 105
CC.2.G.3

Name _____

1. How much of the shape is shaded?

○ a whole
○ a fourth
● a third
○ a half

3. How much of the shape is shaded?

○ a half
○ a third
● a fourth
○ a whole

2. Which of these has a half of the shape shaded?

4. Which of these has a third of the shape shaded?

PROBLEM SOLVING *REAL WORLD*

5. Circle all the shapes that have a third of the shape shaded.

Lesson 106

COMMON CORE STANDARD CC.2.G.3
Lesson Objective: Solve problems involving wholes divided into equal shares by using the strategy *draw a diagram*.

Name _____

Problem Solving • Equal Shares

Two gardens are the same size. Each garden is divided into halves, but the gardens are divided differently. How might the gardens be divided?

Unlock the Problem

What do I need to find?	**What information do I need to use?**
how the gardens are divided	There are __2__ gardens. Each garden is divided into __halves__.

Show how to solve the problem.

Draw to show your answer.

Possible answers are given.

1. Sophie has two pieces of paper that are the same size. She wants to divide each piece into fourths. What are two different ways she can divide the pieces of paper?

Lesson 106
CC.2.G.3

Name _____

1. Dana divides a square into halves like this.

Which is another way she can divide the square into halves?

2. Ben divides a rectangle into fourths like this.

Which is another way he can divide the rectangle into fourths?

3. Mr. Jones cut a sandwich into fourths. Each piece is a triangle. Which way did he cut the sandwich?

4. Helen divides her garden into thirds like this.

Show another way she can divide her garden into thirds.

Check children's work. Possible answer is given.

Common Core State Standards

Operations and Algebraic Thinking

CC.2.OA

Represent and solve problems involving addition and subtraction.

1. Use addition and subtraction within 100 to solve one- and two-step word problems involving situations of adding to, taking from, putting together, taking apart, and comparing, with unknowns in all positions, e.g., by using drawings and equations with a symbol for the unknown number to represent the problem.

Add and subtract within 20.

2. Fluently add and subtract within 20 using mental strategies. By end of Grade 2, know from memory all sums of two one-digit numbers.

Work with equal groups of objects to gain foundations for multiplication.

3. Determine whether a group of objects (up to 20) has an odd or even number of members, e.g., by pairing objects or counting them by 2s; write an equation to express an even number as a sum of two equal addends.

4. Use addition to find the total number of objects arranged in rectangular arrays with up to 5 rows and up to 5 columns; write an equation to express the total as a sum of equal addends.

Number and Operations in Base Ten

CC.2.NBT

Understand place value.

1. Understand that the three digits of a three-digit number represent amounts of hundreds, tens, and ones; e.g., 706 equals 7 hundreds, 0 tens, and 6 ones. Understand the following as special cases:

   a. 100 can be thought of as a bundle of ten tens — called a "hundred."

   b. The numbers 100, 200, 300, 400, 500, 600, 700, 800, 900 refer to one, two, three, four, five, six, seven, eight, or nine hundreds (and 0 tens and 0 ones).

2. Count within 1000; skip-count by 5s, 10s, and 100s.

3. Read and write numbers to 1000 using base-ten numerals, number names, and expanded form.

4. Compare two three-digit numbers based on meanings of the hundreds, tens, and ones digits, using $>$, $=$, and $<$ symbols to record the results of comparisons.

Number and Operations in Base Ten (*continued*)   CC.2.NBT

Use place value understanding and properties of operations to add and subtract.

5. Fluently add and subtract within 100 using strategies based on place value, properties of operations, and/or the relationship between addition and subtraction.

6. Add up to four two-digit numbers using strategies based on place value and properties of operations.

7. Add and subtract within 1000, using concrete models or drawings and strategies based on place value, properties of operations, and/or the relationship between addition and subtraction; relate the strategy to a written method. Understand that in adding or subtracting three-digit numbers, one adds or subtracts hundreds and hundreds, tens and tens, ones and ones; and sometimes it is necessary to compose or decompose tens or hundreds.

8. Mentally add 10 or 100 to a given number 100–900, and mentally subtract 10 or 100 from a given number 100–900.

9. Explain why addition and subtraction strategies work, using place value and the properties of operations.

Measurement and Data   CC.2.MD

Measure and estimate lengths in standard units.

1. Measure the length of an object by selecting and using appropriate tools such as rulers, yardsticks, meter sticks, and measuring tapes.

2. Measure the length of an object twice, using length units of different lengths for the two measurements; describe how the two measurements relate to the size of the unit chosen.

3. Estimate lengths using units of inches, feet, centimeters, and meters.

4. Measure to determine how much longer one object is than another, expressing the length difference in terms of a standard length unit.

Common Core State Standards

Measurement and Data (continued) CC.2.MD

Relate addition and subtraction to length.

5. Use addition and subtraction within 100 to solve word problems involving lengths that are given in the same units, e.g., by using drawings (such as drawings of rulers) and equations with a symbol for the unknown number to represent the problem.

6. Represent whole numbers as lengths from 0 on a number line diagram with equally spaced points corresponding to the numbers 0, 1, 2, ..., and represent whole-number sums and differences within 100 on a number line diagram.

Work with time and money.

7. Tell and write time from analog and digital clocks to the nearest five minutes, using a.m. and p.m.

8. Solve word problems involving dollar bills, quarters, dimes, nickels, and pennies, using $ and ¢ symbols appropriately.

Represent and interpret data.

9. Generate measurement data by measuring lengths of several objects to the nearest whole unit, or by making repeated measurements of the same object. Show the measurements by making a line plot, where the horizontal scale is marked off in whole-number units.

10. Draw a picture graph and a bar graph (with single-unit scale) to represent a data set with up to four categories. Solve simple put-together, take-apart, and compare problems using information presented in a bar graph.

Geometry CC.2.G

Reason with shapes and their attributes.

1. Recognize and draw shapes having specified attributes, such as a given number of angles or a given number of equal faces. Identify triangles, quadrilaterals, pentagons, hexagons, and cubes.

2. Partition a rectangle into rows and columns of same-size squares and count to find the total number of them.

3. Partition circles and rectangles into two, three, or four equal shares, describe the shares using the words *halves*, *thirds*, *half of*, a *third of*, etc., and describe the whole as two halves, three thirds, four fourths. Recognize that equal shares of identical wholes need not have the same shape.